THE CAMINO PORTUGUÉS

THE CAMINO PORTUGUÉS

FROM LISBON AND PORTO TO SANTIAGO – CENTRAL, COASTAL AND SPIRITUAL CAMINOS

by Kat Davis

JUNIPER HOUSE, MURLEY MOSS,
OXENHOLME ROAD, KENDAL, CUMBRIA LA9 7RL
www.cicerone.co.uk

© Kat Davis 2023
Second edition 2023
ISBN: 978 1 78631 196 2
First edition 2018

Printed in Turkey by Pelikan Basim using responsibly sourced paper
A catalogue record for this book is available from the British Library.
All photographs are by the author unless otherwise stated.

Route mapping by Lovell Johns www.lovelljohns.com
Contains OpenStreetMap.org data © OpenStreetMap
contributors, CC-BY-SA. NASA relief data courtesy of ESRI

Front cover: View of the Basílica de Santa Luzia at sunset from the Pousada in Viana do Castelo (Coastal Camino Stage 3)

CONTENTS

Symbols used on route maps

〰	route		woodland
‑‑‑	alternative route		urban areas
Ⓢ	start point		regional border
Ⓕ	finish point		international border
ⓈⒻ	start/finish point	▬■▬	station/railway
▲	peak		
■ 🏠	building/Albergue de Peregrinos		
🍴 ☕	restaurant/café		
♀	church or chapel		
♣	cathedral or convent		
† ⊞	stone cross/cemetery		
🏰	castle or fort		
≍	bridge		
• Ⓦ	water feature/waterfall		
✳	viewpoint		
🛏	picnic area		
❶	tourist office		
🚌	bus stop or bus station		
•	other feature		
⛴	ferry		

Relief
in metres

600–800	
400–600	
200–400	
0–200	

SCALE: 1:100,000

```
0 kilometres   1        2
|_____|_____|
0 miles              1
```

Contour lines are
drawn at 50m intervals
and highlighted at
200m intervals.

GPX files

GPX files for all routes can be downloaded for free at www.cicerone.co.uk/1196/GPX.

View of Porto from the Mosteiro da Serra do Pilar

Cathedral of Santiago de Compostela

ROUTE SUMMARY TABLES

Central Camino

Stage no.	Start	Finish	Distance (km)	Distance from Lisbon (km)	Distance from Santiago (km)	Page
Stage 1	Lisbon	Alpriate	21.8	21.8	599.7	43
Stage 2	Alpriate	Vila Franca de Xira	19	40.8	580.7	48
Stage 3	Vila Franca de Xira	Azambuja	19.5	60.3	561.2	54
Stage 4	Azambuja	Santarém	32.5	92.8	528.7	59
Stage 5	Santarém	Golegã	34.2	127	494.5	65
Stage 6	Golegã	Tomar	30.4	157.4	464.1	72
Stage 7	Tomar	Alvaiázere	32.5	189.9	431.6	81
Stage 8	Alvaiázere	Rabaçal	31.7	221.6	399.9	87
Stage 9	Rabaçal	Coimbra	28.7	250.3	371.2	94
Stage 10	Coimbra	Sernadelo	25	275.3	346.2	103
Stage 11	Sernadelo	Águeda	23.6	298.9	322.6	109
Stage 12	Águeda	Albergaria-a-Velha	16.1	315	306.5	115
Stage 13	Albergaria-a-Velha	São João da Madeira	29	344	277.5	119
Stage 14	São João da Madeira	Grijó	18.8	362.8	258.7	127
Stage 15	Grijó	Porto	15.5	378.3	243.2	131
Subtotal Lisbon to Porto			**378.3**	**378.3**	**243.2**	
Stage 16	Porto	Vairão	25	403.3	218.2	139
Stage 17	Vairão	Barcelos	30.4	433.7	187.8	145
Stage 18	Barcelos	Ponte de Lima	33.5	467.2	154.3	154
Stage 19	Ponte de Lima	Rubiães	17.9	485.1	136.4	162
Stage 20	Rubiães	Tui	19.5	504.6	116.9	167
Stage 21	Tui	Mos	23.1	527.7	93.8	176
Stage 22	Mos	Pontevedra	29.1	556.8	64.7	183
Stage 23	Pontevedra	Caldas de Reis	21.2	578	43.5	194
Stage 24	Caldas de Reis	Padrón	18.6	596.6	24.9	200
Stage 25	Padrón	Santiago	24.9	621.5	0	208
Subtotal Porto to Santiago			**243.2**	**621.5**	**0**	
Total km			**621.5**			

Coastal Camino joining the Central Camino at Redondela

Stage no.	Start	Finish	Distance (km)	Distance from Porto (km)	Distance from Santiago (km)	Page
Stage 1	Porto	Vila do Conde	28	28	237.3	219
Stage 1A	Porto	Vila do Conde	33	33	237.3	228
Stage 2	Vila do Conde	Esposende	23.8	51.8	213.5	233
Stage 3	Esposende	Viana do Castelo	25.5	77.3	188	242
Stage 4	Viana do Castelo	Caminha	26.8	104.1	161.2	250
Stage 5	Caminha	Mougás	25	129.1	136.2	258
Stage 6	Mougás	A Ramallosa	16	145.1	120.2	265
Stage 7	A Ramallosa	Vigo	21.5	166.6	98.7	271
Stage 8	Vigo	Redondela	14.5	181.1	84.2	279
Continue on Central Camino						
Stage 22	Redondela	Pontevedra	19.5	200.6	64.7	183
Stage 23	Pontevedra	Caldas de Reis	21.2	221.8	43.5	194
Stage 24	Caldas de Reis	Padrón	18.6	240.4	24.9	200
Stage 25	Padrón	Santiago	24.9	265.3	0	208
Total km			**265.3 (or 270.3 via Stage 1A)**			

Coastal Camino joining the Central Camino at Valença/Tui

Stage no.	Start	Finish	Distance (km)	Distance from Porto (km)	Distance from Santiago (km)	Page
Stage 1	Porto	Vila do Conde	28	28	225.1	219
Stage 2	Vila do Conde	Esposende	23.8	51.8	201.3	233
Stage 3	Esposende	Viana do Castelo	25.5	77.3	175.8	242
Stage 4	Viana do Castelo	Caminha	26.8	104.1	149	250
Link route 3	Caminha	Tui	32.1	136.2	116.9	290
Continue on Central Camino						
Stage 21	Tui	Mos	23.1	159.3	93.8	176
Stage 22	Mos	Pontevedra	29.1	188.4	64.7	183
Stage 23	Pontevedra	Caldas de Reis	21.2	209.6	43.5	194
Stage 24	Caldas de Reis	Padrón	18.6	228.2	24.9	200
Stage 25	Padrón	Santiago	24.9	253.1	0	208
Total km			**253.1**			

Link routes between the Central and Coastal Caminos

Route no.	Start	Finish	Distance (km)	Page
Link route 1	Vila do Conde	São Pedro de Rates	13.7	284
Link route 2	São Pedro de Rates	Esposende	17.2	287
Link route 3	Caminha	Tui	32.1	290

Spiritual Variant (Variante Espiritual)

Stage no.	Start	Finish	Distance (km)	Distance from Pontevedra (km)	Distance from Santiago (km)	Page
Stage 1	Pontevedra	Armenteira	20.4	20.4	82.4	298
Stage 2	Armenteira	Vilanova de Arousa	23.5	43.9	58.9	304
Stage 3	Vilanova de Arousa	Padrón (by foot)	34	77.9	24.9	309
Stage 3	Boat passengers disembark in Pontecesures, 2.2km from Padrón					
Total walking km (boat option)			**46.1**			
Total walking km (all walking)			**77.9**			

13

Painting of St James on the ceiling of Igreja de
Santiago, Castelo do Neiva (Coastal Camino Stage 3)

INTRODUCTION

Starting in Portugal's capital, Lisbon, and ending in Santiago de Compostela in Spain, the 621km Portuguese Camino – 'Caminho Português' in Portuguese and 'Camino Português' in Spanish – has attracted pilgrims for many centuries. Count Henrique and Dona Teresa, the parents of Portugal's first king, visited the Apostle's tomb in 1097 (they later ordered an inn to be built for 'pilgrims, the poor and the sick' in Albergaria-a-Velha on the Central Camino); Queen (later Saint) Isabel undertook the journey in 1325 and 1335; while Jérôme Münzer (1494, a doctor from Nuremberg) and Giovanni Battista Confalonieri (1594, an Italian priest) wrote accounts so detailed that modern-day hikers will recognise shared experiences. There have been countless other voyagers, both the faithful and the intrepid, across the years.

The Camino follows Roman roads and crosses ancient bridges; it passes through villages, farmland and forests (and provides memorable Atlantic views on the Coastal Camino). Along the way there are four sites that are now designated UNESCO World Heritage Sites – Tomar's magnificent Knights Templar castle, Coimbra University (one of Europe's oldest), and the old towns of Porto and Santiago. Conímbriga Roman site with its exceptional mosaics is also a must-see. Walkers with time to spare might take a scenic river cruise down the Douro in Porto before continuing north and into the Minho region. There's a wonderful *albergue* (hostel) in Ponte de Lima, Portugal's oldest village, and

before leaving Portugal there's a chance to marvel at Valença's ancient fort with panoramic views of medieval Tui over the River Minho in Spain.

The Coastal Camino passes through historic shipbuilding and fishing ports, important during Portugal's 'Age of Discoveries'. On this route, hikers can enjoy fresh seafood and experience an Atlantic sunset from Mt Santa Luzia above Viana do Castelo, one of the best views of the Camino.

On the approach to Santiago, many people visit the Roman altar stone believed to be that which the boat carrying the body of St James moored up against in Padrón. Then it's a case of catching your breath and reflecting on your journey as you enter the old town of Santiago de Compostela, finishing at the steps of the magnificent cathedral in Praza do Obradoiro.

The list of cultural highlights is extensive, but often it's encounters with other people that make the longest-lasting memories; the Portuguese are friendly, genuine and kind-hearted – so don't be surprised if you're invited for coffee and a *pastel de nata* (sweet pastry) soon after being introduced!

ST JAMES AND THE BEGINNINGS OF SANTIAGO DE COMPOSTELA

St James the Great (Sant Iago), son of Zebedee and Salome, brother of John was a fisherman and disciple of Jesus. He is believed to have left Jerusalem to preach in the Iberian Peninsula but after

*Leaving Porto along Rua das Flores
(Central Camino Stage 16)*

In 997 the Moorish Caliph Almanzor attacked Santiago, stole the church's bells and forced Christian slaves to transport them to the mosque in Cordoba (they were returned in the 13th century). The church was rebuilt, then in 1075, during the reign of Alfonso VI, work began on the grand-scale cathedral that exists today. The spectacular Romanesque Pórtico da Gloria by Maestro Mateo was completed in 1188; the cathedral was consecrated in 1211 and Santiago de Compostela became a place of holy pilgrimage alongside Jerusalem and Rome.

PORTUGUESE HISTORY AND THE CAMINO

Prehistoric finds including petroglyphs (outside of Pontevedra on Stage 1 of the Spiritual Variant/*Variante Espiritual*) and megalithic tombs (Dolmen of Barrosa at Vila Praia de Âncora, Stage 4 of the Coastal Camino) pre-date the arrival of the Celts who came to the Iberian Peninsula around 1000BC and built fortified hilltop settlements (Viana do Castelo and A Guarda, Stages 3 and 5 of the Coastal Camino). The Romans arrived around 218BC and after initial

returning to the Holy Land was murdered by King Herod Agrippa in AD44. His disciples brought his body back to Spain by boat, landing at Iria Flavia (present-day Padrón), near where he had preached. His body was then transported by ox and cart and buried on Mt Libredón.

In the ninth century (believed to be around 813–820) a hermit named Pelayo discovered the tomb by following stars shining down on a field. He notified Teodomiro, the Bishop of Iria Flavia, who sent word to King Alfonso II of Asturias. Alfonso travelled from Oviedo to the tomb in the field of stars, '*campus stellae*', and ordered a church to be built on top. This was replaced with a grander church by Alfonso III, consecrated in 899.

*Roman mosaics, Conímbriga
(Central Camino Stage 9)*

resistance from the Lusitanian tribes they flourished, building bridges and a major road network. They introduced new salting techniques to preserve fish (seen in Praia de Angeiras, Stage 1A of the Coastal Camino) and cultivated wine, olive oil and cereals to export back to Rome. One of the best examples of Roman civilisation in Portugal is found in Conímbriga (Stage 9 of the Central Camino) – a key Roman settlement with spectacular mosaics. Portugal's name derives from the Roman name for Porto, Portus Cale.

Barbarian invasions accelerated the downfall of the Romans from the fifth century with the arrival of Alans, Vandals, Suevi and Visigoths, the latter being displaced by the Moors in the eighth century. Under Moorish rule Christians, Jews and Muslims lived alongside each other – although non-Muslims were taxed. The Moors left a lasting legacy which can be seen in place names (such as Alvaiázere and Alvorge), decorative 'azulejo' tiles, castles and food items such as citrus fruit and rice. The long Christian Reconquest reached a pivotal moment when Afonso Henriques captured Ourique in 1139, declaring himself King of the Portuguese nation. He went on to capture Santarém and Lisbon in 1147 and was formally recognised by Pope Alexander III as King of Portugal in 1179.

Portugal's 'Age of Discoveries' reached its peak under King Manuel I when explorer Vasco da Gama discovered a sea route to India (1498) and Pedro Álvares Cabral discovered Brazil (1500). The Monarchy lasted until Manuel II 'The Unfortunate' abdicated in 1910 and a Republic was declared.

Praça da República, Tomar (Central Camino Stage 6)

Igreja de Bom Jesus da Cruz in Barcelos (Central Camino Stage 17)

CHOOSING YOUR CAMINO

There are several options when it comes to choosing the route of your Camino, depending on the length of time you have at your disposal and your personal interests or preferences.

Central Camino (Caminho Central)

This historic route often follows Roman roads (Via XVI connecting Lisbon to Braga and Via XIX connecting Braga to Astorga) and the itineraries of medieval pilgrims such as Jérôme Münzer (a German doctor, 1494) and Giovanni Battista Confalonieri (an Italian priest, 1594), passing through the Ribatejo, Beira Litoral, Douro and Minho regions before crossing into Galicia in Spain.

To reach Santiago:
- from Lisbon (621km), allow 25 days plus a few rest days to enjoy Tomar, Coimbra and Porto

- from Porto (243km), allow 10 days plus a rest day to explore Pontevedra
- from Tui (117km), just across the border in Spain, allow 5 days. This is a popular starting point for pilgrims with limited time but who want to complete the minimum 100km walking distance to be eligible for the Compostela.

Coastal Camino (Caminho da Costa)

Starting from Porto, the 'younger' Coastal route doesn't always hug the coastline although it's spectacular when it does. King Manuel visited Azurara and Vila do Conde (Stage 1) in 1502 on his pilgrimage (modern-day hikers can visit the churches he instructed to be built). Further north, the Church of Santiago in Castelo do Neiva (Stage 3) has the oldest inscription dedicated to Santiago outside of Spain, dated 862. In

Viana do Castelo (also Stage 3) there's the opportunity to visit the old pilgrim hospital, opened in 1468. On reaching the border in Caminha (Stage 5) there's a choice: either cross the River Minho by boat into Spain then continue to follow the coast to Vigo, connecting with the Central Camino in Redondela; or follow the Minho east and join the Central Camino in Valença.

To reach Santiago:
- from Porto (253/263km), allow 10 to 12 days depending on where you rejoin the central route. If you have time for rest days, consider choosing Viana do Castelo then Vigo to visit the Cíes Islands.
- from Vigo (100km), allow 4 to 5 days. This is the minimum walking distance required to be eligible for the Compostela.

Seaside Path (Senda Litoral)
This seaside route along the Portuguese coastline is a work in progress consisting of sections of boardwalks, esplanades and cycle paths. Although it's not currently possible to follow these paths all the way from Porto to Caminha, the Coastal Camino utilises them on a few occasions.

Spiritual Variant (Variante Espiritual)
An exceptionally scenic route between Pontevedra and Padrón, culminating in an optional boat ride following the maritime *Translatio* route which the boat carrying St James' body and his disciples is believed to have sailed along in AD44.
- Distance (taking the boat): 46.1km – allow 2–3 days, depending on the boat schedule
- Distance (all walking): 77.9km – allow 3 days

Other routes
The following Portuguese routes are not described in this guide:

Fátima route – Caminho de Tejo and Caminho Nascente
The Central Camino from Lisbon follows both blue Fátima waymarks and yellow Santiago waymarks until

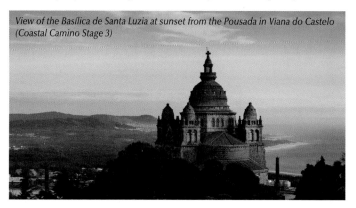

View of the Basílica de Santa Luzia at sunset from the Pousada in Viana do Castelo (Coastal Camino Stage 3)

Santarém, where the two routes split. It's possible to walk from Santarém to Fátima in two days (58km) then one day from Fátima to Tomar (29.5km), rejoining the Central Camino for Stage 7. This is a beautiful yet challenging mountainous Camino; for more information see www.caminho.com.pt

Braga route – Caminho de Braga

This route starts in Porto and travels to the Roman city of Braga, home to Portugal's oldest cathedral, before joining the Central Camino in Ponte de Lima (Stage 18).

Interior route – Caminho Interior

Starting in Viseu, the interior route travels north through Chaves, crossing into Spain near Verín, then connects with the Camino Sanabres leg of the Vía de la Plata.

Other factors

There are other factors to take into consideration when choosing your Camino.

Budget

The number of albergues is increasing year on year and there are plenty from Porto onwards. Between Lisbon and Porto some nights in a private hostel or *pension* will be unavoidable. Expect to pay between €8 and €15 for albergues and between €10 and €35 for hostels and budget accommodation. Food is generally cheaper in Portugal than Spain and if you're travelling as a couple you may even be able to share evening meals as portions are large.

Physical fitness

With just a few exceptions, there is no great elevation gain; there is, however, a considerable amount of walking on

Pastel de nata: *sweet pastries, difficult to resist along the Camino!*

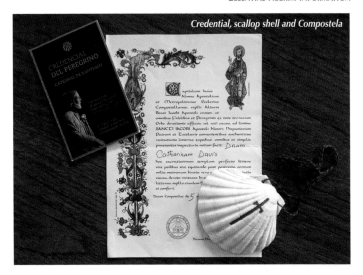

Credential, scallop shell and Compostela

paved and cobbled paths/roads which can be hard on your feet – especially when walking for 6–7 hours, day after day. Some stages may require you to walk more than 25km per day on consecutive days, so a general level of fitness is required. Try to build up your fitness at home by walking on consecutive days and carrying your full pack; this way you can address any niggles and sore spots before starting. The most common problems are blisters, dehydration and back-ache from carrying too much weight, but these issues can be remedied by stopping as soon as you feel a hot spot and applying a plaster, keeping your fluids up and packing as light as possible. Always listen to your body and rest when you need to.

Credential and stamps

Typically, pilgrims collect stamps (*carimbo/sello*) in a *credential*, which is required in order to stay in albergues, and also acts as proof of your pilgrimage, enabling you to receive the Compostela (certificate of completion of pilgrimage) in Santiago.

The all-important credential is available in the following places:

Lisbon
- cathedral, open Mon–Sat 10am–6pm (Oct–Mar); Mon–Sat 9.30am–7pm (Apr–Sep)
- Basílica dos Mártires on Rua Serpa Pinto, open Mon–Fri 9am–6.30pm, Sat–Sun 10am–6.30pm

Porto
- cathedral, open daily 9am–6.30pm

Tui
- cathedral, open daily 10.45am–2pm & 4–8pm (Jul–Sep); Mon–Sat 10.45am–2pm & 4–8pm, Sun 9am–12.45pm & 4–8pm (Apr–Jun); Mon–Sat 10.45am–2pm & 4–7pm, Sun 9am–12.45pm & 4–7pm (Oct–Mar)

If you want to leave home equipped with a credential, contact the pilgrim association nearest you. There is a directory of associations at www.caminodesantiago.gal (English-language option available). You can also purchase one from the store on this popular Camino forum: www.santiagodecompostela.me

You need to collect at least one stamp per day (two during the last 100km) in your credential to be eligible for the Compostela. Stamps can often be obtained from albergues, churches, *turismos* (tourist offices), Junta de Freguesia (parish board)/Câmara Municipal (city hall) in Portugal, museums, cafés, bars, restaurants, government buildings and many other businesses.

Shell

This is a symbol of St James that is carried by many pilgrims, often attached to backpacks. In book five of *The Codex Calixtinus*, the first ever 'Pilgrim's Guide' written in the 12th century about the Camino Frances, there is a record of shells being sold to pilgrims outside Santiago Cathedral. There are many legends relating to how and why the shell became the symbol of St James; one states that as the boat carrying his martyred body approached Galicia, it hit a storm and he was washed overboard only to be found on a beach covered in scallop shells. It is also thought pilgrims used the shell as a scoop for food and water.

If desired, shells can be obtained from various places, including in Porto at the Arte Sacra shop opposite Clérigos Tower, Rua da Assunção no.36; Tui at the Baixo Minho shop on Rúa Ordóñez; or online from www.santiagodecompostela.me

Compostela

This is the official certificate confirming your pilgrimage, provided you fulfil the following requirements: you walked at least the last 100km to Santiago (from Tui on the Central Camino or Vigo on the Coastal Camino); you have a stamped credential (with at least two stamps per day in the last 100km); your motivation for walking was spiritual or religious. Pilgrims with different motivations will receive a document called the 'certificado'.

The Compostela is available in Santiago from the Pilgrim's Office, Rúa Carretas no.33.

Pilgrim etiquette

It's worth remembering at the end of a long day when you're possibly tired, hungry, aching and longing for a bed, that many of the people working in albergues are volunteers who have given up their time to help you. Perhaps the albergue is full and you have to keep walking, but don't despair: the Camino has a way of providing and you may end up with a great story to tell. Respect your fellow pilgrims and the locals, and

Arco da Rua Augusta, Praça do Comércio in Lisbon

cherish the incredible friendships that you'll no doubt form.

Lisbon

By air
Lisbon's Humberto Delgado airport is 7km from the city centre. Its website (www.aeroportolisboa.pt) gives details of flight operators from destinations across the world. Transport from the airport includes:

- metro – a journey of about 20 minutes, at €1.85 (including 50 cents for the 'Viva Viagem' rechargeable card). Take the red line to Alameda then change onto the green line for Rossio (depending on where you're staying). See www.metrolisboa.pt

- bus – the local bus 744 runs every 15 minutes, at €2. You can purchase a ticket from the driver.
- taxi – expect to pay €15–20 to the city centre

By rail
Santa Apolónia or Parque das Nações are the two stations you're likely to arrive at if coming from Porto or abroad. Santa Apolónia is closest to the centre but both have metro connections: see www.cp.pt.

By bus
Bus stations vary by company, the main ones being Sete Rios in the north west of Lisbon (closest metro Jardim Zoologico on the blue line) and Gare do Oriente bus station in the Parque das Nações area. See Eurolines (www.eurolines.com), Rede Expressos (www.rede-expressos.pt), Avanza

23

(www.avanzabus.com) and InterNorte (www.internorte.pt).

Porto

By air

Porto's Francisco Sá Carneiro airport (www.aeroportoporto.pt) is 20km from the city centre. Transport from the airport includes:

- metro – about 30 minutes, at €2.75 (including 60 cents for the 'Andante' rechargeable card). Take the purple line 'E' and get off at Trindade (depending on where you're staying). See www.metrodo-porto.pt
- bus – the local 601 bus runs every 30 minutes and takes 30 minutes, at €2.15 (buy a ticket onboard). Get off at the last stop 'Cordoaria' next to Clérigos Tower.
- taxi – expect to pay €25–35 to the city centre

By rail

Campanhã station is the arrival point for long-distance and international trains, and there are four metro lines connecting this station to the centre. See www.cp.pt

By bus

Bus stations vary by company. See Rede Expressos (www.rede-expressos.pt), InterNorte (www.internorte.pt), Eurolines (www.eurolines.com) and Alsa (www.alsa.es).

Porto and Ponte D Luís I

Blossoms on a country lane near Ansião (Central Camino Stage 8)

Tui

By air

Vigo-Peinador airport (www.aena.es) is the closest airport to Tui, 24km away. From the airport, take a taxi to Vigo or Redondela (about €25), then take a train (www.renfe.com) to Tui. There is also a local bus between the airport and Vigo centre (line L9A, www.vitrasa.es) requiring you to either walk or take a taxi to Vigo Urzaiz train station for onward trains to Tui.

By rail

Tui's train station is 1.3km from the cathedral; see www.renfe.com for information.

By bus

Alsa (www.alsa.es) connects Tui with Porto and Spanish destinations. Monbus (www.monbus.es) connects Tui with Pontevedra.

Leaving Santiago

By air

Santiago's Lavacolla airport (www.aena.es) is 10km from the city. To reach it, there are the following options:

* bus – the local bus 6A departs from Praza de Galicia every 25–30 minutes and takes about 50 minutes, at €1. See www.tussa.org
* taxi – taxis take approximately 15 minutes and cost around €23

Airports in A Coruña (70km north) and Vigo (90km south) are accessible by train then bus/taxi.

By rail

The train station is 1.2km south of the cathedral. There is a Renfe ticket counter inside the pilgrim's office. See www. renfe.com

By bus

The bus station is at Praza de Camilo Díaz Baliño, 1.6km north-east of the cathedral; see www.tussa.org. There's an Alsa ticket counter inside the pilgrim's office (www.alsa.es).

See Appendix C for a list of all transport contacts.

WHEN TO GO

April to October is the most popular time, with peak numbers in July and August which are also the hottest months. Spring brings wildflowers and comfortable walking temperatures but you may also experience days of rain. In summer (with temperatures reaching over 30°C), coastal accommodation is extremely busy and requires advanced booking. In winter many albergues and some coastal hotels close, so plan ahead and expect rain. Although typically drier in the summer months, Galicia is known for its wet weather, so pack a rain jacket or poncho no matter the time of year.

For detailed climate information, see www.ipma.pt (for Portugal) and www.aemet.es (for Spain).

Festivals and annual events

Timing your Camino to coincide with (or avoid) one of the many festivals held in Portugal and Spain may be just as important to you as deciding on where to begin, so the following table should provide a handy reference. There may be additional regional holidays observed.

Month	Day	Festival	Location
Portugal			
January	1	**New Year's Day**	**National**
February/March		Carnival Shrove Tuesday	National
February/March		International Film Festival	Porto
March	19	St Joseph's Day	Santarém
March/April		**Good Friday**	**National**
April	**25**	**Liberty Day**	**National**
May	**1**	**Labour Day**	**National**
	Early	Festival of the Crosses, municipal holiday	Barcelos
	Mid	End of university year 'Burning of the Ribbons'	Coimbra
	Late	May Fair	Azambuja
May/June		**Corpus Christi**	**National**
June	Early	National and Agricultural Fair	Santarém
	10	**Portuguese National Day**	**National**
	12, 13	St Anthony's Day	Lisbon
	23, 24	St John's Day	Porto, Vila do Conde
	Late	Horse fair	Ponte de Lima

Month	Day	Festival	Location
July	Early	Red Waistcoat Festival	Vila Franca de Xira
	Whole month	Agit Águeda Art Festival	Águeda
	Early	International Short Film Festival	Vila do Conde
	4	Saint Isabel Festival and Municipal Holiday	Coimbra
	2023	Festival of the Trays	Tomar
August	**15**	**Feast of the Assumption**	**National**
	Mid	Pilgrimage of Our Lady of Agony	Viana do Castelo
	Whole month	Expect coastal towns to be busy	Coastal Camino
September	Mid	New Fair	Ponte de Lima
	Late	Annual Fair	Vila Franca de Xira
October	**5**	**Republic Day**	**National**
	First half	October Fair	Vila Franca de Xira
	Mid	Beginning of university year 'Can Festival'	Coimbra
	Late Oct/early Nov	National Gastronomy Festival	Santarém
November	**1**	**All Saints Day**	**National**
	First half	National Horse Fair	Golegã
December	**1**	**Independence Day**	**National**
	8	**Feast of the Immaculate Conception**	**National**
	25	**Christmas Day**	**National**
Spain			
January	**1**	**New Year's Day**	**National**
	6	**Epiphany Day**	**National**
March	End	Reconquest of Vigo	Vigo
April	Early	Oyster Festival	Arcade
	Mid	Festivities of San Telmo	Tui
May	**1**	**Labour Day**	**National**
	Mid	Cuttlefish Festival	Redondela
	6	Festivities of St John of Lightning	Padrón
	25	Ascension Festival	Santiago
June	5	Virgin of the Sea Festival	Oia
	13	Rose Festival	Mos
	24	St John's Day	Caldas de Reis
July	11	St Benedict's Day	Pontevedra, O Porriño
	18	St Marina's Day	Baiona
	25	St James Day	Santiago

Month	Day	Festival	Location
August	7	Festivities of San Mamede	Mos, Oia
	15	**Feast of the Assumption**	**National**
	16	Festivities of San Roque	Santiago, Caldas de Reis, Vigo
	Mid	Festivities of the Virgin Pilgrim	Pontevedra
September	25	Festivities of Santísimo Cristo de la Agonía	O Porriño
	26	Festivities of San Cosme and San Damián	Baiona
October	**12**	**National Day**	**National**
November	**1**	**All Saints Day**	**National**
December	**6**	**Spanish Constitution Day**	**National**
	8	**Feast of the Immaculate Conception**	**National**
	25	**Christmas Day**	**National**
		bold denotes national holiday	

To confirm festival dates and for detailed information, contact the local tourist office – see Appendix C.

Holy Year
A Holy or Jubilee year is every year that St James Day (25 July) falls on a Sunday. This occurs every six, five, six and 11 years. The next will be in 2027 and then 2032. During a Holy year, the Holy Door (*Porta Santa*) of Santiago Cathedral is opened and pilgrims may pass through it.

ACCOMMODATION

As a general rule, all accommodation except albergues can be pre-booked and phone numbers/websites are listed in this guide where available. However, the listed options are not exhaustive, and additional accommodation can be found through websites such as www. booking.com as well as local tourist offices (see Appendix C). During peak holiday/festival times and summer, expect small towns and coastal towns along the Coastal Camino to book up.

Albergue
This is accommodation often run by a pilgrim organisation/church/municipality, available only for pilgrims carrying the credential. Albergues usually feature dorm-style accommodation (bunk beds) with communal bathrooms, a place to hand-wash clothes (although increasingly they have washing machines), and most have kitchen facilities. Disposable sheets may be provided and sometimes a pillow, but you are expected to bring a sleeping bag.

Unless privately owned, bookings are not permitted and beds are allocated on a first-come basis. 'Lights-out' is 9 or 10pm, depending on the season, and you are expected to leave by 8am. Some operate on a '*donativo*' (donation) basis, in which case a minimum donation of

Bunks in an albergue at Rubiães (Central Camino Stage 19)

*Albergue de Peregrinos in Alpriate
(Central Camino Stage 1)*

€8–10 is appreciated. Others may be from €8–15, depending on whether they are run by the council or private. Staying in albergues is a great way to get to know your fellow pilgrims and lasting memories can be made through cooking and sharing meals together.

Hostel

These are privately run, often with private rooms in addition to dorm-style accommodation, with communal facilities. They are not exclusive to pilgrims. Prices generally start from €10 and bookings are permitted.

Pousadas de Juventude

Not to be confused with Pousadas (see below), these are youth hostels and are often in great locations, with terrific facilities. They can be used by people of any age or nationality. Prices range from €14–20pp for dorm rooms and some offer discounts to pilgrims with a credential; see www.pousadasjuventude.pt.

Pensão and residencial

Low-budget private accommodation (sometimes rooms in a house or apartment), often with communal bathrooms. Prices vary from €20–40 per room, depending on location.

29

Bombeiros Voluntários (Volunteer Firefighters)

As pilgrim numbers increase, this service has been declining; however, some fire stations still allow pilgrims to use their lodging overnight. Facilities may be basic and/or you may need your own mattress. Enquire at the local tourist office for details. Beds may be free of charge or offered on a donation basis.

Quinta

A *quinta* is a large country house that has accommodation, often similar to a B&B. Prices tend to start from €35 per room.

Pousada and Parador

At the top end of the scale is the restored luxury accommodation in historic castles, convents or palaces. These are called Pousadas in Portugal (www.pousadas.pt) and Paradors in Spain (www.parador.es). Outside of peak periods you may be surprised to find luxurious rooms available from €50; otherwise expect upwards of €75 per room.

FOOD AND DRINK

Portugal

Breakfast (*pequeno almoço*), often served from 7.30am, typically consists of a sweet pastry followed by a coffee. Served in a café, cake shop (*pastelaria*) or bakery (*padaria*), it will cost you €3–4 in a city and less in smaller towns. Lunch (*almoço*) is from 12–2.30pm and for locals tends to be a leisurely three-course meal of the day (*menu do dia*) in a restaurant or pastelaria, costing €10–15. If you want a sit-down meal but not the three courses, there's the plate of the day (*prato*

do dia) at €4–7. Typical main meals include fish/pork/beef with potatoes, rice and vegetables. For a quick lunch, toasted sandwiches (*tosta mista* for ham and cheese, for example) are a cheap and filling option. Dinner (*jantar*), served from 7–9.30pm, can be eaten at BBQ restaurants (*churrasqueira*), bars (*cervejaria*) and seafood restaurants (*marisqueira*) for €8–15. If you're on a budget, a bowl of soup (*sopa*) and basket of bread (*pão*) will set you back about €2–4, or if travelling as a couple, one portion (*dose*) shared between two will usually suffice as portion sizes are large. Half-portions may be available – ask for *meia dose*.

Almost every Portuguese town has their own speciality when it comes to sweet pastries but the most famous of all is the *pastel de nata* (custard tart). The national dish is salted cod (*bacalhau*) and it's said there are more than 365 ways of cooking it! Drinks include wine (*vinho verde* and *Albarinho* from the Minho region are very popular), *Licor Beirão* (a sweet digestif), *ginjinha* (cherry brandy) and port, among others.

Cover charge (couvert)

Unlike free *tapas* in Spain, when you sit down in restaurants in Portugal you are often served small plates of food (olives, cheese, bread, meats) that you haven't ordered. This acts as a cover charge and you will be charged for what you eat, or simply ask for them to be taken away (and you won't be charged).

Spain

Breakfast (*desayuno*), served from 8am, usually consists of a croissant, *churros* (sugary fried stick of dough, often accompanied by a hot chocolate) or toast. A hot drink and pastry/toast will cost around €3–4. Lunch (*almuerzo*), from 1.30–3pm, varies from a sit-down meal of the day (*menú del día*, €8–15) or single-course dish (*plato combinado*, €5–8) in a restaurant, to a filled roll (*bocadillo*) or slice of tortilla in a café/bar. Bakeries (*panadería*) and cake shops (*pastelaría*) also sell savoury snacks, including slices of *empanada* (like an English pastie but filled with seafood/beef/pork/chicken) which cost €3–5. Dinner (*cena*) is usually served from 8–10pm. Many bars offer free small tapas when you buy a drink, and *raciones* are larger portions of tapas, good for sharing with a group.

You'll encounter regional specialities including oysters (*ostras*) in Arcade, cuttlefish (*chocos*) in Redondela, empanadas (Pontevedra's speciality is *empanada de maiz*, made with corn flour), Galician-style octopus (*pulpo a la Gallega*), Padrón peppers (*pimientos de Padrón*) and Santiago almond tart (*tarta de Santiago*). Local drinks include wine (Albarino, Ribeiro, Godello, Mencia and more), *aguardiente* (also known as *orujo* – distilled liqueur with flavours including herbal, coffee, cream and honey), Estrella Galicia beer and Nordés Galician gin, among others.

Pilgrim menus
These are popular in cafés/restaurants along the Camino, often involving a three-course meal including soup/salad, main meal, dessert and wine/water for about €10–15.

Vegetarians
Meat and seafood dominate menus in both Portugal and Galicia, so vegetarians may feel their choices lacking in comparison to those of meat-eaters. Most restaurants serve salads and soup (although note that *caldo verde* comes with sliced chorizo in Portugal), and typical sides include potato, rice and vegetables (often cabbage). Staying in albergues/hostels with communal kitchen facilities will allow you to cook your own meals.

USEFUL INFORMATION

Via Lusitana
Via Lusitana (www.vialusitana.org) is a friendly pilgrim organisation in Portugal with a 24-hour helpline: (+351) 915 595 213. To volunteer as a *hospitalero* or to donate to the association, visit their website for details.

Bedbugs
They may not be a nice thought, but often a topic of conversation along all Caminos is the dreaded bedbug – *percevejos* in Portuguese, *chinches* in Spanish. They live in bedding, are mainly active at night and feed on blood. Check the sheets and around the mattress for signs of rusty/reddish stains, tiny black spots, or eggs. If you think you've been bitten (usually in a row of three, itchier/longer-lasting than a mosquito bite):
• inform the owner of the accommodation where you are (and where you came from if they developed during the day)
• place all of your clothes and sleeping bag in a hot dryer (the hottest setting possible without melting your belongings) for a minimum of two hours

	Portugal	Spain
National emergency number	112	112
International dialling code	+351	+34
Currency	Euro	Euro
Electrical power	220V	220V
Time	GMT (winter), GMT +1 (summer)	GMT +1 (winter), GMT +2 (summer)
Language	Portuguese	Spanish (*Castellano*) is the main language. The Camino enters Spain in Galicia, which also has a regional language called *Galego*
Drinking water	You can fill up your water bottle at accommodation, cafés/bars and *fontes* (springs) unless there is a sign stating the water is non-potable: Portuguese – *água não potável*; Spanish – *agua no potable*	
Internet	Wi-Fi is widely available in cafés, bars, restaurants, accommodation and tourist offices	
Money/banks	Albergues, budget accommodation and many cafés accept cash only. Banking hours are Monday to Friday 8.30am–3pm, but you will find ATMs in most towns	
Museums	Mostly closed on Mondays. Many offer free entrance Sunday mornings	Mostly closed on Mondays
Pharmacy	Typically open Monday to Friday 9am–7pm, and Saturdays 9am–1pm	Typically open Monday to Friday 9.30–2pm and 4.30–8pm, Saturdays 9.30am–2pm
Phones	Some public payphones take coins but many use a phone card, available from post offices and news-stands. Another option is to purchase a prepaid sim card on arrival (Vodafone has shops at Lisbon and Porto airports), or use your existing sim on roaming (check your network charges for this option)	
Post	CTT (Correios, Telégrafos e Telefonos) hours are generally Monday to Friday 9am–6pm. Some city locations may be open at the weekend	Correos hours vary greatly; for smaller locations expect opening times to be Monday to Friday 8.30am–2.30pm and Saturday 9.30am–1pm. For city centre locations hours can be Monday to Friday 8.30am–8:30pm, Saturdays 9.30am–1pm

- place your backpack and anything else that may have come into contact with the bed in a garbage bag and put it in the sun or a hot room if available

- seek advice from the accommodation owners as they may have their own methods of treatment

Some people recommend using a bed-bug liner and bed-bug sleep sheet, but it's no guarantee you won't get bitten.

LANGUAGE

Walking the Portuguese Camino means travelling through Portugal (where Portuguese is the national language) and entering Spain in Galicia, where the regional Galician (*Galego*) language is used in addition to Spanish (*Castellano*). Although English is widely spoken throughout Portugal, the Camino passes through many small villages with an ageing population and you may have difficulty making yourself understood. If you can speak Spanish and speak slowly you will often be understood in Portugal, but the reverse doesn't necessarily apply if you're trying to speak Portuguese and be understood in Spain. English is not as commonly spoken in Galicia as it is in Portugal, so if you don't speak Spanish you may find communication more taxing. Learning a few basic phrases before you set off could make for a smoother journey.

Throughout both Portugal and Spain, most bars and cafés have Wi-Fi, so if travelling with a smartphone you can enlist the help of an online translation tool. Or you can refer to the glossary in Appendix B of this guide, or carry one of the many pocket phrasebooks published by Lonely Planet, Collins, Berlitz and others. If you'd like to do some learning in advance, the BBC has free language lessons at www.bbc.co.uk/languages.

Foreign terms used in this guide

Some foreign words used throughout this guide and their translations include:

Portuguese: *azulejo* (decorative tile), *capela* (chapel), *convento* (convent), *fonte* (drinking fountain), *igreja* (church), *igreja matriz/paroquial* (mother/parish church), *jardim* (garden), *mercado* (market), *moinho de vento* (windmill), *mosteiro* (monastery), *museu* (museum), *parque* (park), *ponte* (bridge), *praça* (plaza), *quinta* (farmhouse).

Galician: *igrexa* (Spanish: *iglesia*/ English: church), *auga* (*agua*/water), *capela* (*capilla*/chapel), *convento* (convent), *fonte* (*fuente*/drinking fountain), *hórreo* (granary), *mosteiro* (*monasterio*/ monastery), *muíño* (*molino*/mill), *museo* (museum), *parque* (park), *ponte* (*puente*/ bridge), *praza* (*plaza*/plaza), *xardín* (*jardín*/garden).

For a more comprehensive list of Portuguese and Spanish terms, see Appendix B.

PREPARATION AND TRAINING

Walking a Camino is a rewarding experience but it can be physically and mentally challenging. Consider taking these few steps before you leave, for a more enjoyable time:

1   If you're buying new shoes or boots, break them in at home
2   Make sure your pack fits comfortably and start wearing it as soon and as much as possible
3   If you're new to walking, start with short distances and increase the distance week by week, then walk longer distances back-to-back at the weekends

If you've had no time to train before leaving for your Camino, remember to take it easy at the beginning and allow your body to adjust.

WHAT TO TAKE

Pack light, as you can buy most things along the way; however, you may find drugs like painkillers and anti-inflammatories more expensive so bring your own. The following is a general guide based on travelling between spring and autumn. If walking in winter, pack a warmer sleeping bag, warmer clothes and good-quality wet-weather gear.

Essential items: passport, travel insurance, credit cards and cash, credential (the credential is also available in Portugal/Spain).

Footwear: whether you wear hiking shoes or light hiking boots, make sure they're broken in and comfortable. You will be walking on earthen tracks, pavements, roads and cobbles. Lightweight sandals or flip-flops are useful for showering in and wearing in the evenings.

Clothes: three sets of socks and underwear is a handy rule that will allow you to wear one, wash one and have a spare. One long-sleeved quick-drying shirt is all you need for walking (long-sleeves provide sun protection), along with an evening top to change into while you wash the walking shirt. One pair of trousers/shorts/skirt is also enough. A fleece is useful for cooler days, early mornings and evenings. Many people wear base-layers or lightweight clothing to sleep in. Stay away from cotton; lightweight and quick-drying synthetics or merino is best and worth the investment.

Raingear: a good rain jacket and rain trouser combination or poncho is essential almost all year round. If you use a rain jacket and rain trousers, consider using a pack cover as well as a dry-bag

liner inside your pack. With a poncho, a dry-bag inside your pack should be sufficient to keep your belongings dry.

Sleeping bag: a lightweight two-season sleeping bag will be fine unless you're walking in winter when you should consider something warmer.

Backpack: along with your footwear, this is the most important thing you'll be taking on the Camino, so it's essential you have a good-fitting, comfortable pack. A 40-litre pack is enough. For evenings, a lightweight daypack or cloth bag is useful.

Water: whether you like to use a bladder or Nalgene bottle, ensure you have something to carry water in.

Headlamp and spare batteries: useful in albergues or starting early to avoid the summer heat. Use the red infrared setting, if possible, in albergues when others are sleeping.

Towel: take a lightweight, quick-drying compact towel.

Electronics: take a European travel adaptor if coming from abroad, and although common-sense, never leave anything unattended while it's charging.

First aid kit: take a compact kit including plasters, painkillers, anti-inflammatories, antihistamines, antiseptic cream, scissors, tweezers, Imodium and any medicine you require on a daily basis.

Toiletries: you'll need shampoo (travel-size bottles or a shampoo bar), multi-purpose soap (for clothes and body), toothbrush, toothpaste, tissues, sunscreen, lip-balm, brush/comb and any sanitary products.

Other gear: consider also taking trekking poles, hat, sunglasses, buff/scarf, antibacterial hand-gel, zip-lock bags (for rubbish), utensils (spork and cup), ear plugs, eye mask, camp-pillow, safety pins (for hanging wet clothes on your pack), needle and thread (for blisters or sewing), clothes pegs.

Luggage transfers
Companies operating a luggage transport service, from accommodation to accommodation, include Tuitrans www.tuitrans.com and Camino Facil www.caminofacil.net (Porto–Santiago) or Paq Mochila through the Spanish postal system, www.elcaminoconcorreos.com (Tui–Santiago).

WAYMARKING AND GPS

If starting from Lisbon, you'll be following blue Fátima arrows as well as yellow Santiago arrows until Santarém when the two routes split. After Santarém, if you're ever unsure whether you're going the right way and you haven't seen a yellow arrow, look behind – if you see a blue Fátima arrow (heading south) you'll know you're on the right track.

For the most part, the Camino is well waymarked with yellow arrows and scallop shell markers, or an 'X' meaning wrong way. *Desvio* means detour and will often be accompanied by a map displaying the available options.

Extra detailed descriptions have been given in this guide for entering/exiting cities as the arrows (on street lamps, behind road signs, painted on the pavement) can easily be hidden behind cars, posters etc. Outside of built-up areas, arrows may be painted on rocks, trees, signs... you'll get used to looking for them everywhere! There

Various waymarks along the Camino; the blue boot signals left for Fátima, right for Santiago

are new brown waymarks on the pavement through many towns on the Coastal Camino in Portugal, although they're not as obvious as the blue/yellow waymarks so you may need to look more carefully.

A GPS is not required, although GPX tracks are available online if you would like to download them to a smartphone or tablet: www.cicerone.co.uk/1196/GPX.

In an effort to move the Central route away from busy roads and highways, the route has been changing and improving with pilgrim-friendly infrastructure each year. Every effort has been made to provide up-to-date, accurate and clear directions, and further updates will be posted online at www.cicerone.co.uk/1196/updates.

USING THIS GUIDE

Each stage begins with an information box giving the start/finish points, distance, total ascent/descent, difficulty rating (easy, moderate or hard – based on a combination of distance, ascent and walking time), duration, details of any cafés and accommodation, and special notes. Distances for cafés and accommodation are cumulative; for example, 'Coimbra (28.7km)' indicates that from the start of the stage to the accommodation in Coimbra is 28.7km, and 'Conímbriga (12km +210m)' indicates that the accommodation is a 210m detour off the Camino.

Following the information box is a short introduction with an overview of the stage, and then detailed route directions. Stage maps are provided at a scale of 1:100,000, as well as elevation profiles. Points of interest along the way are noted, as are any facilities that you may pass. (Prices were updated in spring 2023. Accommodation prices when stated are based on starting prices for one person, and star ratings are 'official' regional ratings rather than recommendations.) Keywords in **bold** in the route description relate to features that you will also see on the map for that stage, so you can cross-reference where you are. The following abbreviations are used: 'KSO' – keep straight on, 'LHS' – left-hand side, 'RHS' – right-hand side, and 'NM' – national monument.

In the route descriptions, distances in brackets (**2.2km**) within paragraphs measure from the previous given distance, while distances at the end of paragraphs – for example **6.2km/22.8km** – represent first the total distance described in that paragraph (6.2km) and then the total cumulative distance for the stage (22.8km).

Throughout the route description, as well as on road signs and many maps, Portuguese national highways have the prefix 'N' followed by the highway number (N1, for example), and 'M' is used for municipal roads (M538). You may also see the same roads denoted with 'En' (*Estrada Nacional*), 'Em' (*Estrada Municipais*) or CM (*Caminho Municipais*).

The Galician spelling of names for places such as churches, chapels and bridges, which differs slightly from the Spanish, is used in the Galician section of the route description as this is what you'll encounter first on signs in that region.

LEAVE NO TRACE

Pilgrim numbers have been increasing year-on-year and the Portuguese Camino is now the second most-walked Camino after the Camino Frances – which, sadly, also means an increase in rubbish along the way. Zip-lock bags are handy for disposing of tissues/rubbish. Leave only footprints!

CENTRAL CAMINO

Cloister in Convento de São Francisco, Santarém (Central Camino Stage 4)

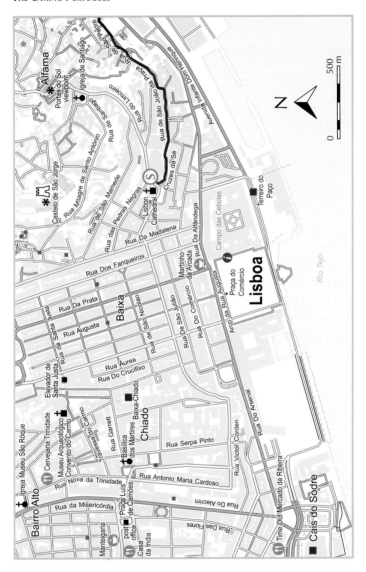

LISBON, 2M, POP. 547,733

View of Castelo de São Jorge from Miradouro de São Pedro de Alcântar

Europe's westernmost capital, Lisbon is a hilly cosmopolitan city by the River Tagus with deep historical roots. Known as 'Olisipo' to the Phoenicians, it was designated a municipium under Julius Caesar, called Felicitas Julia. In 1147 Afonso Henriques 'recaptured' Lisbon from the Moors, and it became the capital from 1255. The city was extensively destroyed on All Saints Day in 1755 by a devastating earthquake (and subsequent fires and tsunami) and rebuilt by the Marquês de Pombal; the Convento do Carmo serves as a haunting reminder.

A ship with two ravens adorns lamp posts, street tiles and Lisbon's coat of arms; it's believed to be from the 12th century when the remains of Lisbon's Patron Saint, St Vincent were brought from the Algarve by ship, followed by two ravens. Lisbon actually has two Patron Saints, St Vincent and the more popularly known St Anthony.

No trip to Lisbon would be complete without visiting the picturesque suburb of Belém, where the caravels set sail on their voyages around the world. Some 8km west of Lisbon's Praça do Comércio, it is home to the UNESCO World Heritage Mosteiro dos Jerónimos and Torre de Belém. It's also the location of the MAAT Museum, Pastéis de Belém (custard tarts) and much more.

Tourist office: Praça do Comércio, tel 210 312 810, and Jardim do Regedor, Rua Jardim do Regedor 50, tel 213 472 134. Both open daily, www.visitlisboa.com.

Visit Lisbon: cathedral (Sé de Lisboa, NM), built after Afonso Henriques captured Lisbon; the first bishop was the English crusader, Gilbert of Hastings. Successive kings added to the cathedral, contributing to its Romanesque, Gothic and Baroque styles. Archaeological excavations in the Gothic cloister have uncovered Iron Age remains dating back to the eighth century BC, as well as Roman streets and Moorish foundations. Open Mon–Sat 10am–6pm (Oct–Mar); Mon–Sat 9.30am–7pm (Apr–Sep), Mass held Sunday 11.30am. Winding up the hill from the cathedral is the church of Igreja de Santiago; originally 12th century, it was largely rebuilt after the earthquake. Castelo de São Jorge (NM), a Moorish castle then royal palace dating from the 13th to 19th centuries; the site includes a museum, archaeological finds dating from the seventh century BC, a restaurant and terrific views – **www.castelodesaojorge.pt**, open daily, €15. Elevador de Santa Justa (NM, 1902), a Neo-Gothic iron elevator designed by an apprentice of Eiffel; open daily, €5.30. Praça do Comércio (NM) was rebuilt by Pombal after the earthquake; the large riverfront square was known as Terreiro do Paço and housed the Royal River Palace (moved from the castle by King Manuel in 1511). The equestrian statue in the middle of the square is King José I and the triumphant Arco da Rua Augusta (completed in 1875) includes statues of Pombal and Vasco da Gama, among others. There's also a tourist office, Lisboa Story Centre (interactive museum recounting Lisbon's history – **www. lisboastorycentre.pt**, €7), Lisbon's oldest café 'Martinho da Arcada' (1778) and ViniPortugal wine-tasting rooms (**www.viniportugal.pt**) in the square. Convento do Carmo (NM) was built by Nuno Álvares Pereira in the 14th century; the Carmelite Convent was all but destroyed in the earthquake, and it now houses an archaeological museum (**www.museuarqueologicodocarmo.pt**). Miradouro de São Pedro de Alcântara, castle and city viewpoint. Igreja de São Roque, dating from the 16th century, is a lesson in not judging a book by its cover: the inside dazzles and it has to be seen to be believed. *Fado*, a style of folk-music meaning 'fate,' involves women dressed in black singing melancholic themes of *saudade* – longing and heartbreak – accompanied by a Portuguese guitar. It's a great night out and there are often some upbeat songs thrown into the mix. Casa de Linhares (**www.casadelinhares.com**) and Clube de Fado (**www.clube-de-fado.com**) are two well-known Fado restaurants in Alfama. Follow Your Destination have walking tours and a variety of other interesting tours: **www. followyourdestination.com**.

Visit Belém: from Lisbon's Praça do Comércio, take the number 15 tram (€3, about 35 minutes) or bus 714 (€2, about 30 minutes).

Mosteiro dos Jerónimos (NM), an awe-inspiring and beautiful monastery, was begun in 1501 under King Manuel I (on top of an existing Order of Christ

Torre de Belém

church) to house the Order of St Jerome and provide spiritual support for seafarers before they set sail. It oozes the King's maritime 'Manueline' style in addition to late Gothic and Renaissance styles. Among the many tombs is Vasco da Gama's opposite the poet Luís de Camões. Allow a few hours at least: **www.mosteirojeronimos.gov.pt**, closed Mondays, entrance €10 (the church alone is free), or €12 for a combined ticket including Torre de Belém. The *torre* (tower, NM) – built as a fortress in the Tagus and commemorating Vasco da Gama's advantageous voyage – was completed in 1520 and drips in Manueline style with twisted ropes, knots, armillary spheres and the cross of the Order of Christ: **www.torrebelem.gov.pt**, closed Mondays, entrance €6. Pastéis de Belém are the best custard tarts (in the world) and use a secret Jerónimos Monastery recipe. Even if you have to queue, it's worth it! Rua de Belém 84–92, **www. pasteisdebelem.pt**. MAAT is the Museum of Art, Architecture & Technology: **www.maat.pt**.

Specialities: *bacalhau* (cod) has been a staple of the Portuguese diet since at least the Age of Discoveries. It was originally fished in Newfoundland, then salted and dried to preserve it for the long sea journeys. Today it is still salted and dried but mostly imported from Norway. One of the many (supposedly 365) ways to cook it is as croquettes called *pastel de bacalhau*. *Ginjinha* is cherry brandy; try it at the original small tavern on Largo de São Domingos, with or without cherries. *O Melhor do Mundo Bolo de Chocolate*, 'the world's best chocolate cake', is sold in slices from a green kiosk of the same name on Av da

Liberdade just before Rua das Pretas. If you can't get to Pastéis de Belém, try the second-best custard tarts at Manteigaria opposite Praça Luís Camões, near Baixa-Chiado metro.

Where to eat: try Time Out Market in Cais do Sodre or Casa da India near Praça Luís de Camões for traditional Portuguese food. At Cervejaria Trindade you can eat in a beer hall in a former 13th-century monastery surrounded by *azulejos* (tiles); touristy but worth it!

Accommodation: Largo da Se Guest House (Calçada do Correio Velho 3, tel 218 861 393, 8 rooms, opposite the cathedral). Lisbon Destination Hostel (Rossio Train Station, second floor, tel 213 466 457, www.followyourdestination.com, shared and private rooms). Lisbon Story Guesthouse (Largo de São Domingos 18, tel 218 879 392, www.lisbonstoryguesthouse.com, 12 rooms, next to Praça Rossio).

Lisbon Cathedral and the start of the Camino

STAGE 1

Lisbon to Alpriate

Start	Lisbon Cathedral
Finish	Albergue de Peregrinos, Alpriate
Distance	21.8km
Total ascent	161m
Total descent	170m
Difficulty	Easy
Time	5–6hr
Cafés	Lisbon, Parque das Nações (7.5km), Sacavém (12.7km), Granja (20.2km +130m), Alpriate (21.8km)
Accommodation	Lisbon, Parque das Nações (7.5km), Alpriate (21.8km)
Note	You can get a credential from Lisbon's cathedral or Basílica dos Mártires. The albergue in Alpriate has limited space (12 beds).
Waymarking	Follow both blue Fátima and yellow Santiago waymarks until Santarém (Stage 4)

Starting at Lisbon's cathedral, this initial stage takes you past the Fado and tile museums before arriving in Parque das Nações with nearby Oriente train station and accommodation – a convenient stop-off if you want more time to explore the city's delights. The route then continues along a scenic esplanade by the River Tagus where you can look out for flamingos, before following the Trancão tributary and ending in Alpriate.

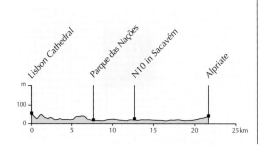

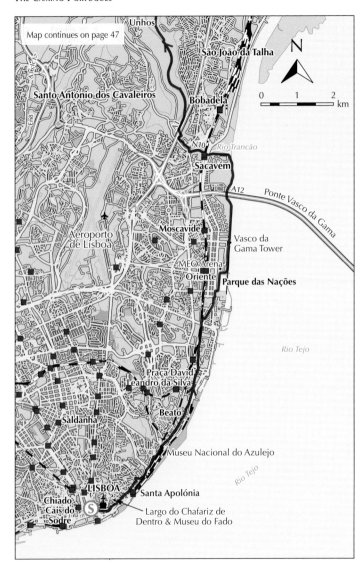

Map continues on page 47

Unhos

São João da Talha

N

Santo António dos Cavaleiros

Bobadela

0   1   2 km

N10   Rio Trancão

Sacavém

A12   Ponte Vasco da Gama

Aeroporto de Lisboa

Moscavide

Vasco da Gama Tower

MEO Arena

Oriente

Parque das Nações

Rio Tejo

Praça David Leandro da Silva

Beato

Saldanha

Museu Nacional do Azulejo

Rio Tejo

LISBOA

Chiado
Cais do Sodre

Santa Apolónia

Largo do Chafariz de Dentro & Museu do Fado

Find the yellow arrow on the bottom right corner of the cathedral entrance facade and take the street to the right, Cruzes da Sé, heading east. Continue into Rua de São João da Praça, through Largo de São Rafael, take the right fork at the orange building onto Rua de São Pedro, then keep right into **Largo do Chafariz de Dentro (580m)**. ▸ Cross the square onto Rua dos Remédios, go uphill and straight into Rua do Paraiso, under an arch, into Rua do Mirante then downhill. KSO across a junction into Rua da Cruz de Santa Apolónia, passing Café Santa Clara (RH corner), and go straight onto Calçada da Cruz da Pedra, passing the Santa Apolonia container terminal (RHS) then taking the right fork onto Rua Madre de Deus. Shortly after, pass the **Museu Nacional do Azulejo**. **2.7km**

The Museu do Fado is across the road: **www. museudofado.pt**, closed Mondays, €5.

This **decorative tile museum** is housed in the opulent 16th-century Mosteiro da Madre de Deus and includes a panoramic Lisbon pre-earthquake cityscape. (Rua da Madre de Deus 4, www. museudoazulejo.pt, closed Mondays, €5.)

Continue under the railway line into Rua de Xabregas, Calçada Dom Gastão, Rua do Grilo, Rua do Beato, then pass old warehouses on Rua do Açúcar. Keep right at the leafy **Praça David Leandro da Silva** opposite the former splendid wine warehouse Abel Pereira da Fonseca (**2.2km**). ▸ Go straight into Rua Fernando Palha. At the next junction cross Av Infante Dom Henrique, turning left then **immediately right** onto Rua do Vale Formoso. Follow this for 1.2km before going through an underpass then take the first right onto Rua Gaivotas em Terra, then left onto Av Fernando Pessoa. Pass a Pingo Doce supermarket (LHS) before reaching a roundabout at the beginning of the **Parque das Nações**. **4.8km/7.5km**

Built in 1917, grapevines surround the large wine barrel-like round windows.

Developed for the 1998 World Expo, **'Nations Park'** includes an Oceanarium, Casino, Vasco da Gama Tower, cable car, gardens, monuments and the impressive Oriente station, designed by Santiago Calatrava.

Accommodation nearby: Pousada de Juventude-Parque das Nações (Rua de Moscavide, tel 218 951 006, **www.pousadasjuventude.pt**, shared and private rooms, kitchen, €17+, +2.1km). Meliã

Lisboa Oriente (Av Dom João II, tel 218 930 000, **www.melialisboaoriente.com**, +1km). ***Hotel Ibis Lisboa Parque das Nações (Rua do Mar Vermelho, tel 210 730 470, **www.ibis.com**, +1.1km). ****VIP Executive Arts Hotel (Av Dom João II 47, tel 210 020 400, **www.viphotels.com**, +1.4km).

Cross the roundabout, passing the large Pavilhão do Conhecimento (science and technology museum, RHS), then turn right through the trees towards the Oceanarium and the River Tagus. ◄ Turn left to follow the river for the next 4km through the expo development. (For Oriente station and Vasco da Gama Mall with shops, supermarket and food court, turn left at the MEO Arena.) Pass the sail-shaped **Vasco da Gama Tower**. Vasco da Gama (1460–1524) was the first explorer to sail from Europe to India. The observation tower (145m) is Lisbon's tallest building. About 800m further

This is the longest waterway in Portugal and Spain, running for approximately 1007km from Spain's Serra de Albarracín to the Atlantic Ocean.

Vasco da Gama tower, Parque das Nações

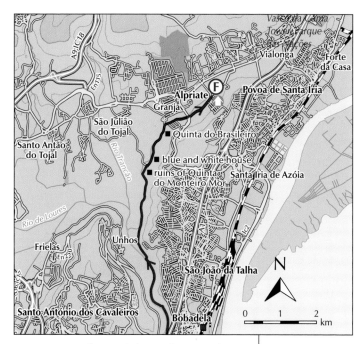

on, pass a statue of Queen Catherine of Braganza then join a wooden boardwalk and go under **Ponte Vasco da Gama** (17km long!). After 1.1km reach the Trancão tributary and turn left, following the tributary under the IC2 and railway tracks (Sacavém station is on the LHS) to reach the N10 in **Sacavém**. ▶ **5.2km/12.7km**

> The slightly hidden petrol station (LHS) sells water and there is a café diagonally left behind the park.

Turn right and cross the bridge, turning left immediately onto a dirt path and down to the river past a Toyota dealership (RHS). Shortly after, turn left onto a paved road, following as it bends right, then left and under a green pipe. Go under the A1 and follow the dirt road then path beside the tributary for 2.7km until the path veers right, away from the river and becomes a dirt road. After a further 2.6km pass the ruins of the large **Quinta do Monteiro Mor** (RHS, 17th century, with occasional obscene graffiti). **6.2km/18.9km**

Veer right here, then in 1.2km pass the dilapidated red **Quinta do Brasileiro** (RHS, with tower) and pass the small bridge (new arrows detour you over the bridge and through **Granja** but don't cross it unless you're going to the café in **Granja** +130m). Join a paved road passing factories then KSO across the roundabout and for a further 850m into Largo de Alpriate, ending the stage at the blue-and-white painted Albergue de Peregrinos (RHS) in **Alpriate**. **2.9km/21.8km**

ALPRIATE, 38M

A peaceful hamlet with two cafés and a welcoming albergue run by Via Lusitana volunteers.

Where to eat: Café Grillus +50m, turn right after the albergue. Also a café +280m, opposite the soccer field.

Accommodation: Albergue de Peregrinos (Largo de Alpriate 13, tel 915 595 213, www.vialusitana.org, 12 beds, kitchen, €8). As at spring 2023, the albergue had not re-opened following the 2022 season. Other options: continue along the camino to Póvoa de Santa Iria and rather than crossing the bridge over the railway tracks, walk to Póvoa train station for frequent services back to Oriente, Parque das Nações; VIP Executive Santa Ira (Estrada Nacional 10, tel 210 032 300, www.viphotels.com, +3.4km).

STAGE 2
Alpriate to Vila Franca de Xira

Start	Albergue de Peregrinos, Alpriate
Finish	Vila Franca de Xira train station
Distance	19km
Total ascent	118m
Total descent	140m
Difficulty	Easy
Time	5hr
Cafés	Alpriate, Póvoa de Santa Iria (3.8km), Praia dos Pescadores (5.2km), Alverca (9.4km), Alhandra (15km), Vila Franca de Xira (19km)
Accommodation	Alpriate, Vila Franca de Xira (19km)
Notes	The route passes Alverca, Alhandra and Vila Franca de Xira train stations, providing options for alternative stages

This stage follows quiet back roads, dirt paths, peaceful boardwalks through wetlands and a short section along the N10 highway before joining a delightful riverside path for the approach to Vila Franca de Xira.

Leaving the albergue, follow the arrows in front of the yellow house then turn right onto Rua da Vinha. After 850m take the right fork onto a farm track and follow this to a paved road then turn right. Just before the tunnel, turn left onto a dirt track. KSO to reach a road (with a car yard in front) and turn right then go under the A1. Continue for 1km to a large roundabout (with a fountain) on the edge of **Póvoa de Santa Iria**. **3.8km**

Take the diagonal right onto the N10 and pass Café Estrela do Tejo (RHS) then take the next left (or KSO to Póvoa train station +700m), crossing a bridge over the railway tracks. KSO across a roundabout onto a dirt path, turning left to cross a wooden bridge then passing abandoned

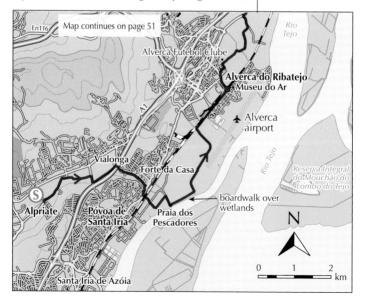

Map continues on page 51

Joining the boardwalk in the Tagus Estuary Riverside Park

This is the beginning of the Tagus Estuary Riverside Park, with a café, picnic area, information boards and boardwalks.

buildings. Follow the footpath as it bends right into **Praia dos Pescadores** (**1.4km**). ◀ Join a boardwalk with the Tagus on the RHS. After passing a bird hide (RHS) cross the bridge, now walking along a path with a canal on the LHS. Cross two more bridges before joining a dirt road parallel to the railway tracks. Go through an underpass and KSO to reach Alverca train station opposite the **Museu do Ar** (Air Museum, open Mondays). **5.6km/9.4km**

Cross over the tracks through the station (café and ATM inside) and KSO onto Av Infante Dom Pedro, passing more cafés before turning right at an apartment block, then immediately left onto Rua 20 de Maio passing a small fountain.

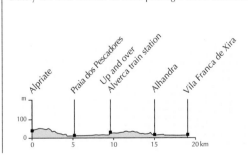

Turn right at the end, then left at the end onto a dirt path behind a school. Shortly after this, turn right to cross the canal and pass behind **Alverca Futebol Clube**, then continue onto a farm track. At a T-junction, turn right onto a dirt road then left onto a paved road at the beginning of an industrial area. After 650m turn left at a T-junction then KSO to a roundabout, turning right onto the N10. **2.7km/12.1km**

Carefully follow the N10 for 2.3km, passing a **Pingo Doce supermarket** and under two industrial chutes, then as the road begins to climb, turn right and cross a bridge over the railway tracks towards the cement works. Alhandra train station is on the RHS.

Turn right at the end of the road towards the 'B.V.A' initials then left at the end onto Av Batista Pereira, passing Restaurant Voltar Ao Cais in **Alhandra**. ▶ **2.9km/15km**

For cafés and services take the second left on Av Sousa Martins.

Continue along the river esplanade then join the red 'Ribeirinho' path with benches, drinking fonts and colourful artwork. After 3.1km pass the Praça de Touros Palha Blanco

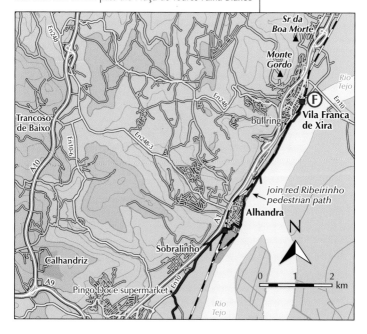

51

Bullfighting monument, Vila Franca de Xira

bullring – across the tracks; built in 1901 and named after its founder – and shortly afterwards pass Vila Franca de Xira's uber-modern municipal library. Continue into Jardim Municipal Constantino Palha until you reach the steps of **Vila Franca de Xira station** (cross the tracks for all services). **4km/19km**

VILA FRANCA DE XIRA, 11M, POP. 122,908

Known throughout Portugal for horse and bull breeding as well as bullfighting, Vila Franca de Xira is a pleasant town with excellent facilities. The two annual celebrations (July and Sep/Oct) include the running of the bulls through the streets.

Tourist office: Rua Alves Redol 7, tel 263 285 605, www.cm-vfxira.pt, closed Sundays.

Visit: Mercado Municipal (1929), a market with beautiful *azulejo* (tile) facade, closed Sundays. Train station (1856) – azulejos line the inside of the station and platforms.

Specialities: Shad river fish, Leziria and Garraios sweet pastries.

Where to eat: Churrasqueira A Canoa for delicious BBQ, a one-minute walk from the town hall. Restaurante O Retiro (slightly further) for traditional meals. Pastelaria Franca Leziria near the station for all things sweet.

Accommodation: Guesthouse Vilatejo, formerly 'Pensão Ribatejana' (Rua da Praia 2A, tel 925 912 679, shared & private rooms, €15+, next to the station). Hostel DP (Rua António Palha 2, tel 926 070 650, shared and private rooms, €20+, modern accommodation near the market). Hospedaria Maioral (Travessa do Terreirinho 2, tel 263 274 370, 10 rooms, €30+, next to the tourist office).

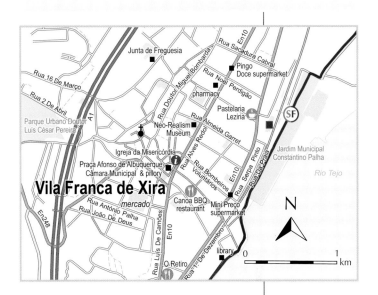

STAGE 3
Vila Franca de Xira to Azambuja

Start	Vila Franca de Xira train station
Finish	Praça do Município, Azambuja
Distance	19.5km
Total ascent	80m
Total descent	75m
Difficulty	Easy
Time	5hr
Cafés	Vila Franca de Xira, Castenheira do Ribatejo station (4.5km) Carregado (7.3km), Vila Nova da Rainha (12km), Azambuja (19.5km)
Accommodation	Vila Franca de Xira, Azambuja (19.5km)
Note	The Camino has been re-routed off the highway in many places; make sure to follow the new arrows

This relatively short stage follows small busy roads, quiet dirt roads parallel to railway tracks, a short section along the N3, and passes no fewer than five train stations. Look out for wildflowers in season.

From the station steps, continue to the end of the municipal gardens, turning right then left onto a minor road. Go under the N10, then after 750m pass the turnoff for the **Sim Tejo factory** (RHS) and take the second right onto a dirt road

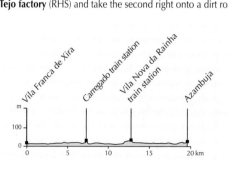

bringing you parallel to the railway tracks. After 1.1km veer right then left around the **electric sub-station**, continuing parallel to the tracks along dirt then paved roads and passing **Castenheira do Ribatejo station** (café inside). **4.5km**

After 1.6km go straight across a roundabout then at the T-junction turn left, then left at the multi-coloured wall and go up and over the tracks at **Carregado station** (**2.8km**). Exiting the station (cafés left and right), turn right, then turn left at the end and follow a canal for 850m before turning right to cross a bridge over the canal. Carefully follow the road for 3.4km (passing the **Carregado Thermoelectric Power Plant**, going under the A10 and past the **Fátima 100km marker**) to reach the N3 in **Vila Nova da Rainha**. **7.3/11.8km**

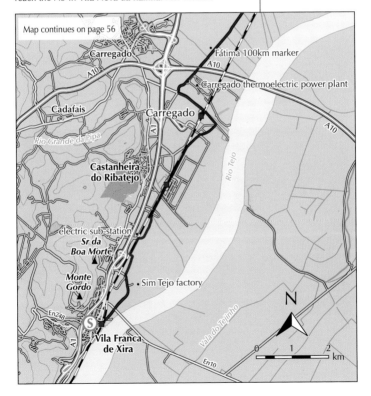

Map continues on page 56

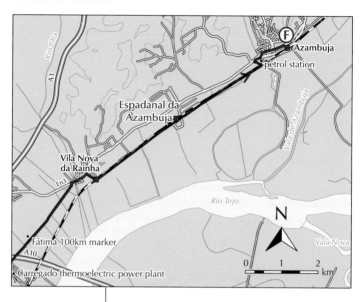

Praça do Município, Azambuja

Turn right onto the N3, pass the popular truck-stop Restaurant O Velhote (RHS) then turn right at traffic lights, following the 'Apeadeiro' sign to Vila Nova da Rainha station. Cross the tracks and turn left onto a dirt road through the gate (going around it if it's locked) and KSO. After 2.8km pass **Espadanal da Azambuja station**, then after a further 2.7km (having passed a water treatment plant and before the next underpass) turn left onto a paved path and go under the railway tracks. On reaching the N3, turn right and pass a **petrol station** with Ouro Hotel behind then turn left at the roundabout. Turn right at the next roundabout onto Av do Valverde, passing the bullring, then KSO onto Rua Eng Moniz da Maia, passing the library and tourist office before arriving at Praça do Município (LHS) in **Azambuja**. **7.7km/19.5km**

AZAMBUJA, 17M, POP. 20,837

Officially settled in the 13th century, the compact town of Azambuja has a small albergue and also celebrates the running of the bulls during its annual May Fair.

Tourist office: Rua Eng Moniz da Maia 29, tel 263 400 476, www.cm-azambuja.pt, open daily.

Visit: Azambuja Municipal Museum, Av do Valverde, www.cm-azambuja.pt, closed Mon–Tues. Igreja Matriz: 16th-century church with 17th-century *azulejos* (tiles) lining the inside walls and a Baroque altarpiece.

Specialities: Stewed or fried eel (*enguias*); delicious *queijadinhas* (almond/lemon tart) from Favorita.

Where to eat: Favorita, opposite the tourist office (closed Mondays). Restaurant Flor de Sal in Atrium Azambuja.

Accommodation: Albergue de Peregrinos (Rua Vitor Cordon 69, tel 914 103 807 (no reservations), 14 beds, kitchen, €10, open 3pm. Ouro Hotel (Antigo Campo da Feira, tel 263 406 530, 37 rooms, €50+, behind the Ouro Negro petrol station). Residencial Flor da Primavera (Rua Conselheiro Frederico Arouca 19, tel 263 402 545 & 965 306 634, www.flordaprimavera.pt, 8 rooms, €35+, on the Camino).

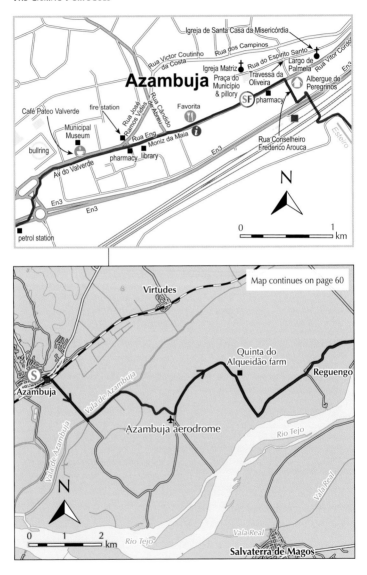

Igreja de Santa Casa da Misericórdia

Rua Victor Coutinho da Costa

Rua dos Campinos

Rua do Espírito Santo

Rua Vitor Cordo

Azambuja

Igreja Matriz

Praça do Município & pillory

Travessa da Oliveira

Largo de Palmela

Albergue de Peregrinos

Café Pateo Valverde

fire station

Favorita

SF

pharmacy

Municipal Museum

Rua José Ramos Vides

Rua Cândido de Abreu

bullring

Rua Eng Moniz da Maia

En3

Esteiro

pharmacy   library

Av do Valverde

Rua Conselheiro Frederico Arouca

En3

En3

N

0   1
km

petrol station

Map continues on page 60

Virtudes

Quinta do Alqueidão farm

Reguengo

S

Azambuja

Vala de Azambuja

Azambuja aerodrome

Rio Tejo

Vala de Azambuja

Vala Real

N

0   1   2
km

Rio Tejo

Vala Real

Salvaterra de Magos

STAGE 4
Azambuja to Santarém

Start	Praça do Município, Azambuja
Finish	Largo Cândido dos Reis, Santarém
Distance	32.5km
Total ascent	212m
Total descent	118m
Difficulty	Medium
Time	8hr
Cafés	Azambuja, Reguengo (10.6km), Valada (13km), Porto de Muge (17.3km), Santarém (32km)
Accommodation	Azambuja, Valada (13km), Porto de Muge (17.9km), Santarém (32.5km)
Note	There are limited services on this stage

This longer stage is mostly along quiet farm tracks (watch out for trucks during harvest time) through Ribatejo's agricultural heartland. Depending on the season, you may see tomatoes, melons, barley, wheat, corn or grapevines. While mostly flat, it finishes on top of a hill in Santarém.

▸ Continue along Rua Eng Moniz da Maia and take the second right onto Rua Conselheiro Frederico Arouca, passing Residential Flor da Primavera (no.19, RHS). Cross the pedestrian bridge over the N3 and railway tracks, then turn left onto a paved road and follow this beside a canal (RHS) and past a picnic area. After 1.4km cross a bridge over the **Vala de Azambuja** canal and immediately turn left onto a dirt path, veering right onto a dirt road beside the canal. Follow this main dirt road for 3.2km, passing fields to reach a paved road and the blue-and-white building of **Azambuja Aerodrome** (RHS). **5km**

Turn left onto the road and after 2.6km pass the farm of **Quinta do Alqueidão** (LHS). After a further 3km pass Café Campino in the small village of **Reguengo** (**5.6km**), then continue beside the concrete/grassy flood wall for 2.1km

Jérôme Münzer (1494) noted that the 'valley between Lisbon and Santarém is very fertile in all productions, especially oil, wine and salt.'

59

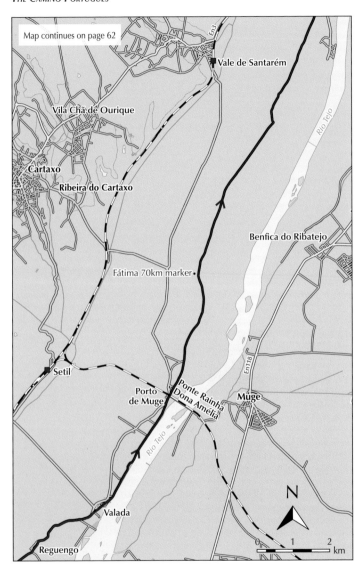

Map continues on page 62

Vale de Santarém

Vila Chã de Ourique

Cartaxo

Ribeira do Cartaxo

Rio Tejo

Benfica do Ribatejo

Fátima 70km marker •

En118

Setil

Porto de Muge

Ponte Rainha Dona Amélia

Muge

Rio Tejo

N

Valada

Reguengo

0   1   2 km

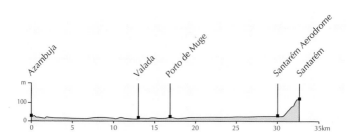

before taking the right fork just before a BP petrol station into **Valada**. If the café in Porto de Muge (4km away) is closed, this is your last chance for provisions until Santarém in 20km. **8km/13km**

VALADA, 12M, POP. 822

A pleasant riverside village with cafés, a post office, ATM and 13th-century church.

Accommodation: Albergue Dois Caminhos (Rua Dom Diniz 4, tel 915 657 651, 6 beds, kitchen, €20 including breakfast).

Pilgrims walking along the flood wall, Valada

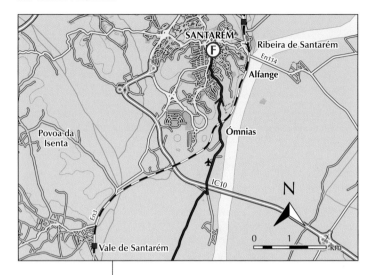

Walk along the concrete flood wall, passing the church at the end of town. After 900m keep left, passing a water treatment plant (RHS), then continue straight for 2.3km before going under Ponte Rainha Dona Amélia in **Porto de Muge (3.7km)**. Café Cardoso (closed Sundays, the last café before Santarém) is 600m further along the Camino, then after a further 600m pass the charming **Quinta da Burra**. Continue, now on a dirt road passing fields (and the **Fátima 70km marker**) for 7km (!) before turning left at a Camino waymark, still surrounded by fields. After a further 3.5km reach a T-junction and turn right, passing a white building (LHS), then turn left onto a paved road and pass a stone flood marker before going under the IC10. **15.7km/28.7km**

Pass **Santarém Aerodrome** then go through **Ómnias** and veer left under the railway tracks to start the 1.6km climb up into Santarém. Pass Fonte da Junqueira half-way (LHS, 1835, ruins) then at the top of the hill veer left (opposite Café Botequim) then turn right onto Rua Pedro de Santarém. Soon after, reach the large roundabout (with W shopping centre and the Santa Casa da Misericórdia building) on the edge of Santarém's old town, Largo Cândido dos Reis. **3.8km/32.5km**

SANTARÉM, 118M, POP. 63,563

Known as Scallabis to the Romans (Roman ruins can be seen next to the Portas do Sol gardens), the name 'Santarém' originates from Santa Iria after the martyred nun's body washed up on the banks of the Tagus from Tomar in the seventh century. After four centuries of Moorish rule (eighth to 12th centuries) Santarém was conquered in 1147 by Portugal's first king, Afonso Henriques. It is now considered the Gothic capital of Portugal, owing to a number of churches from this period.

Tourist office: Rua Capela Ivens 63, tel 243 304 437, www.cm-santarem.pt, open daily.

Painted ceiling of Santarém's cathedral

Visit: cathedral and museum, built in the 17–18th century on top of the ruins of the royal palace (interestingly, one lonely Manueline window remains above a shop opposite the cathedral), featuring a magnificent painted ceiling, Praça Sá da Bandeira – www.museudiocesanodesantarem.pt, open daily, €4. Convento de São Francisco, 13th century, Gothic, beautiful cloister. Igreja de Nossa Senhora da Graça, 14th century, Gothic, stunning rose window, contains the tombstone of Brazil's discoverer, Pedro Alvares Cabral. Igreja de Nossa Senhora de Marvila, striking Manueline facade, the interior is covered in 17th-century azulejos (tiles). Igreja de Santa Maria da Alcáçova, a Roman site later used as the Knights Templar headquarters then a Royal Chapel. Mercado Municipal (1930), covered in a set of 63 azulejo panels. Jardim das Portas do Sol, Roman ruins, castle walls and River Tagus viewpoint.

Specialities: fish soup (*sopa de peixe*), eels (*enguias*). Sweet: Celestes of Santa Clara, Arrepiados of Almoster (delicious almond biscuit).

Where to eat: Taberna Sebastião in the old town. Café Bijou near the cathedral for all things sweet.

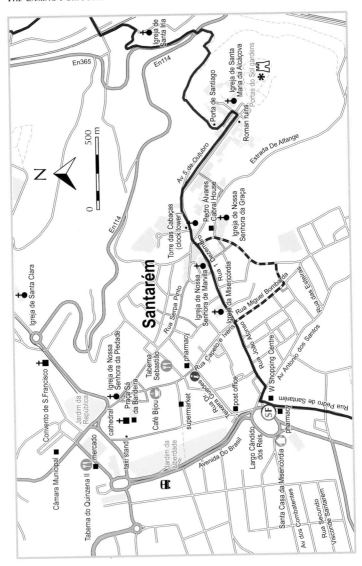

STAGE 5 – SANTARÉM TO GOLEGÃ

Accommodation: Villa Graca (Rua 1º de Dezembro 7, tel 243 327 127, www.villagraca.pt, shared and private modern accommodation, kitchen, €25+). Santa Casa da Misericórdia (Largo Cândido dos Reis, tel 243 305 260, private rooms with shared bathrooms, €5, checkout at 6.30am – the accommodation was temporarily closed as at spring 2023, so check in advance). N1 Hostel, apartments and suites (west of the old town on Av dos Combatentes 80, tel 243 350 140, www.n1hostelapartments.com, shared and private modern accommodation, €20+). Casa da Alcáçova (Largo da Alcáçova 3, tel 936 080 100, www.alcacova.com, 8 rooms in a 16th-century manor house, entrance next to Portas do Sol gardens).

STAGE 5
Santarém to Golegã

Start	Largo Cândido dos Reis, Santarém
Finish	Igreja Matriz, Golegã
Distance	34.2km
Total ascent	158m
Total descent	270m
Difficulty	Medium
Time	8–9hr
Cafés	Santarém, Vale de Figueira (11.5km), Pombalinho (22km), Azinhaga (26.6km), Golegã (34.2km)
Accommodation	Santarém, Azinhaga (26.6km), Golegã (34.2km)
Note	If arriving during Golegã's Annual November Horse Fair, pre-book accommodation (months in advance) or change the stage accordingly
Waymarking	The waymarks split in Santarém; blue lead to Fátima and yellow to Santiago

After departing Santarém through the ancient Santiago Gate and following an initial steep descent, this stage meanders along low-lying farm tracks, passing agricultural fields and stud farms. Although it is a long stage, there is only one climb up into Vale de Figueira.

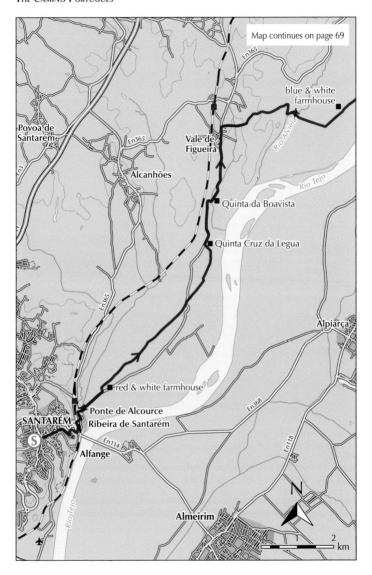

Map continues on page 69

En365

blue & white
farmhouse

Povoa de
Santarém

En365

Rio Alviela

Vale de
Figueira

Alcanhões

Rio Tejo

Quinta da Boavista

Quinta Cruz da Legua

Alpiarça

En365

red & white farmhouse

Ponte de Alcource
Ribeira de Santarém

SANTARÉM

En368

En118

En114

Alfange

Rio Tejo

N

Almeirim

2

1

km

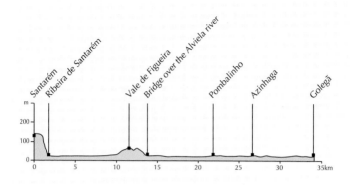

From Largo Cândido dos Reis, follow the 'Portas do Sol' signs
and turn left onto Rua João Afonso. Follow the arrows right
down Rua Miguel Bombarda for a short alternative route, or
more simply KSO and pass the Igreja da Misericórdia then
Igreja de Marvila, then turn right at the end onto Rua de S.
Martinho. Pass the Torre das Cabaças then shortly afterwards
go through the avenue of trees on Av 5 de Outubro. Just
before reaching Jardim das Portas do Sol, turn left onto Largo
da Alcáçova then left onto Travessa de Santiago. Go through
the Porta da Santiago then downhill on a steep woodland
path for 380m, taking the left at the fork and ignoring the
X on the metal bollard. At the road turn left, then take the
lower right fork. Arrows are lacking but take the first right
onto an old road, going downhill and doubling back, then
turn left at the end and follow the railway tracks into **Ribeira
de Santarém**. 1.6km

Turn right at the railway crossing then turn left at the
end, and shortly afterwards cross the white 14th-century
Ponte de Alcource. Continue right onto a paved road and
after 700m turn left at the **red-and-white farmhouse** (LHS),
then turn right onto a farm track behind the house. Walk
through fields and grapevines for 3.3km before joining the
paved road again briefly, then turn right onto a dirt road.
Continue through fields for 1.6km to a T-junction and turn
left (still on a dirt road), then reach the paved road and turn
right to pass an old *quinta* ('Cruz da Legua' farmhouse, RHS).
Follow the road for 1.2km past the grand entrance of **Quinta**

da Boavista (RHS) then for a further 3km and uphill into **Vale de Figueira**. **9.9km/11.5km**

This blue-and-white parish council building next to the church provides stamps and has an ATM.

Pass the Junta de Freguesia (LHS). ◄ Pass Café Val Doce opposite (delicious toasted sandwiches), then turn right at Café O Sibuca (RHS) onto Rua do Sobral. On reaching a fork with a green gate, veer left then turn right at the end and descend the hill along a forest road. After 1km veer left then right around a white building (with red roof, RHS) then after a further 530m cross a bridge over the **River Alviela**. **2.8km/14.3km**

Once again in fields, 920m after crossing the bridge turn left through two posts then pass a **blue-and-white farmhouse** (LHS). After another 2km reach a T-junction and turn left onto a dirt road, then after a further 1.3km turn right at a cross-roads onto a small road (**5km**). Follow this for 940m, turning right at the end onto the N365. Carefully follow the N365, passing **Ponte Sobre a Alverca de Fernão Leite** with picnic area, before entering **Pombalinho**. **7.7km/22km**

Statue of José Saramago, Largo da Praça, Azinhaga

Pass a few cafés before taking the right fork at **Igreja de Santa Cruz** onto Rua Manuel Monteiro Barbosa, passing Jardim Pombalinho. After 650m take the diagonal right at a junction onto a dirt road and continue for 3.1km before join-ing a paved road beside the peaceful River Almonda. Follow the arrows for a further 600m to Largo da Praça with cafés, ATM and José Saramago statue in **Azinhaga**. **4.6km/26.6km**

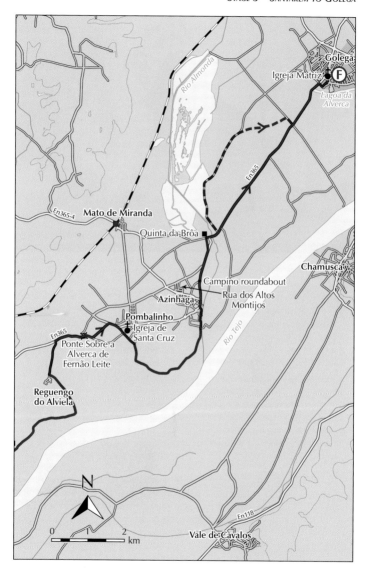

Carlos Relvas studio-house, Golegã

AZINHAGA, 27M, POP. 1620

Still a 'small village', as the Italian priest Giovanni Battista Confalonieri described it after his pilgrimage in 1594, Azinhaga is the birthplace of Portugal's famous author and Nobel Laureate, José Saramago (1922–2010). The José Saramago museum is on Largo das Divisões, www.josesaramago.org, closed Sun–Mon. Cafés and an ATM surround Largo da Praça.

Accommodation: Albergue de Peregrinos de Azinhaga (Rua do Espírito Santo 19, tel 919 209 621, 4 beds, donation, a friendly new albergue on the Camino with a communal dinner). Casa da Azinhaga (Rua da Misericórdia 26, tel 249 957 146, 7 rooms, €30+, ivy-covered building on the Camino). Casa de Azzancha (Rua dos Altos Montijos 68, tel 919 187 773, shared (€30+) and private rooms (€65+), 1km west of the Camino).

Follow Rua da Misericórdia, passing Casa da Azinhaga guest house (LHS), then continue out of town and straight across the roundabout (with traditional *campino* herdsman statue) onto the verge of the N365. After 1.2km, pass the stately **Quinta da Brôa** then cross a bridge over the Almonda. Now you have a choice: either carefully KSO along the N365 for the next 5km, or take the next left to avoid 3.6km on the N365 (1.2km longer, no waymarks) along a small road and farm track.

To detour on small road and farm track
Turn left onto Estrada dos Lazaros CM1. After 3.2km take the right fork onto a farm track, then after 1.4km reach a T-junction and turn right. Shortly afterwards turn left onto the N365 and continue for the final 1.7km into Golegã.

After passing **Alverca Lagoon** (picnic area, kiosk and WC) turn right at the crossroads onto Rua do Campo. Follow this left and uphill to the impressive Igreja Matriz in **Golegã**. **7.6km/34.2km**

GOLEGÃ, 33M, POP. 5710

Horse signs, stables, an equestrian centre and the National Horse Fair (since the 16th century) are testament to Golegã's status as Portugal's horse capital. Historically a stop along the Royal Road to Coimbra, Napoleon's troops also stayed here in 1808 on their way to capture Lisbon. Surrounding the Igreja Matriz are cafés, an ATM, a pharmacy and a tourist office.

Tourist office: Rua Dom Afonso Henriques (behind the Igreja Matriz), tel 249 979 002, **www.cm-golega.pt**, closed weekends.

Visit: Igreja Matriz (NM), 15–16th century, Gothic with an elaborate Manueline entrance and beautiful *azulejos* (tiles). Carlos Relvas studio-house, a striking 19th-century iron and glass home/photographic studio of the wealthy farmer born in Golegã in 1838, Largo D Manuel I – closed Mondays, guided tours only.

Specialities: *Torreiros* (bullfighter) sweets from Café Central, *abafado* fortified sweet wine.

Where to eat: Páteo Da Gallega (opposite the square) and Adega Ribatejana (near Hotel Lusitano) for great value Portuguese food.

Accommodation: Albergue Solo Duro & Casa da Tia Guida (Rua José Relvas 84/86, tel 935 640 550, albergue with kitchen €15+, B&B rooms €35+). Inn Golegã (Rua Dr Rafael da Cunha 17, tel 964 327 312, shared and private rooms, kitchen, €18+). ****Hotel Lusitano (Rua Gil Vicente 4, tel 249 979 170, **www.hotellusitano.com**, 24 rooms, €100+).

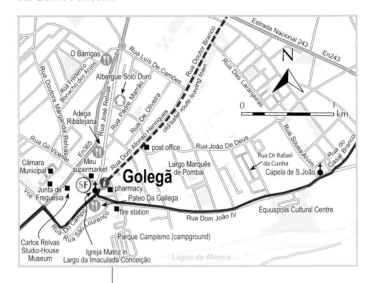

STAGE 6

Golegã to Tomar

Start	Igreja Matriz, Golegã
Finish	Praça da República, Tomar
Distance	30.4km
Total ascent	425m
Total descent	397m
Difficulty	Medium
Time	8–9hr
Cafés	Golegã, Atalaia (10.8km), Asseiceira (19.2km), Casal Marmelo (25.3km), Tomar (30.4km)
Accommodation	Golegã, São Caetano (5.8km), Atalaia (10.8km), Tomar (30.4km)

Small but busy roads bring us to the land of the Knights Templars and the intriguing Quinta da Cardiga. After leaving Atalaia, the route climbs through a eucalyptus forest and then descends into Asseiceira before following the N110, but only for 2km. It then passes through more small hamlets before arriving in the incredible city of Tomar.

On leaving Golegã there are two options:

New waymarks along busy roads
Turn right at the Igreja Matriz onto Rua D João IV. After 950m pass the Equuspolis cultural centre then take the next left fork onto Rua do Casal Branco. KSO across a roundabout onto the CM1183 and carefully follow this for 4.2km to reach the **Terra de Templarios monument**.

Old waymarks along backroads (200m shorter)
Go through the square to the left of the Igreja Matriz onto Rua D Afonso Henriques, passing the tourist office. After 840m carefully cross the N243 onto a dirt road, then after 500m KSO across a minor road. Reach the CM1183 after 1.3km and turn left, rejoining the Camino. After 2.7km reach the **Terra de Templarios monument**.

The monument, which commemorates the surrounding land that was donated to the religious military Order of the Knights Templars by King Afonso Henriques in 1169, is at the entrance to the peaceful hamlet of **São Caetano** (**5.8km**). ▸ Shortly after the hamlet, reach **Quinta da Cardiga**. **0.7km/6.5km**

Bar (irregular hours) and Albergue Casa São Caetano (Largo São Caetano 30, tel 914 951 076, 3 rooms, €20+, dinner available on request for €10).

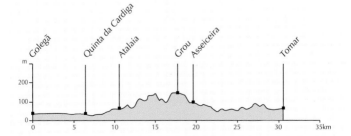

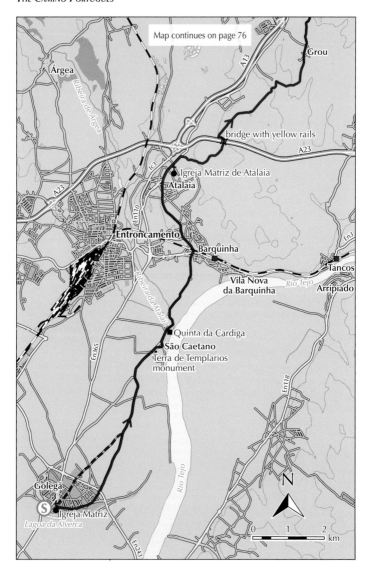

Map continues on page 76

Grou

Árgea

Ribeira de Árgea

A13

bridge with yellow rails

A23

Igreja Matriz de Atalaia

Atalaia

IC3

En110

A23

Entroncamento

Barquinha

Tancos

Vila Nova
da Barquinha

Rio Tejo

Arripiado

En3

Ribeira da Atalaia

En365

Quinta da Cardiga

São Caetano
Terra de Templarios
monument

En118

Rio Tejo

N

Golegã

S Igreja Matriz

Lagoa da Alverca

En243

0   1   2
km

Originally a castle, Quinta da Cardiga was built by the Knights Templars to defend the Tagus in the 12th century; the reformed 'Order of Christ' took ownership in the 14th century, then in the 16th century additional buildings were added including a royal chapel and cloister. Confalonieri ate here in 1594, describing it as a 'royal palace, with good possessions, belonging to the Friars of Tomar'.

Quinta da Cardiga between Golegã and Tomar

Pass the *quinta* and cross the bridge, turning left. Follow the dirt road for 2km then pass a school and KSO across the N3 (on the edge of Vila Nova da Barquinha) and across the railway tracks, turning left. Take the diagonal right at the roundabout onto Rua D Afonso Henriques, then after 1.4km pass Café Monteiru (RHS, closed Sundays) and turn left onto Rua Paulino José Correia. Keep right, passing a small fountain. ▶ Continue into **Atalaia. 4.3km/10.8km**

Take the left fork for Restaurante Stop, +270m, at the end on the LH corner, Rua Patriarca Dom José 90–92, tel 249 710 691, closed Tuesdays.

Merge right onto Rua Patriarca Dom José (N110), passing Casa do Patriarca (RHS, no.134, tel 249 710 581, 6 rooms in a 17th-century house, €30+) then the **Igreja Matriz** (NM, 16th century, Renaissance, lined with early 17th-century *azulejo* tiles). Leaving Atalaia, KSO for 550m before

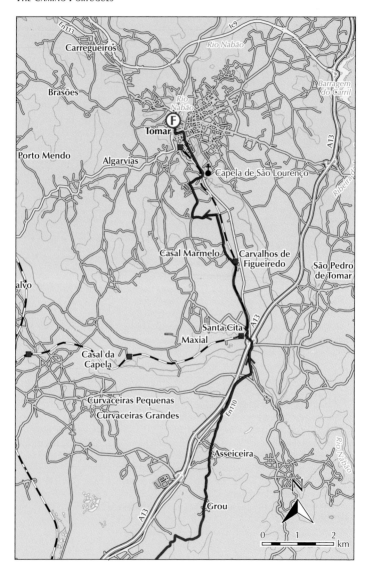

turning right onto a forest road, then veer left and uphill into the eucalyptus forest. ▶ After 700m KSO across a dirt road, downhill then after 600m cross a **bridge with blue rails** over the A23. Follow the dirt road (initially bending left) for 200m, then turn right and climb up a rocky track. After 1.2km reach a junction (149m altitude) and turn left then immediately right, and downhill for 1.2km to reach a junction with a wire fence (LHS). Turn right here onto a dirt road, going uphill past a farmhouse (RHS), then veer left and after 1.1km enter the hamlet of **Grou**. Continue past its modern-looking church and downhill for 1.5km to the next village, passing Café Terraça in **Asseiceira**. **8.4km/19.2km**

Look carefully for the arrows on trees, poles and rocks.

Soon afterwards pass Café Moço and KSO through Asseiceira. Reach the N110 and turn right, carefully walking along the shoulder for 2.2km until you reach a roundabout. Turn left, go under the A13 then continue straight across the next roundabout. Take the first right then cross a bridge over the railway tracks (**Santa Cita station** is on the left) and after 60m turn right onto a dirt road. Follow this parallel to the railway tracks for 1.8km then KSO onto a paved road, uphill into **Casal Marmelo**. **6.1km/25.3km**

After a further 1.2km turn left at a T-junction, heading gradually uphill. Turn right at the crossroads then carefully follow this road for 1km before turning right at a sign for S. Lourenço, going downhill to the railway tracks. Go through the underpass and turn left onto the N110 (be careful on this corner), passing **Capela de São Lourenço** (NM).

Dating from the 16th century, the **capela**'s side azulejo panel celebrates the 14th-century meeting of two Portuguese armies on their way to the Battle of Aljubarrota against the Crown of Castile. The Portuguese were victorious, assuring their independence.

Note the monument to 'Festa dos Tabuleiros', when women carry tall heavy reed baskets filled with bread and flowers on their heads.

KSO for another 1.3km to the second roundabout. ▶ Turn left here onto Av Dr. Cândido Madureira, then take the second right onto Rua de Infantaria 15 and KSO to Igreja de São João Baptista opposite Praça da República in **Tomar**. **5.1km/30.4km**

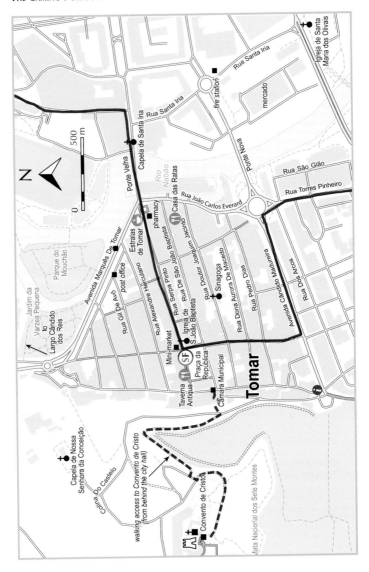

TOMAR, 71M, POP. 40,677

Known as Seilium to the Romans, the Tomar we see today is an enchanting city beside the River Nabão, watched over by the Knights Templar Castle. Gualdim Pais, the first Master of Portugal's Order of the Knights Templars, founded Tomar in 1160, building the castle which would become their headquarters. In the early 14th century the Order was disbanded by the Pope and reformed as the Order of Christ under King Dinis. Münzer (1494) noted that Tomar had a superb castle that Prince Henry had decorated well, and Confalonieri (1594) described it as one of the most beautiful he'd ever seen.

Tourist office: Av Dr. Cândido Madureira, tel 249 329 823, **www.cm-tomar.pt**, open daily.

Visit: Convento de Cristo, UNESCO World Heritage, former Knights Templar Castle. The highlight is the breathtaking 12th-century *charola* (rotunda), possibly influenced by Jerusalem's Church of the Holy Sepulchre and added to by successive kings. In the 15th century Prince Henry (the Navigator) built his court in the convent, then in the early 16th century King Manuel I added new buildings. Of particular note is the chapter house window (Janela do Capítulo) decorated with 'Manueline' maritime motifs. Another addition to the convent was the 6km aqueduct with 180 arches, completed in 1619. **www. conventocristo.gov.pt**, open daily, €6. Access: go up the stairs behind the Câmara Municipal (city hall) and onto a woodland path to the top of the hill. Igreja de São João Baptista, 15–16th century, facing the main square and built on 12th-century ruins, with a Gothic facade, clock tower, intricate Manueline doorways and 16th-century paintings by the artist Gregorio Lopes. Sinagoga (NM), 15th century, the oldest in Portugal, was closed in the late 15th century following the expulsion of Jews and became a jail then warehouse, now a museum. Igreja de Santa Maria dos Olivais (NM), 13th century, Gothic, built on top of a former Benedictine monastery. Gualdim Pais and later Masters of the Order are buried here. Capela de Santa Iria, 16th century, honouring Tomar's legendary Patron Saint Iria (the nun who was murdered in the seventh century and thrown into the Nabão, giving Santarém its name). Parque do Mouchão is a peaceful island with castle views.

Specialities: *beija-me depressa* sweets and *estralas de Tomar*, almond tart from Estralas de Tomar, Rua Serpa Pinto.

Where to eat: Casa das Ratas, great value Portuguese food in atmospheric surroundings. Taverna Antiqua, medieval-themed restaurant opposite the square.

Igreja de São João Baptista, Praça da República, Tomar

Accommodation: Hostel 2300 Thomar (Rua Serpa Pinto 43, tel 927 444 144 & 249 324 256, **www.hostel2300thomar.com**, shared and private rooms, kitchen, €20+, centrally located friendly hostel). Residencial União (Rua Serpa Pinto 94, tel 249 323 161, 18 rooms, €35+, central location). Thomar Story Guest House (Rua João Carlos Everard 53, tel 249 327 268, **www.thomarstory. pt**, 12 rooms, €45+, modern rooms in a converted 19th-century building). ****Hotel dos Templários (Largo Cândido Dos Reis 1, tel 249 310 100, **www. hoteldostemplarios.pt**, 176 rooms, €69+).

STAGE 7
Tomar to Alvaiázere

Start	Praça da República, Tomar
Finish	Igreja Matriz, Alvaiázere
Distance	32.5km
Total ascent	736m
Total descent	478m
Difficulty	Medium
Time	8–9hr
Cafés	Tomar, Soianda (8.6km), Calvinos (10.6km), Tojal (22.5km +180m), Alvaiázere (32.5km)
Accommodation	Tomar, Cortiça (25.8km), Alvaiázere (32.5km)

This stage includes the greatest elevation gain yet, so have a hearty breakfast, pack some snacks and get ready for undulating paths as the Camino moves into a changing landscape dotted with olive groves, forest and sections of the Via XVI Roman road.

From Praça da República, turn right onto the pedestrianised Rua Serpa Pinto and cross Ponte Velha over the River Nabão. Take the second left onto Rua do Centro Républicano then take the right fork, uphill on Rua da Fábrica de Fiação. Shortly afterwards there are two sets of arrows painted on a pole (both options are waymarked and the same length).

Winter route along roads
Turn right onto Av Dr Egas Moniz then after 450m turn left at the bullring and immediately right, uphill on António Duarte Faustino. Go through the car park, and straight across the road, pass an Infantry Regiment then take the right fork at a white apartment building (with two cafés underneath) onto Rua da Vincennes. Take the first left, downhill then the second left onto Rua Ponte de Peniche which after 800m brings you to **Ponte de Peniche (3.2km)**.

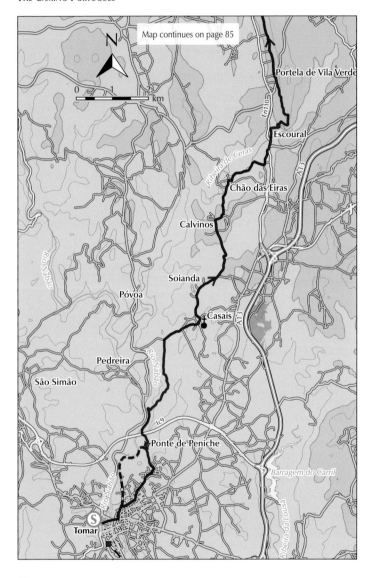

Map continues on page 85

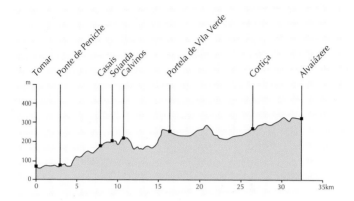

Summer route along a riverside track (muddy after rain)
KSO into Rua Ponte da Vala, beside a canal (LHS) then onto
a dirt road which becomes a peaceful woodland path beside
the Nabão. Follow the arrows painted on trees for 2.2km
until you reach a dirt road, then turn left and shortly after
reach **Ponte de Peniche (3.2km)**.

Cross the bridge then KSO uphill along the dirt road and
under the IC9. After 700m, pass a house then an abandoned

*A pilgrim crossing
Ponte de Peniche,
between Tomar
and Casais*

building (LHS) and turn right, doubling back, and uphill. Follow the dirt road for a further 2.3km to a paved road. Turn right, downhill and take the right fork into **Casais**. Turn left at a pharmacy then pass the church and continue for 800m into the next village, reaching Café Balrôa in **Soianda**. **5.4km/8.6km**

Continue through Soianda then take the left fork, following signs to Calvinos. After a rollercoaster downhill then up, follow the arrows through **Calvinos** (**2km**) and just before leaving, pass Café Cabeleira (LHS). Go downhill and follow undulating roads through the next village of **Chão das Eiras**, and on reaching the N110 (**3.4km**) turn left onto a parallel road. Soon afterwards, join the N110 briefly before turning right onto Rua Lagar da Boucha, then cross a small bridge and turn right onto Estrada Romana. Turn right onto Rua das Azenhas then veer left at the sign 'Camino Portela' and uphill along a forest road for 800m, before turning left and starting to descend. Soon join a paved road and follow this through **Portela de Vila Verde**. **8km/16.6km**

Turn left at a bus stop onto Estrada das Galegas then KSO for 2.1km before merging right onto Estrada da Daporta, uphill. After 600m turn left onto Rua do Casal dos Grilos then turn right onto a forest road, and after 350m take the upper right fork. After a further 900m turn left (293m altitude), descend for 800m, then pass behind a church (LHS) and keep right along a grassy track and through a cork oak forest.

Portugal is the world's largest **cork producer**. Harvesting occurs every 9–10 years and is done by peeling the bark, exposing a red undercoat. Numbers painted on the trees indicate the next year of harvest.

Or KSO along the N110, +180m for Café Tojal Douro, opposite the petrol station.

On reaching the N110, turn right then left at the crossroads onto the N348. ◄ Follow this for 3.3km, passing olive groves, until you reach the noticeable tower of **Quinta da Cortiça** (Rua do Caminho de Santiago 88, tel 926 923 994, www.quintadacortica.pt, 14 beds, €20+, kitchen, premade meals/ingredients available for purchase) in **Cortiça**. **9.2km/25.8km**

Turn right at the *quinta* then after 800m turn left onto a cobbled road at a sign for Outeirinho. Continue along

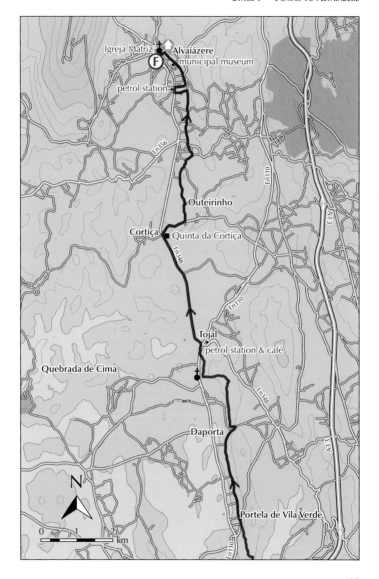

Igreja Matriz — Alvaiázere
F — municipal museum
petrol station

En356

Outeirinho

Cortiça — Quinta da Cortiça

En348

En110

Tojal
petrol station & café

Quebrada de Cima

En348

Daporta

N

0   1   km

Portela de Vila Verde

En110

A13

En110

85

Cork oak forest before Cortiça

cobbled, paved and dirt roads for 2.4km through **Outeirinho** and to the N356, turning left then immediately right onto Rua do Sobreiral. Continue straight for 1.4km to a concrete barrier, perhaps replaced by steps as the Camino continues straight on. If not, turn left onto Rua Rego de Água then right onto the N348, and after passing the **petrol station**, turn right. On reaching the roundabout (where you could've come down had it not been for the barrier, saving 800m), turn left. KSO for 1.1km, passing the **Municipal Museum** (LHS) and Restaurant & Residencial O Bras (RHS). Reaching Albergaria Pinheiro (above the laundrette), turn left to end the stage at the **Igreja Matriz. 6.7km/32.5km**

ALVAIÁZERE, 320M, POP. 8438

Alvaiázere's Arabic name comes from its Moorish rule from the eighth century. There's not a lot to see except for the Municipal Museum (closed Mondays), which has a fascinating archaeological collection dating back to the Palaeolithic era. There are cafés, a pharmacy, and an ATM on the N348.

Tourist office: inside the town hall next to the church, Praça do Município, www.cm-alvaiazere.pt, closed weekends.

Specialities: olive oil, *chicharo* (chickpea).

Where to eat: Restaurant O Bras on the Camino serves a hearty meal. Café Flor da Serra, on the Camino.

Accommodation: Residencial O Bras (Rua 15 de Maio no.18, tel 236 655 405, www.residencialobras.com, 11 rooms, €15+, rooms above the restaurant). Albergaria Pinheiro (Rua Dr Acurcio Lopes 1, tel 915 440 196, shared and private rooms, kitchen, €15+, special stamps).

STAGE 8
Alvaiázere to Rabaçal

Start	Igreja Matriz, Alvaiázere
Finish	Igreja Matriz, Rabaçal
Distance	31.7km
Total ascent	672m
Total descent	800m
Difficulty	Medium
Time	8–9hr
Cafés	Alvaiázere, Ansião (12.8km), Venda do Brasil (19km), Alvorge (22.8km), Rabaçal (31.7km)
Accommodation	Alvaiázere, Ansião (12.8km), Alvorge (22.8km), Rabaçal (31.7km)

The Camino now enters the Terra de Sicó region, known for its limestone, oak trees and olive groves. After an initial climb to 474m, the stage gently undulates through scrubland, along woodland lanes and through quiet hamlets. Ansião is the largest town with all facilities.

Turn right in front of the church onto the N348 and after 300m turn right up the steep Rua da Quintinha. Cross the N350 into Rua da Igreja Velha and KSO for 2.4km through **Laranjeiras**, going uphill and passing eucalyptus trees to reach a T-junction. Turn left into **Vendas** (**3.3km**) then take

87

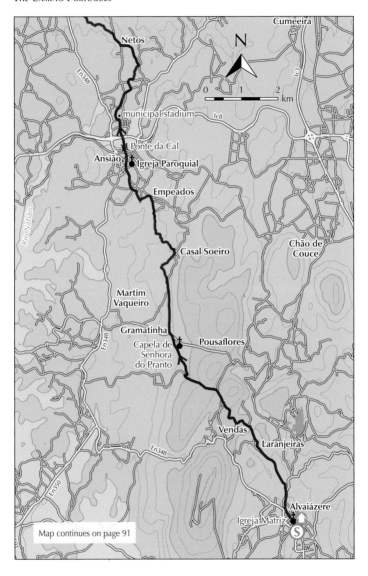

Cumeeira

Netos

N

0   1   2
km

municipal stadium

Ponte da Cal
Ansião
Igreja Paroquial

Empeados

Chão de
Couce

Casal Soeiro

Martim
Vaqueiro

Gramatinha
Pousaflores
Capela de
Senhora
do Pranto

Vendas
Laranjeiras

Alvaiázere
Igreja Matriz

Map continues on page 91

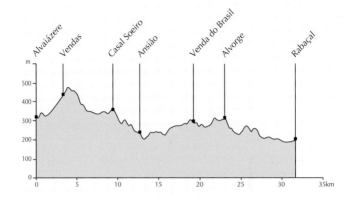

the first right onto Rua Fonte das Vendas, passing houses. Continue uphill for 700m before starting to descend, then KSO and after 1.5km leave the paved road by turning right onto a wide gravel road through tall scrub, continuing downhill. After 900m join a cobbled road and pass **Capela de Senhora do Pranto** (17th century). **3.2km/6.5km**

Reach the end of the road and merge left onto Estrada dos Moinhos, taking the first right onto a dirt road through olive groves and scrub. As the road bends left, continue straight onto a lane, then on reaching a paved road, turn right. Soon after, turn left onto another woodland lane and follow the arrows painted on rocks for 1.2km to reach a cobbled road in the hamlet of **Casal Soeiro** (**2.9km**). Leave on the dirt Rua d'Alem, heading towards Ansião with views over the scrubland. After 700m reach a dirt T-junction and turn right towards **Empeados**, then after 1.1km (having passed through Empeados) reach the main road (CM1094) and turn left onto the parallel dirt path, passing a wayside shrine (RHS). Join a forest road for 300m before entering Ansião by crossing the wide Av Américo Santo onto Rua da Mina. Pass the library (RHS, stamp) shortly before reaching the town centre and **Igreja Paroquial**. **6.3km/12.8km**

Continue along Rua Conselheiro António José da Silva, passing the pillory (17th century). ▶ Pass a Mini Preço supermarket then cross the Nabão beside **Ponte da**

Turn left here for Adega Típica.

ANSIÃO, 213M, POP. 13,719

Situated near the source of the River Nabão and with all town services, Ansião would make a pleasant overnight stop or coffee/lunch break. The Camino goes through the centre of town, passing the few sights.

Tourist office: Praça do Município, tel 236 670 206, www.cm-ansiao.pt, closed weekends.

Specialities: Terras de Sicó red wine, honey, olive oil and cheese.

Where to eat: Pastelarias Diogo (opposite the Igreja Paroquial), lunch-buffet Mon–Sat 12–3pm. Adega Típica, pilgrim menu.

Accommodation: Adega Típica (Rúa Combatentes da Grande Guerra, tel 236 677 364, www.adegatipicadeansiao.com, 18 rooms, €30+, rooms above the popular restaurant). Solar da Rainha (Alto dos Pinheiras 394, tel 236 676 204, 14 rooms, €20+, +1km along the Camino).

Queen Isabel is believed to have bathed in one of the tanks under the bridge on her journeys.

Cal. ◄ Go under the IC8, pass Solar da Rainha, then follow the road left. Turn right onto Rua do Estádio, passing the **municipal stadium** (RHS), and continue straight onto Travessa da Fonte Santa. Cross the next junction then turn left onto a dirt path and follow the arrows along winding lanes and roads for 1.5km, heading uphill into **Netos**. **3.8km/16.6km**

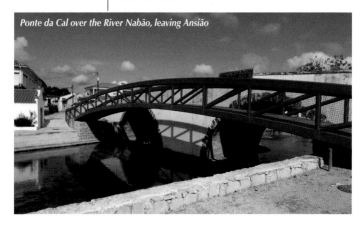

Ponte da Cal over the River Nabão, leaving Ansião

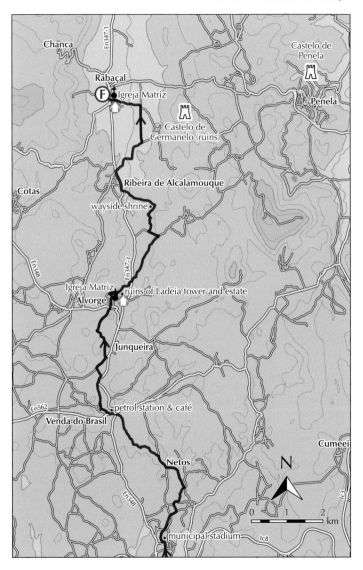

Turn right at the T-junction then left onto a gravel road at the old house with a blue door and enter woodland. After 2km reach a crossroads in **Venda do Brasil** and go straight across the N348, passing a **petrol station** with café (RHS), then turn right onto the cobbled Rua do Comareiro. Follow small roads then a woodland path back to the N348 and turn left, then soon after take a parallel dirt path on the LHS. Turn right at the T-junction onto a paved road and before the next hamlet of **Junqueira** turn left onto a dirt road, going uphill and turning right at the T-junction then continuing to Largo do Cruceiro in **Alvorge**. 6.2km/22.8km

ALVORGE, 300M, POP. 1227

A quiet village first referenced in 1141 when the land (including a tower, which Alvorge is named after) was donated to Coimbra's Santa Cruz Monastery. It has a small albergue and interesting ruins that are passed on leaving. There is a café, mini-market and ATM surrounding Largo do Cruceiro.

Accommodation: Albergue de Peregrinos (10 beds, donation. Get the key at Café Cruceiro (now called Café Tira Peles) in the square. Access: continue along the Camino, turning right at the Igreja Matriz. The albergue is on the ground floor of the Centro Paroquial building, entrance at the back). Restaurante Albergue 'O Lagareiro' (Rua das Boiças 52, tel 913 132 477, 12 beds, €15).

Dating from the 15th century, there is a coat of arms from 1693 visible at the chapel entrance above the stairs.

The 12th-century Castelo de Germanelo (ruins) are visible on top of the conical hill, RHS.

Go straight through the square onto Rua David Miguel Namora, and after passing the **Igreja Matriz** (16th century) turn left then right at the end of the car park, going downhill on a woodland path. Pass a picnic area then start uphill, passing the intriguing **ruins of Ladeia tower and estate** (RHS). ◄ Take the next right, heading downhill to the road (N347–1), and turn left briefly then right onto a dirt road, passing olive groves. After 1.5km reach a paved road and turn left, then after 300m turn right, back onto a dirt road. Continue for a further 900m to a T-junction and **wayside shrine** (LHS) and turn left. After 1km, reach the N347–1 and turn right, passing a few old buildings in **Ribeira de Alcalamouque**. 5.2km/28km

Some 570m later, turn right onto the cobbled Rua Ribeira de Baixo. Follow this left onto a dirt road, pass an old windmill (up left) and after the road bends right, turn left, passing grapevines and olive groves. ◄ After a further 610m

Wayside shrine on the way to Rabaçal

turn left again (this is the Roman XVI road), then after 1km join a paved road and take the first left, continuing for 900m to Rabaçal's **Igreja Matriz**. 3.7km/31.7km

Mosaic at the Roman Villa, Rabaçal

RABAÇAL, 194M, POP. 291

Known for its cheese and the nearby Roman villa (with sand-covered mosaics), Rabaçal has a terrific private albergue and the few services are all just minutes away. Confalonieri (1594) stayed and attended mass here.

Visit: Museu Villa Romana, near the church, includes a movie recreating the Roman villa. Guided visits to the site (1.2km away) are possible, Rua da Igreja, www.cm-penela.pt, closed Mondays, €2.25.

Specialities: Rabaçal cheese (made using sheep's and goat's milk), honey, walnuts, wine.

Where to eat: Café/restaurant Bonito.

Accommodation: Albergue O Bonito (Rua da Igreja, tel 916 890 599 & 239 104 665, 30 beds, kitchen, €12.50+, opposite the church).

STAGE 9
Rabaçal to Coimbra

Start	Igreja Matriz, Rabaçal
Finish	Largo da Portagem, Coimbra
Distance	28.7km
Total ascent	467m
Total descent	625m
Difficulty	Medium
Time	8–9hr
Cafés	Rabaçal, Conímbriga Museum (11.1km), Cernache (17.4km), Cruz dos Morouços (24.3km), Mesura (26.3km), Santa Clara (27.6km), Coimbra (28.7km)
Accommodation	Rabaçal, Conímbriga (12km +210m), Cernache (17.4km), Santa Clara (27.6km), Coimbra (28.7km)

The Camino climbs up out of the Rabaçal valley, leaving the Ribatejo and Estremadura regions to enter the Beiras. It passes the renowned Roman ruins of Conímbriga (a must-see, open from 9am) then follows residential roads to Cernache before climbing three small hills then descending to Coimbra, described by Confalonieri (1594) as 'a small but beautiful city with a beautiful bridge, it is walled and the city of study'.

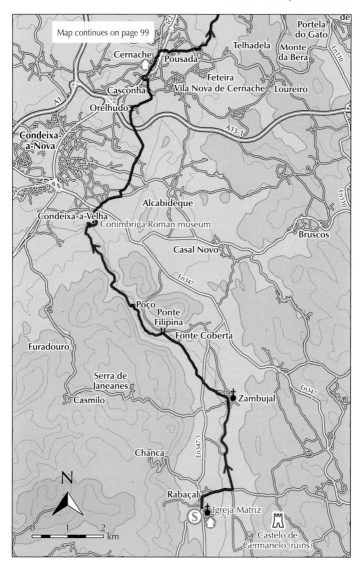

Map continues on page 99

95

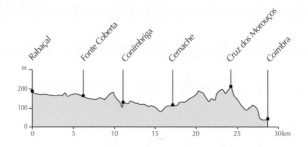

*Roman mosaics,
Conímbriga*

Turn right at the Igreja Matriz onto the N347–1 through Rabaçal, then turn right again, following a sign for Penela. After 900m turn left onto a dirt road (the Roman XVI road), passing olive groves, then after 1km turn left then right and follow the dirt road for 1.5km into **Zambujal** (**3.8km**). Pass the church (RHS, ransacked by Napoleon's troops) and turn left onto Rua do Jogo da Bola, going downhill, over a stone bridge and straight across the N347–1. After 1.3km enter the old hamlet of **Fonte Coberta** with colourful information panels. ▶ **6km**

In the hamlet pass a reproduction of a painting that Pier Maria Baldi painted in 1669 when accompanying Cosimo III of Medici on his pilgrimage to Santiago.

At the end of the village pass a picnic area (with *fonte*) and turn left onto a dirt road. Continue onto a narrow path beside a riverbed for 1.2km before passing the few stone houses of **Poço**. Turn left then right onto a dirt road, gradually climbing through a eucalyptus/pine forest. After 2.6km turn right then go downhill, followed by a steep uphill to reach **Conímbriga** (NM). **5.1km/11.1km**

Inhabited since at least the ninth century BC, the Romans arrived at **Conímbriga** in the second century BC and built a city which would flourish until the Swabian invasion in 468. Astonishingly, the site is only 17% excavated, but within it you can see impressive mosaics, baths, a forum, amphitheatre and more. The site also includes a museum and café, and provides a stamp. (Open daily (except major holidays) from 9am, €4.50.)

Continue around the museum then car park, turning right onto an old road. Go through the underpass (IC3) and carefully cross the next road, passing Bar Triplo Jota. (For Albergue de Peregrinos de Conímbriga +210m, take the next left and it's at the end of the street: Rua da Lagoa 15, tel 962 870 633, 8 beds, €15+, open 5pm, supermarket +600m.) After 600m turn left then right at the end and KSO, over a canal and across the M605. KSO, passing vegetable fields, then after 1.2km cross a bridge over the A13–1 and enter **Orelhudo** (**4.2km**). Follow the arrows down then up into **Casconha**, and after passing the primary school (LHS) turn left then cross a bridge over the IC2, turning right at the roundabout onto Rua Cruz. After 550m pass the albergue (LHS) in **Cernache**. **6.3km/17.4km**

CERNACHE, 126M, POP. 3929

The albergue in Cernache continues a tradition of welcoming pilgrims that began in the 15th century when a local hero, Álvaro Anes de Cernache, founded a pilgrim hospital and shelter. The Igreja Matriz (off the Camino, turn left at the square then follow Rua Nossa Senhora dos Milagres for 180m) retains 13th- to 14th-century Romanesque foundations and has Renaissance and later additions. There's a pharmacy, supermarket and café in the square. Café/Pastelaria Moleirinho (open daily, 7am–9pm) is +180m along the Camino.

Accommodation: Albergue de Cernache (LHS, Rua Alvaro Anes 37, tel 968 034 708, 14 beds, kitchen, €8) – call ahead to confirm.

KSO, passing the small square, onto Rua do Cabo, then after passing Café/Pastelaria Moleirinho turn right at the roundabout and go under the N1. Turn left at the crossroads (with a stone cross) then keep right and straight on through **Pousada**. Turn left at the church then right onto Rua da Palmeira and left at the end onto a dirt road, following the arrows for 2.1km up and over a hill. Reach a paved road and continue downhill, passing workshops, then turn left at the end onto Estrada Principal. After 380m take the right fork uphill through **Palheira (4.6km)**, then go downhill initially before climbing again along a dirt road for 500m, and then keep left onto a paved road into the parish of Antanhol. Take the next left, then follow the road down to a pedestrian bridge over the IC2. Cross the bridge and turn right, then follow the road as it becomes cobbled. KSO across a busy road and uphill, then after 340m turn right onto Rua D'Alem, soon passing Café Araújo in **Cruz dos Morouços. 6.9km/24.3km**

Turn left in front of the viewpoint (with views of Coimbra) and go downhill, straight across a junction then left at the end. Follow this road across a bridge over the N1 and through an arch of the **Santa Clara Aqueduct. ◄** Turn right at the roundabout into **Mesura (2km)** and pass Café Primavera, an Intermarche supermarket, then continue straight across the large roundabout, turning left onto Calçada de Santa Isabel with panoramic Coimbra views. Go downhill, passing Albergue 'Rainha Santa Isabel' (Alto de Santa Clara, tel 239 441 674, open 2–10pm, register at

Started in 1783 to provide water for Santa Clara Monastery from a spring in Cruz dos Morouços, a portion was removed to build the highway.

the gift shop, 18 beds, kitchen, €10), which is attached to **Mosteiro de Santa Clara-a-Nova** (**3.3km/27.6km**).

> This **'new' monastery** was built in the 17th century to replace the older, constantly flooded monastery beside the River Mondego. Queen Saint Isabel rests in a brilliant silver tomb on the main altar. Join a guided visit to see the intricately carved 14th-century tomb she commissioned and the staff given to her by the Archbishop of Santiago after her pilgrimage in 1325. There's a beautiful statue of Isabel carrying her pilgrim purse and scallop shell in front of the church. (Igreja da Rainha Santa Isabel, www.rainhasantaisabel.org, open daily, entrance €2+.)

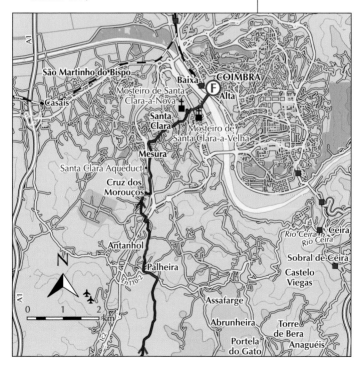

Largo da Portagem and a statue of Joaquim António de Aguiar (former Prime Minister), Coimbra

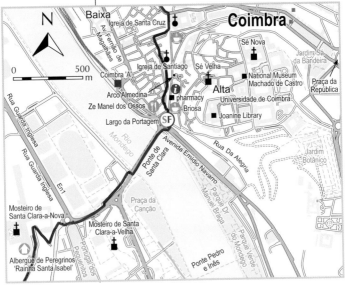

Continue down the hill, across a roundabout, past **Mosteiro de Santa Clara-a-Velha**.

Now a National Monument, the **'old' monastery** was founded by Queen Isabel in 1314. The last nuns moved out and into the new monastery up the hill in 1677. (Rua das Parreiras, also www.rainhas-antaisabel.org, closed Mondays, entrance €5.)

Cross Ponte de Santa Clara over the River Mondego to reach Largo da Portagem in **Coimbra**. **1.1km/28.7km**

Coimbra University's clock tower

COIMBRA, 40M, POP. 148,443

The city was called 'Aeminium' by the Romans, who established a forum on top of the hill. The forum's cryptoportico can still be seen in the National Museum's basement. The Almedina arch and tower are remnants of the Moorish period, and after the Christian Reconquest King Afonso Henriques established the royal court here. Coimbra became the capital of Portugal during the 12–13th centuries and in 1537 the university was transferred from Lisbon, and is now a UNESCO World Heritage Site.

Coimbra is the setting for the tragic love story of Pedro and Inês: Pedro, the son of King Afonso IV, moved in with his lover Inês de Castro after the death of his wife, but the king, worried about an uprising, ordered her assassination in 1355. Once Pedro became king he avenged her death by having her assassins brutally murdered in front of Santarém's Royal Palace. The 'fountain of tears' in the grounds of Coimbra's Quinta das Lagrimas (now a luxury hotel) is supposedly where Pedro and Inês would meet.

Tourist office: Rua Ferreira Borges 20, tel 239 857 186, **www.cm-coimbra.pt**, open daily.

Visit: Coimbra University – don't miss the 18th-century Joanine Library with illusionist ceiling paintings in each room. Bats are released at night to protect the books from insects. Also impressive is Saint Michael's Chapel (16th century) with Manueline entrance, Largo da Porta Férrea, www.uc.pt, open daily, entrance (including the library) €13.50. Sé Velha (Old Cathedral), 12th century, Romanesque with a 13th-century Gothic cloister, Largo da Sé Velha, open daily, €2.50 entrance. Igreja de Santa Cruz, Romanesque, founded in 1131, rebuilt in 1520; visit the stunning Manueline cloister and elaborate tombs of King Afonso Henriques and his son (Sancho I) €3 for entrance to the cloister. The café next door is part of an old chapel so you can experience the vaulted Manueline ceilings and stained-glass windows while having a coffee, Praça 8 de Maio, open daily. National Museum Machado de Castro (named after the famous sculptor, 1731–1822) was built on top of the Roman Forum which would then become the Bishop's Palace (12th century to 1910), Largo Dr José Rodrigues, www.patrimoniocultural.gov.pt, closed Mondays, €6+. Igreja de Santiago, 12th century, Romanesque, Praça do Comércio, open daily (closed August). Sister Lucia's Memorial: one of the three children to witness the apparitions of Fátima and the last survivor, Sister Lucia lived in the Carmel of Coimbra Convent from the age of 41 until she died at the age of 97 in 2005, Av Marnoco e Sousa 54, www.coimbra.carmelitas.pt. Fado Centro (in Coimbra's style of *Fado* only men sing), a 50-minute show daily at 6pm including port tasting, €14, Rua do Quebra Costas 7, www.fadoaocentro.com, booking advised.

Specialities: *Pastel de Santa Clara* and *Briosa* (sweet custard/egg pastries) from Café Briosa, Largo da Portagem.

Where to eat: Ze Manel Dos Ossos, popular BBQ restaurant serving large portions at bargain prices. Arrive early or prepare to stand in a long queue, Beco do Forno (close to the square).

Accommodation: Portagem Hostel (Rua da Couraça Estrela 11, tel 962 296 479, www.portagemhostel.com, kitchen, €22+, great location behind the old tourist office). Serenata Hostel (Largo da Sé Velha 21/23, tel 239 853 130, www.serenatahostel.com, 40 beds, kitchen, €15+, next to the old cathedral). *Residencial Larbelo (Largo da Portagem 33, tel 239 829 092, central location). ***Hotel Astória (Av Émidio Navarro 21, tel 239 853 020, www.astoria-coimbra.pt, 62 rooms, historic building overlooking the river).

STAGE 10
Coimbra to Sernadelo

Start	Largo da Portagem, Coimbra
Finish	Albergue Hilário, Sernadelo
Distance	25km
Total ascent	302m
Total descent	295m
Difficulty	Easy
Time	6–7hr
Cafés	Coimbra, Adémia de Baixo (6.1km), Trouxemil (9.4km), Adões (10.3km), Sargento Mor (11.4km), Santa Luzia (13.2km), Mala (17.6km), Lendiosa (18.6km), Mealhada (23.4km)
Accommodation	Coimbra, Fornos (8.1km), Mealhada (24km), Sernadelo (25km)

This is a relatively easy stage along small roads with two short forest sections (and a brief section along the N1), and with cafés in most of the villages. Mealhada is the *leitão* (suckling pig) capital, and Sernadelo, where the stage ends, is surrounded by leitão restaurants – so arrive hungry!

Find Pastelaria Briosa (RHS) in Largo da Portagem and go down the steps opposite, onto Rua dos Gatos, following bronze Camino tiles on the ground. Continue straight through Praça do Comércio, past Igreja de Santiago (RHS), taking the diagonal left exit through the square, then take the right fork along the narrow Rua Eduardo Coelho. Cross Largo do Poço, turn right onto Rua da Louca then turn left into Praça 8 de Maio, reaching Igreja de Santa Cruz. **500m**

Turn left onto the busy Rua da Sofia for 370m then turn left onto Rua Dr Manuel Rodrigues. Turn right at the end onto Av Fernão de Magalhães and KSO for 540m. After passing the bus station (LHS) next to McDonald's, take the next left and go under the IC2 and railway tracks, turning right onto a path beside a canal (LHS). KSO, across a roundabout, past a car park (RHS) then turn right onto a paved road (the canal

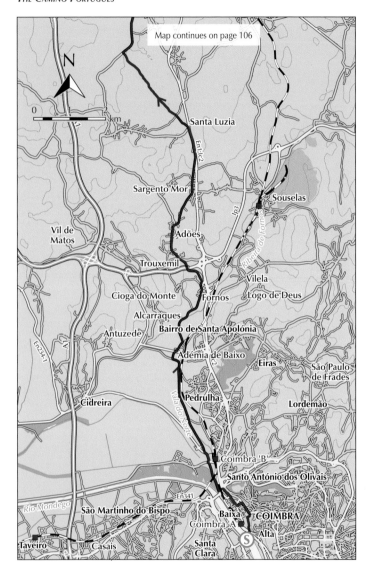

Map continues on page 106

N

0   1 km

Santa Luzia

En112

Sargento Mor

Souselas

Vil de
Matos

Adões

Ribeiro de Fornos

Trouxemil

Vilela

Ip3

Cioga do Monte

Fornos

Logo de Deus

Alcarraques

Antuzede

Bairro de Santa Apolónia

Adémia de Baixo

Eiras

São Paulo
de Frades

Vala do Norte

Cidreira

Pedrulha

Lordemão

Coimbra 'B'

Santo António dos Olivais

Rio Mondego

São Martinho do Bispo

En341

Baixa

COIMBRA

Taveiro

Casais

Coimbra A

Alta

Santa
Clara

is now on the RHS). After 2.8km cross the canal and enter **Adémia de Baixo**. **5.6km/6.1km**

Go straight across the N111 into Rua de São João, passing Restaurant Adega do Leite, then take the first left. Turn left at the T-junction then after 640m keep right, passing a small red footbridge (RHS). After a further 900m take the left fork and soon after, in **Fornos**, pass Casa Morais Turismo Rural (RHS). ▶ Leave Fornos across a roundabout and walk uphill for 1km, before passing a statue of St James in front of Igreja de Santiago with Café Milfrutas opposite, in **Trouxemil**. **3.3km/9.4km**

Rua da Capela, tel 239 431 061, 7 rooms, €40+, a 16th-century pilgrims' inn.

Continue through the village, keeping right at the stone cross (LHS), and go straight on to the next village, passing Café Central in **Adões**, then keep right and pass a chapel

St James statue outside Igreja de Santiago, Trouxemil

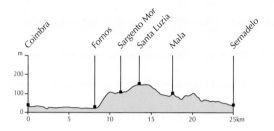

(LHS). After 1km turn left at a T-junction onto Rua do Lagar and pass a church and two cafés in **Sargento Mor**. After 850m reach the N1 and turn left, uphill, carefully walking along the shoulder for 770m. Leave the highway at traffic lights onto a parallel road (left), passing Restaurant Manuel Julio in **Santa Luzia**. **3.8km/13.2km**

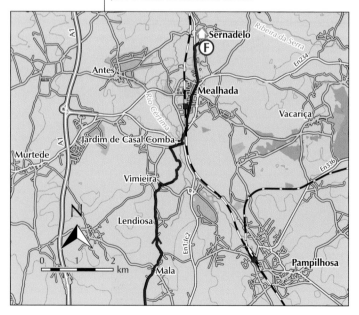

The road becomes a dirt road through eucalyptus forest; follow the waymarks on posts (almost in a straight line) for 2.3km to reach a paved road, then turn right. KSO for 1.5km, taking the left fork at a chapel, then take the next right and pass Café Nossa Senhora das Candeias in **Mala**. Take the next left, going downhill, then follow the road left, over a bridge and past Café One Way in **Lendiosa**. **5.4km/18.6km**

After a further 1km enter **Vimieira** and take the right fork, then shortly afterwards pass a chapel (LHS). Reach a T-junction and turn right, then take the next left onto Rua Areias, which becomes a dirt track. Carefully follow the arrows through olive groves and grapevines for 1km until you reach the paved Rua Catarossa. Turn right, then as the road bends left, KSO, passing **Jardim de Casal Comba** and café (LHS). Turn left at the end and go straight across the roundabout (with Bacchus God statue) then up the N1 and over the railway tracks. Take the first left and pass an Intermarche supermarket, then take the right fork at the *fonte* onto Rua Visconde Valdoeiro. ▶ KSO into the pedestrianised shopping street, Rua Dr José Cerveira Lebre in the centre of **Mealhada**. **4.8km/23.4km**

Or KSO +400m for Mealhada train station with connections to Coimbra and Porto.

MEALHADA, 59M, POP. 20,751

Known throughout Portugal for the gastronomic speciality 'Leitão da Bairrada,' Mealhada is also situated in the Bairrada wine region which produces red and sparkling white wines.

Specialities: Leitão de Bairrada (spit-roasted four- to six-week-old suckling piglets) and Bairrada wines.

Where to eat: Hotel & Restaurant Oasis (delicious meals with a daily menu), or try the highly rated Rei dos Leitões on the N1 in Sernadelo just before the albergue.

Accommodation: Hotel & Restaurant Oasis (Av da Floresta 39, tel 231 202 081, 12 rooms, €22+, +500m along the Camino).

Continue straight into Rua Dr Costa Simões (passing the art deco pharmacy) and after 400m reach the N1 and turn left. Pass the large city park (RHS) and Hotel & Restaurant Oasis opposite. After 800m turn right opposite Rei Dos Leitões restaurant, then reach the end of the stage at the friendly **Albergue Hilário**. **1.6km/25km**

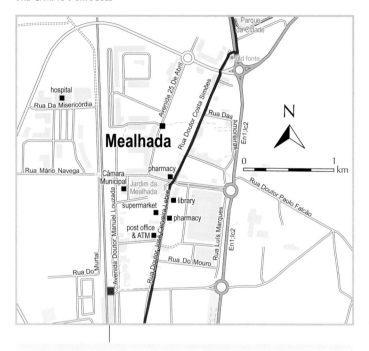

SERNADELO

Just out of Mealhada, Sernadelo is surrounded by leitão restaurants and has an accommodation option.

Accommodation: Albergue & Residencial Hilário (Av da Restauração, 28–30, tel 231 202 117 & 916 191 721, **www.hilario.pt**, albergue €10+, residencial €15+).

STAGE 11
Sernadelo to Águeda

Start	Albergue Hilário, Sernadelo
Finish	Praça da República, Águeda
Distance	23.6km
Total ascent	245m
Total descent	275m
Difficulty	Easy
Time	6–7hr
Cafés	Alféloas (8.5km), Avelãs de Caminho (11.9km), Aguada de Baixo (16.2km), Estrada Real (21.8km), Águeda (23.6km)
Accommodation	Sernadelo, Anadia (6.2km +300m), Águeda (23.6km)

This stage is mainly along roads through villages and industrial zones, but you can try the local specialities by having lunch at Casa Queiroz in Avelãs de Caminho and a few kilometres later, taste the local wines in the cellar at Caves São João.

Continuing on from the albergue, take the next right at the pink house, going uphill on Rua 25 de Abril. Turn left onto Rua do Regato then KSO into Rua da Carvalha, which becomes a dirt road through a pine/eucalyptus forest for 800m before joining a paved road in **Alpalhão**. Reach a

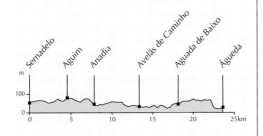

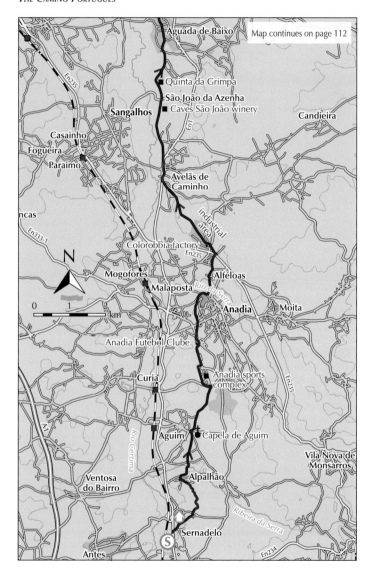

Map continues on page 112

Aguada de Baixo

Quinta da Grimpa

São João da Azenha
Caves São João winery

Sangalhos

Candieira

Casainho
Fogueira
Paraimo

Avelãs de Caminho

industrial area

ncas

En333-1

Colorobbia factory

En235

N

Mogofores

Alféloas

0   1   km

Malaposta

Rio da Serra

Anadia

Moita

Anadia Futebol Clube

Anadia sports complex

Curia

Aguim

Capela de Aguim

Vila Nova de Monsarros

Ventosa do Bairro

Alpalhão

Rio Cértima

Ribeira da Serra

Sernadelo

S

Antes

En234

junction with a chapel in front and veer left then turn right, passing the front of the chapel, and then onto Rua dos Poços. After 1.4km enter **Aguim** and turn right at the **chapel** (RHS) onto Estrada de Vale de Cid, going left at the roundabout. Continue along the road for 1.4km, turning left at a T-junction then right at the roundabout and passing the large **Anadia sports complex** (RHS). **5.2km**

Eucalyptus forest, Sernadelo

At the end of the complex turn left, passing apartment buildings (RHS), then after 400m pass **Anadia Futebol Clube** and turn left at the roundabout with drink/snack vending machines on the LH corner. ▶ Turn right at the next roundabout onto Rua da Bela Vista, passing the cemetery. Cross the avenue and take the left fork, downhill. Turn right at the end onto Rua das Cavadas and pass Igreja de São Paio, then turn right onto Rua da Igreja. Take the first left onto Rua da Calçada and at the top of the hill, reach **Alféloas**. **3.3km/8.5km**

KSO across the roundabout for ***Anadia Cabecinho Hotel +300m, Av Eng. Tavares da Silva, tel 231 510 940, **www.hotel-cabecinho.com**, 51 rooms, €37.50+.

Reach a small roundabout with a stone cross and take the diagonal left onto Rua das Alfelinas, then keep right. Carefully cross the N235, taking the first left. Turn right at the end, then turn left passing the **Colorobbia factory** (LHS) and enter an industrial and forestry area. After 1.6km pass a

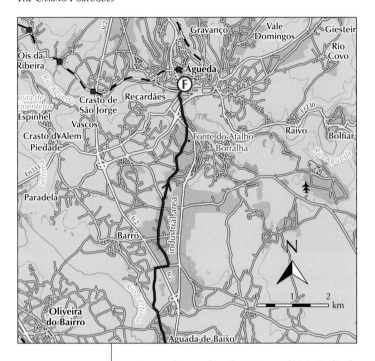

cemetery, and on reaching the N1 turn right into **Avelãs de Caminho**. **3.4km/11.9km**

Take the first right then continue along the parallel road to the N1, Rua da Fonte do Sobreiro. ◄ After 300m carefully cross the N1 and pass Capela de Nossa Senhora dos Aflitos. KSO, and after 1.6km pass **Caves São João** (wine tastings available Mon–Fri). KSO, passing the stately **Quinta da Grimpa**, then after a further 1.8km pass Café Cininha opposite a pharmacy then a tile-covered church in **Aguada de Baixo**. **4.3km/16.2km**

KSO, downhill, across Rua do Certima then take the right fork onto Rua Padre Francisco Dias Ladeira, now uphill. After 1km turn right at the T-junction and go under the IC2, turning left at the roundabout (with orange sculpture) into an industrial area. After 1.9km, at the end of the industrial area, turn right onto Estrada Real. Follow this for 1.5km

Along the N1 are cafés and the excellent Restaurant Casa Queiroz that serves delicious *leitão* (suckling pig, as a sandwich or meal) and home-made desserts, open 12–10pm, closed Tuesdays.

then take the left fork at a wayside shrine and Café Rasteiro (LHS). Descend steeply, passing **Fonte do Atalho** (RHS, 15th century) then carefully cross the N1 into the cobbled and colourful Rua Dr António Breda. Continue straight and cross a wooden footbridge then go under the N333. Turn right at the T-junction onto the N1, cross the bridge over the River Águeda, ending the stage at Praça da República (RHS) in **Águeda**. **7.4km/23.6km**

The colourful pedestrianised Rua Luís de Camões, Águeda

ÁGUEDA, 24M, POP. 49,041

A delightful, quirky city full of interesting street art. Pick up an Urban Art map from the tourist office (opposite the square) to explore. There are cafés, a pharmacy and ATM along the pedestrianised Rua Luís de Camões.

Tourist office: Largo Dr. João Elisío Sucena, tel 234 601 412, **www.cm-agueda. pt**, closed Sunday & Monday.

Visit: Igreja Matriz, 14th century, reconstructed during the 16–18th centuries, views over the city.

Specialities: *Pastéis de Águeda* from Requinte & Categoria (formerly Pastelaria Almendrina) in the square.

Where to eat: Tem-Tem, in the square. Telhas E Canecos, nice Portuguese restaurant on Rua Botaréu.

Accommodation: XPT Águeda AL (Rua Vasco da Gama 37, tel 969 523 545, private rooms, €35+, modern central hostel). ****Hotel Conde d'Águeda (Praça Conde de Águeda, tel 234 610 390, www.hotelcondedagueda.com, 28 rooms, next to the library). Albergue Sto. António & Residencial Celeste (Estrada Nacional N1, tel 234 602 871, www.residencialceleste.com, albergue with kitchen, €15+, residencial rooms €38+, pilgrim-friendly accommodation on the N1, just past the Lidl supermarket. Access: continue along the Camino for 1km until crossing the railway tracks then turn right following the arrows to the albergue, total +1.7km. Or KSO north along the N1 +1.2km).

STAGE 12
Águeda to Albergaria-a-Velha

Start	Praça da República, Águeda
Finish	Praça Ferreira Tavares, Albergaria-a-Velha
Distance	16.1km
Total ascent	267m
Total descent	160m
Difficulty	Easy
Time	4–5hr
Cafés	Águeda, Mourisca do Vouga (4km), Lameiro (9.9km), Serém (10.9km), Albergaria-a-Velha (16.1km)
Accommodation	Águeda, Albergaria-a-Velha (16.1km)

Leaving Águeda, the Camino climbs steeply then enters an industrial area and largely follows (often unknowingly) the Via XVI Roman road. It passes grand 'Casas Brasileiras' houses built in the 19–20th centuries by returning emigrants, and crosses Ponte Velha de Marnel before another climb and a few kilometres through forest to finish at Albergaria-a-Velha with all services.

Leave Praça da República and pass the modern tourist office (LHS), then walk beside the river along Rua 5 de Outubro. After 500m turn right at the church (RHS) onto Largo Nossa

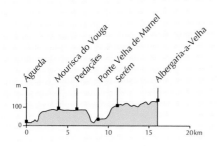

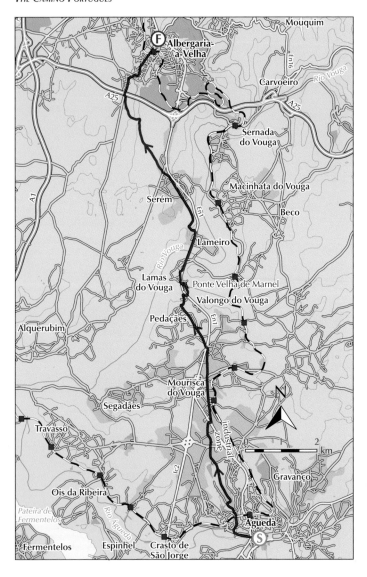

Senhora da Ajuda. Take the first right onto Rua do Ribeiro then the left fork, going uphill. Carefully cross the railway tracks then KSO downhill. After 400m take the right fork onto Rua do Portinho, heading up a steep hill and through an industrial area. After 1.8km KSO at the busy crossroads then take the next right. Carefully cross the N1 onto the road behind, Rua Liberdade, passing an ATM into **Mourisca do Vouga. 4km**

KSO for 2km, passing a pharmacy, cafés and old mansions, then follow the road as it bends left, crossing the N1 into **Pedaçães**. After 1.1km take the right fork at a large pine tree (and old *fonte*), going downhill, then carefully cross the N1 again onto a dirt road and cross **Ponte Velha de Marnel (4km)**. ▸ Go under the N1 then turn right and uphill, passing the white church, before turning left onto the shoulder of the N1. Cross a long bridge over the River Vouga then take the first left, up into **Lameiro** (there's a café up the bank, LHS). Soon afterwards, turn left and go uphill for 1km, reaching a crossroads (Casa Leonel is to the right) in **Serém. 6.9km/10.9km**

Situated on the Via XVI Roman road over the River Marnel, the current construction with five arches dates from the 16th century.

KSO, then after 700m veer right then keep left onto a short bit of dirt road, then go straight across a paved road

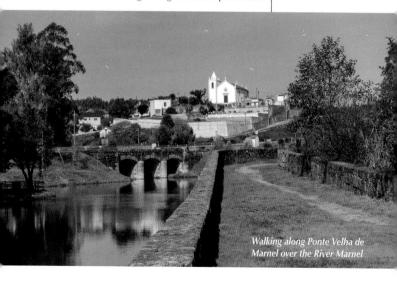

Walking along Ponte Velha de Marnel over the River Marnel

onto another dirt road into a eucalyptus forest with Camino information boards. Follow the arrows almost in a straight line for 1.6km, then bend left on the main dirt track. After a further 900m reach a T-junction and turn right onto a paved road then cross a bridge over the A25. Pass an Intermarche supermarket then reach a roundabout and take the diagonal (second) right, uphill, passing a beige apartment block (RHS). Shortly after, keep left then pass the Misericórdia Hospital and turn right onto Av Bernardino Máximo de Albuquerque. After 300m pass the albergue (LHS, no.14) then cross the roundabout and go over the railway tracks. The stage ends at the next roundabout, at the gardens opposite **Albergaria-a-Velha**'s town hall on Praça Ferreira Tavares. **5.2km/16.1km**

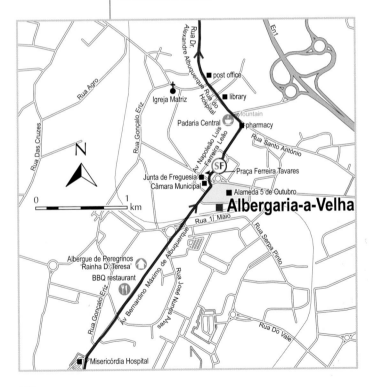

ALBERGARIA-A-VELHA, 128M, POP. 24,638

In 1117, Dona Teresa (the mother of Portugal's first king) requested that an inn should be built here for pilgrims, the poor and the sick – hence Albergaria's name. A stone was inscribed with these wishes in the 17th century and can be seen inside the town hall. Via Lusitana run a wonderful albergue and the town has all the services a hiker could need.

Accommodation: Albergue de Peregrinos 'Rainha D. Teresa' (Av Bernardino Máximo de Albuquerque 14, tel 234 529 754, 21 beds, kitchen, €8, on the Camino). Pensão & Restaurante Parente (Rua Dr Brito Guimarães 11, tel 234 521 271 & 918 149 584, €20+, follow the Camino for 210m then turn right at the fountain).

STAGE 13
Albergaria-a-Velha to São João da Madeira

Start	Praça Ferreira Tavares, Albergaria-a-Velha
Finish	Praça Luís Ribeiro, São João da Madeira
Distance	29km
Total ascent	593m
Total descent	487m
Difficulty	Medium
Time	7–8hr
Cafés	Albergaria-a-Velha, Albergaria-a-Nova (7.2km), Pinheiro da Bemposta (12.4km), Oliveira de Azeméis (20km), Salgueiro (23.6km), Vila de Cucujães (24.5km), São João da Madeira (29km)
Accommodation	Albergaria-a-Velha, Albergaria-a-Nova (6.2km), Oliveira de Azeméis (20km), São João da Madeira (29km)
Note	Take care when walking beside the railway tracks

This is a hilly stage, starting with two short forest sections then following undulating roads through residential areas and crossing two medieval bridges. Oliveira de Azeméis and São João da Madeira have all services.

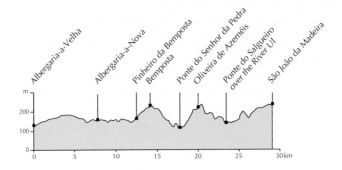

Continue through the gardens into Av Napoleão Luís Ferreira Leão, turning left at the end onto Rua Santo António. Pass a fountain (turn right here for Pensão Parente) and Café Padaria Central (selling delicious cake) and KSO for 800m. Reach a large roundabout and go straight across, following Porto signs, then go downhill and through the underpass. Turn left at the T-junction then take the right fork onto a dirt road behind houses. Follow this for 1.2km before turning sharp left into the forest, and shortly afterwards turn right. On reaching a paved road turn left and after 300m pass a **statue of Nossa Senhora do Socorro**. **3.4km**

KSO for 800m before turning left onto a dirt track, back into the forest. After 1km take the right fork then after 500m emerge from the forest and turn left onto a paved road. Cross the railway tracks and turn right onto the N1, then pass Albergue Albergaria-a-Nova. ◄ Shortly afterwards, turn right to follow the quieter Rua Velha (or KSO along the N1 +180m for 'Pão Regional' bakery, LHS) and once this meets the N1 again, turn right to pass a restaurant and café (RHS, after the traffic lights) in **Albergaria-a-Nova**. **3.8km/7.2km**

EN1, km 252.3, tel 234 547 068, **www. albergaria.eu**, 25 beds, €12+, kitchen, restaurant +1km further along the N1.

When the road soon starts to ascend, turn left onto a parallel road. After 1.7km reach a T-junction and turn right then immediately left onto Rua das Silveiras, towards an old chimney stack (RHS). After 1.3km, reach the railway tracks (just before the N1) and turn left, beside the tracks. KSO, then after passing a primary school (LHS) turn right onto Rua do Lagar de Azeite. Turn right onto Rua dos Soares then shortly

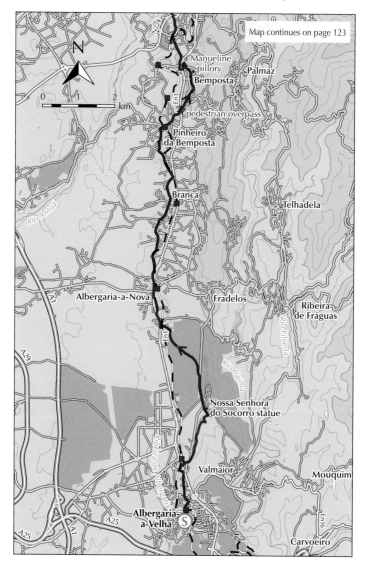

Map continues on page 123

N

0 1 2 km

N224

Manueline
pillory
Bemposta

Palmaz

En1

pedestrian overpass

**Pinheiro
da Bemposta**

Branca

Telhadela

Rio Antuã

A1

Albergaria-a-Nova

Fradelos

En1

Ribeira
de Fráguas

Rio Filveda

A29

Rio Caima

**Nossa Senhora
do Socorro statue**

Albardia de Albergaria

Valmaior

Mouquim

A25

Albergaria-
a-Velha
Ⓢ

En16

A25

A1

Carvoeiro

after crossing the railway tracks, reach a crossroads with cafés opposite the pink 'Brazilian-style' house and a covered stone cross (1604, rebuilt in 1774) in **Pinheiro da Bemposta**. **5.2km/12.4km**

Continue straight, passing a post office (LHS), then reach the N1 and cross it using the **pedestrian overpass**. Continue straight into Rua, pass Café Areosa then take the second right onto Rua de Manuel I. Follow this for 1.3km as it loops around, passing a medieval fountain then a 16th-century **Manueline pillory** next to Bemposta's old town hall, before descending. Carefully cross straight over the N1 and turn left at the roundabout (and bar) onto Av Do Espírito Santo, going downhill, and after crossing the railway tracks turn right. Shortly after, keep left at the fork and continue on Estrada Real. **3.5km/15.9km**

KSO across a bridge over the N224, turning right at the stop sign onto Rua Monte D'Alem. After 630m when you're almost at the top (and the highway wall is in front), turn right to go up a driveway beside a white house (RHS), then carefully turn left through a tunnel beside the railway tracks. KSO onto the cobbled Rua do Senhor da Ponte then go downhill and over **Ponte do Senhor da Pedra (1.9km)**. ◄ Cross the railway tracks then turn right at the T-junction and take the left fork up Rua do Álmeu. KSO for 1.1km then take the diagonal left at a **stone cross** into Rua do Cruzeiro, and soon afterwards pass ****Hotel Dighton in Largo da República, **Oliveira de Azeméis**. **4.1km/20km**

This bridge dates from the 18th century and has an attached shrine.

OLIVEIRA DE AZEMÉIS, 220M, POP. 68,611

Along the Via XVI Roman road, Oliveira de Azeméis is a city with all services, some charming buildings, and a train station with indirect connections to Porto.

Accommodation: ****Hotel Dighton (Largo da República, tel 256 682 191, www.hotel-dighton.com, 93 rooms, €58+).

Pass a Roman milestone opposite the **Igreja Matriz** then KSO, downhill. Turn right at the T-junction then pass a Pingo Doce supermarket (RHS) and turn left at the roundabout onto Rua Dr Silva Pinto. After 1km cross the railway tracks and take the right fork, passing a *hórreo* (granary, LHS). At the top, turn right and cross a bridge over the railway tracks,

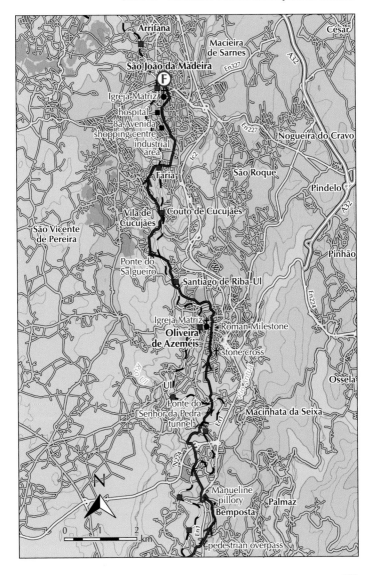

Roman milestone opposite the Igreja Matriz, Oliveira de Azeméis

taking the first left onto Rua do Sardoeira. After 530m turn left at the T-junction then cross the tracks once more before crossing the River Ul on the 14th-century **Ponte do Salgueiro**. **3.3km/23.3km**

Turn right and pass Café Emigrante then follow the road to a T-junction, turning left onto Rua do Mosteiro (N327) through **Vila de Cucujães**. Pass Café Coelho, then after passing a pharmacy and Café Refugio, turn right uphill on Rua D Crisóstomo de Aguiar. After 1.2km (and after descending) cross the railway tracks (**Faria station** is on the RHS), then after 430m enter an industrial zone. At the end of the road, at a roundabout with a Lidl supermarket, turn left onto Av Dr Renato Araújo. Pass **8a Avenida shopping centre** then reach

a roundabout with a fountain and Santander bank and take the diagonal right onto Rua Padre António Maria Pinho. Go uphill, past the **Igreja Matriz** (19th century), then turn left

Igreja Matriz, São João da Madeira

onto Rua Visc de São João da Madeira. KSO into the one-way street, passing a Pingo Doce supermarket to reach Praça Luís Ribeiro in the centre of **São João da Madeira**. **5.7km/29km**

SÃO JOÃO DA MADEIRA, 240M, POP. 21,102

During the 19th century São João da Madeira's main industry was producing hats, then shoes (it's considered the 'shoe capital' of Portugal), and today the city is leading the way in industrial tourism. The plaza has cafés, ATMs, a pharmacy and accommodation. The train station has indirect connections to Porto.

Tourist office: Torre da Oliva, Rua Oliveira Júnior 591, tel 256 200 204, **turismoindustrial.cm-sjm.pt**, open daily, across the car park from the hat museum.

Visit: Museu da Chapelaria (hat museum), Rua Oliveira Júnior 501, **www.museudachapelaria.pt**, closed Mondays, +540m along the Camino.

Where to eat: Tudo aos Molhos, specialising in *Francesinha* (hot sandwich filled with meat and covered in melted cheese and a special sauce). Galito Dourado for BBQ chicken. Both a few minutes from the square.

Accommodation: Solar São João (Praça Luís Ribeiro 165, tel 918 030 000, **solarsaojoao.pai.pt**, 14 rooms, €39+, overlooking the plaza). **Hotel A.S. São João da Madeira (Praça Luís Ribeiro 7, tel 256 836 100, **www.hotel-as-sjmadeira.com**, 36 rooms, €40+, overlooking the plaza). **** Golden Tulip São João da Madeira Hotel (Rua Adelino Amaro da Costa, tel 256 106 700, **sao-joao-madeira.goldentulip.com**, 117 rooms, +1km along Av da Liberdade).

STAGE 14
São João da Madeira to Grijó

Start	Praça Luís Ribeiro, São João da Madeira
Finish	Albergue de Peregrinos, Grijó
Distance	18.8km
Total ascent	273m
Total descent	370m
Difficulty	Easy
Time	5–6hr
Cafés	São João da Madeira, Arrifana (1.4km), Malaposta (7.1km), Souto Redondo (8.9km), Ferradal (10.6km), Vergada (13.4km), Grijó (18.8km)
Accommodation	São João da Madeira, Malaposta (7.1km), Grijó (18.8km)

This short but hilly stage is all road-walking and includes a well-preserved section of Roman road in addition to the N1. Grijó Monastery, opposite the albergue, provides respite with shade and benches.

Head diagonally left through the plaza onto Rua António José de Oliveira Júnior, passing a Novo Banco (RHS). KSO for

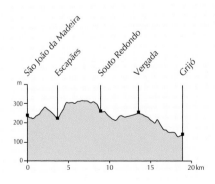

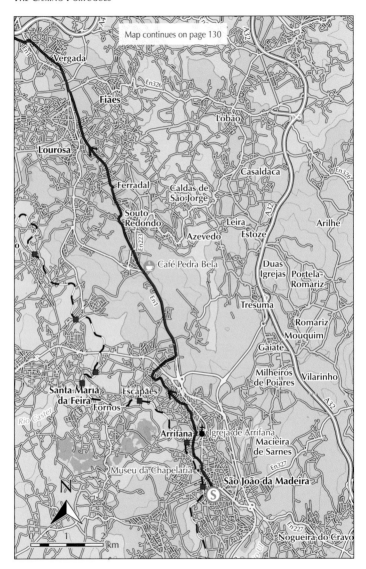

Map continues on page 130

Vergada

Fiães

En326

A4

A32

Lobão

Lourosa

Casaldaca

En326

Ferradal

Caldas de
São Jorge

Souto
Redondo

Leira

Arilhe

Azevedo

Estoze

En223

Café Pedra Bela

Duas
Igrejas

Portela-
Romariz

A32

En1

Tresuma

Romariz

Mouquim

Gaiate

Santa Maria
da Feira

Escapães

Milheiros
de Poiares

Vilarinho

Fornos

Rio Gaster

Arrifana

Igreja de Arrifana

Maceira
de Sarnes

En327

Museu da Chapelaria

São João da Madeira

S

N

0   1   2
km

Nogueira do Cravo

En227

500m, then after passing the **Museu da Chapelaria** (yellow-and-pink building), turn left. Take the right fork onto Rua da Várzea, then on reaching a junction, KSO across onto a cobbled road. Shortly afterwards pass Café Padaria Seara, then at the next junction pass in front of the blue-and-white tiled **Igreja de Arrifana**. 1.6km

> During the second French invasion, Marshal Soult's nephew was killed in battle nearby, and when the locals heard the French were on their way to seek retribution they hid in the church. On 17 April 1809, the French forced the men and boys to leave the church then selected one in five to be shot. This became known as the **'Arrifana Massacre'**.

Take the right fork onto Rua Prof Vicente Reis and after 2km, when the road has levelled out, turn right onto Rua dos Bombeiros Voluntários, passing Café Tarico (RH corner). Take the third right then turn right at the end onto Rua Dr Domingos da Silva Coelho and pass 'Casa da Arvore' kindergarten in **Escapães**. ▸ 2.4km/4km

Pilgrims are welcome to have a short break with access to water, WC and stamp, Mon–Fri.

Continue uphill for 730m, turning left onto the N1 (with footpath). Follow this for 2.4km, and after passing **Café Pedra Bela** (RHS) with ****Hotel Feira Pedra Bela behind (Rua da Malaposta 510 EN1, tel 256 910 350, www.hotelpedrabela. com, 62 rooms, €47+), take the next right then go immediately left onto the parallel Rua da Estrada Romana. KSO along the old Roman road and go straight across the N223, continuing straight until you rejoin a paved road. Shortly afterwards take the right fork, passing a *hórreo* (granary, RHS) then Café Souto in **Souto Redondo**. 4.9km/8.9km

After 700m KSO onto a dirt road then pass a Star petrol station and continue straight, going downhill. Pass a bar then café/mini-market Ferradalense in **Ferradal** and continue for 2.2km to the end of the road. Turn left then right onto the N1. As the N1 bends left, KSO onto Rua Central da Vergada into **Vergada**. 4.5km/13.4km

Continue straight for 1.3km, passing cafés, then turn left onto Rua Joaquim do Porto and carefully cross the N1. Take the first right onto Rua das Centieiras then after 740m carefully cross the busy Rua Central de Goda onto Rua Nossa Senhora dos Aparecidos. Go up then downhill (with views of the Atlantic), turning right onto Rua do Bairro Manuel

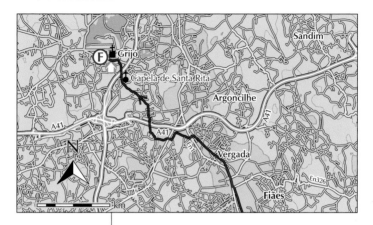

Entrance to Grijó Monastery

Lima. Turn right at the end, go under the A41 then follow a few more twists for 1.4km before passing the blue-and-white tiled **Capela de Santa Rita**. KSO into Rua do Ermo, go under the A1 then turn left at the crossroads following **Grijó Monastery**'s stone wall, soon arriving at the Albergue de Peregrinos S. Salvador (LHS). **5.4km/18.8km**

GRIJÓ, 130M, POP. 10,578

Grijó Monastery, built in the 12th century and reconstructed in the 16th century, houses the 13th-century tomb of D Rodrigo Sanches (NM), the illegitimate son of King Sanches I. Confalonieri stayed at the monastery in 1594. Café/mini-market Adega Padrão is next to the albergue (open Tues–Sun 9am–9pm, Mon 9am–2pm). The monastery entrance is +290m along the Camino and there are more cafés +1km along the Camino.

Accommodation: Albergue de Peregrinos S. Salvador (LHS, Rua Cardoso Pinto 274, tel 913 495 004, 14 beds, kitchen, €7).

STAGE 15
Grijó to Porto

Start	Albergue de Peregrinos, Grijó
Finish	Porto Cathedral
Distance	15.5km
Total ascent	270m
Total descent	322m
Difficulty	Easy
Time	4–5hr
Cafés	Grijó, Perosinho (4.9km), frequent after Rechousa (9km)
Accommodation	Grijó, Porto (15.5km)

This short stage involves a picturesque section of Roman path as the Camino climbs over the Serra de Negrelos, then it's downhill and across the Douro into the charming UNESCO World Heritage city of Porto.

Follow the monastery wall, passing the entrance, then reach a roundabout (cafés) and turn right onto Rua da Guarda. Pass a petrol station, then as the road begins to climb, turn left onto the cobbled Rua de Casal de Baixo. After 600m reach a T-junction and turn left, then turn right at the end onto Rua das Alminhas. Shortly after, take the left fork into

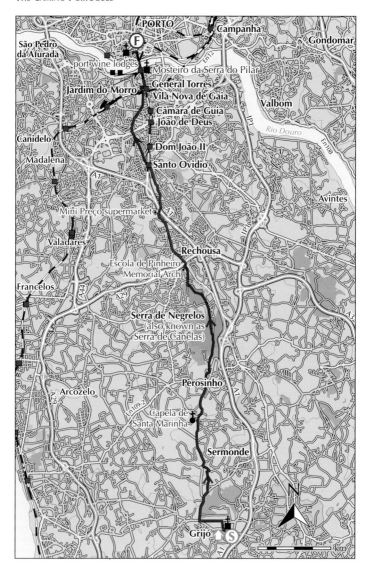

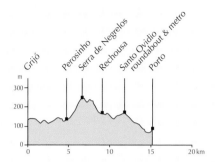

Rua do Parque Desportivo then KSO, passing small pockets of forest. After 1.1km pass behind **Capela de Santa Marinha** (LHS, with benches) and take the right fork onto Rua de Santa Marinha. After a further 1km pass Café Jardim (LHS) in **Perosinho**. **4.9km**

Shortly after passing the café, go straight over the crossroads (with cafés) into Rua da Igreja, passing Perosinho's Igreja Matriz. After 500m KSO into Rua da Bela Vista and onto a section of Roman path climbing over the **Serra de Negrelos** (Serra de Canelas on some maps). Reach the top

A pilgrim walking along the ancient path, Serra de Negrelos

133

of the hill after 600m and turn left then immediately right onto a forest road. Rejoin a road after 450m, passing houses, then as the road bends left, KSO back into the forest. Follow the arrows for 730m to reach a paved road and turn left then right onto the cobbled Rua do Mirante. Continue downhill for 550m, and after passing the **Escola de Pinheiro Memorial Arch** turn left at the roundabout, crossing a bridge over the A29 onto Rua Rechousa into **Rechousa**. **4.1km/9km**

Continue along the busy street for 1.6km, passing cafés, then reach a large **Mini Preço supermarket** (LHS) and take the right fork, going under the A1 and onto Rua Fonte dos Arrependidos. Follow this for 1.3km to the large **Santo Ovidio** roundabout and metro station (**2.8km**). ◀ It's possible to turn right here onto Av da República (N1) and follow the metro tracks for the remaining 3.3km to Porto, but for the traditional route (which is 400m longer) KSO across the roundabout onto Rua Soares Reis for 1.4km until you reach a large roundabout. Take the diagonal right onto Rua Dr Francisco Sá Carneiro, then after 750m cross a bridge over the metro tracks at **General Torres station**. Take the next right onto Rua Luís de Camões and then the first left onto Av da República. Shortly afterwards pass **Jardim do Morro** – popular viewpoint, cable car and metro station – and up the ramp

This is the yellow line 'D' of the Porto metro. São Bento is the closest metro stop to Porto Cathedral.

Porto's cathedral and pillory

opposite is another popular viewpoint from **Mosteiro da Serra do Pilar**.

> The **monastery** is a UNESCO World Heritage site and National Monument. Founded in the 16th century, Confalonieri stayed here in 1594. It belongs to the military after being used as a base during the French invasions and civil war. Closed Mondays, €1+.

As this stage finishes at Porto Cathedral, cross the top deck of the impressive Ponte D Luís I over the sparkling **River Douro**. ▶ (Look back for views of Vila Nova de Gaia's port lodges.) Take the first left up the cobbled Calçada de Vandoma to the imposing Romanesque **cathedral**, 'Sé do Porto'. **6.5km/15.5km**

The 'golden river' is 895km long and flows from Spain's Sierra de Urbión.

PORTO, 80M, POP. 263,131

Known as Portus Cale (Port of Cale) to the Romans, this is Portugal's second largest city and its historical centre is a UNESCO World Heritage site. Roman foundations and mosaics were discovered at Casa do Infante, where Prince Henry 'The Navigator' was born. His parents, King John I and England's Philippa of Lancaster, were married in the cathedral (1387) where Henry was later baptised. The port grew in importance during the 14th century and a second line of defensive walls, 'Muralha Fernandina', were built, and they're still visible today.

It was in the 17th century when at war with France that England started importing wine from its close ally, Portugal. By the time the wine arrived in England it was often spoiled, so brandy was added to fortify it – resulting in port wine, which is now produced exclusively in the Douro Valley.

Tourist office: Porto Cathedral Tourist Office, Terreiro da Sé, tel 223 326 751, **www.visitporto.travel**, open daily, stamp.

Visit: cathedral, 12th-century Romanesque with Gothic and Baroque additions. Highlights include the original rose window, the 14th-century cloister covered in 18th-century blue-and-white *azulejos* (tiles), and the 18th-century side-porch and staircase by Nicolau Nasoni. Next-door is the impressive Episcopal Palace. Terreiro da Sé, tel 222 059 028, open daily 9am–6.30pm, mass daily at 11am, entrance €3. Igreja de São Francisco (highly recommended), NM, 14th-century Gothic with Baroque additions, featuring a stunningly opulent interior with baroque gilt carvings and catacombs, Rua do Infante dom Henrique, **www.ordemsaofrancisco.pt**, open daily and next to the neoclassical Palácio da Bolsa (stock exchange palace), NM, with exceptional interiors, **www.palaciodabolsa**.

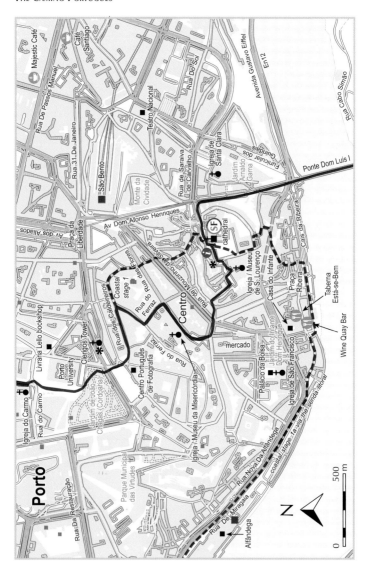

Porto

Majestic Café

Café Santiago

Rua De Passos Manuel

Rua-Da-Restauração

Rua.31-De Janeiro

Rua Do Carmo

Igreja do Carmo

Livraria Lello bookshop

Porto University

Clérigos Tower

Rua dos Caldeireiros

Rua do Ferraz

Centro Português de Fotografia

Jardim de João Chagas (Cordoaria)

Parque Municipal das Virtudes

Teatro Nacional

São Bento

Praça da Liberdade

Av. dos Aliados

Monte da Cividade

Av Dom Afonso Henriques

Rua de Mouzinho da Silveira

Rua das Flores

Coastal stage 1

Ferraz

Centro

Igreja i Museu da Misericórdia

mercado

Rua Do Sol

Rua de Saraiva de Carvalho

Igreja de Santa Clara

Jardim Arnaldo Gama

Funicular dos Guindais

Avenida Gustavo Eiffel

En12

Rua Cabo Simão

Ponte Dom Luis I

SF cathedral

Igreja i Museu de S.Lourenço

Casa do Infante

Praça Ribeira

Taberna Está-se-Bem

Cais da Ribeira

Jardim do Infante Dom Henrique

Palácio da Bolsa

Igreja de São Francisco

Wine Quay Bar

Rua Nova Da Alfândega

coastal stage 1a-via the senda litoral

Rua De Miragaia

Alfândega

N

500 m

0

136

com, open daily, 30-minute guided tours, €12. Igreja de Santa Clara, NM, 15th century with spectacular 18th-century gilded carvings. Look inside São Bento train station, built on top of a former convent, to see 20,000 azulejos depicting Portuguese history, including King João I and Queen Philippa of Lancaster standing beside the cathedral in 1387. Clérigos Tower and church, NM, 18th-century Baroque designed by Nicolau Nasoni; climb the steps to the top of the tower for a panoramic view, open daily, €8+. Livraria Lello bookstore, 1906, neo-Gothic, considered one of the most beautiful bookshops in the world, Rua das Carmelitas 144, **www.livrarialello.pt**, open daily, reserve online for a timed entrance, €5. Cais da Ribeira, lovely riverfront with bars, restaurants and exceptional views. Rua Santa Catarina, shops, Café Majestic and the 18th-century Capela das Almas covered in blue-and-white azulejos. A Casa do Fado, Rua do Infante Dom Henrique 85, tel 927 572 955, *fado* music daily at 7pm, €14 (including port tasting). Taste port at one of the many wine lodges in Vila Nova de Gaia. Enquire at the tourist office for the one-hour 'six bridges' Douro river cruise, or longer cruises that visit the vineyards upstream.

Specialities: *tripas* (tripe) – during the Age of Discoveries, the best cuts of meat were given to the ships and the leftovers, including tripe, were given to the locals, earning them the nickname *tripeiros*. *Francesinha* is a sandwich with steak, sausage and ham, covered in melted cheese and a special sauce. Port is produced in the Alto Douro region 80km upstream and then transported (traditionally by wooden boats down the Douro) to the lodges of Vila Nova de Gaia, where it's aged and bottled.

Where to eat: Café Santiago, said to have the best Francesinha in Porto, Rua Passos Manuel 226 & 198. Taberna Está-Se Bem, atmospheric tapas restaurant, Rua Fonte Taurina 70. Wine Quay Bar, popular tapas and wine bar in an enviable location overlooking the Douro. Café Majestic – it's worth

Livraria Lello bookstore, Porto

a visit to the romantic Art Nouveau café (be prepared for inflated prices) – Rua Santa Catarina 112.

Accommodation: Albergue de Peregrinos do Porto (Rua do Barão de Forrester 954, tel 220 140 515, www.albergueperegrinosporto.pt, 26 beds, kitchen, €15, +2.5km north of the cathedral along the Camino, closest metro station: Carolina Michaelis). Best Guest Porto Hostel (Rua Mouzinho da Silveira 257, tel 222 054 021, www.bestguesthostel.com, private and shared rooms, kitchen, €17+, modern hostel close to the cathedral). Lost Inn Porto Hostel (Rua Escura 23-27, tel 222 081 469, www.lostinn.eu, 50 beds, kitchen, €32, very close to the cathedral). The Poets Inn (Rua dos Caldeireiros 261, tel 223 324 209, www.thepoetsinn.com, 10 rooms, kitchen, near Clérigos Tower on the Camino).

CHOOSING YOUR ONWARD ROUTE

Leaving Porto, you have the following options:

Central Camino: this continues inland along cobbled roads, through rolling hills and historical towns like São Pedro de Rates, Barcelos, Ponte de Lima and Valença before entering Spain.

Coastal Camino: this passes through Vila do Conde and Viana do Castelo before taking a ferry from Caminha to Spain.

Both are well waymarked with ample accommodation. The following routes (described in this guide) connect the Central and Coastal Caminos:

• Link route 1 Vila do Conde to São Pedro de Rates joins the coastal to central
• Link route 2 São Pedro de Rates to Esposende joins the central to coastal
• Link route 3 Caminha to Tui (via Valença) joins the coastal to central

STAGE 16
Porto to Vairão

Start	Porto Cathedral
Finish	Albergue de Peregrinos, Vairão
Distance	25km
Total ascent	354m
Total descent	366m
Difficulty	Easy
Time	6–7hr
Cafés	Porto (0–7km), Araújo (9.5km), Moreira (14.1km), Mosteiro (17.9km), Gião (21.8km), Monte de Santo Ovídio (23.8km)
Accommodation	Porto, Vairão (25km)
Note	If starting from Porto you can get a credential from Porto Cathedral

After the first 16km leaving Porto and its suburbs, the Camino reaches the countryside and passes small villages, stone walls, fields, and lots of cobbled roads. Spending the night in Vairão Monastery's albergue will feel like a million miles from the city.

From the cathedral's main (west) entrance, go down the ramp, passing the tourist office (RHS, inside the tower) then turn left. Go down the steps to Largo do Colégio and pass Igreja/Museu de São Lourenço, turning right onto Rua de Santana then left at the end. Take the right fork onto Travessa da Bainharia then go straight across Rua Mouzinho da Silveira and take the first right into the colourful Rua das Flores. Pass the Igreja/Museu da Misericórdia then take the next left onto Rua do Ferras, going uphill and turning right at the end onto Rua da Vitória. Turn left onto Rua dos Caldeireiros, pass The Poets Inn (LHS, no.261) then turn right at the large square of Campo dos Mártires da Pátria. ▶ **800m**

Cross the road (passing **Clérigos Tower**, RHS) into Jardim da Cordoaria, heading diagonally right towards

Coastal Camino Stage 1 joins the route at this point and follows it to the stone cross of Padrão da Légua.

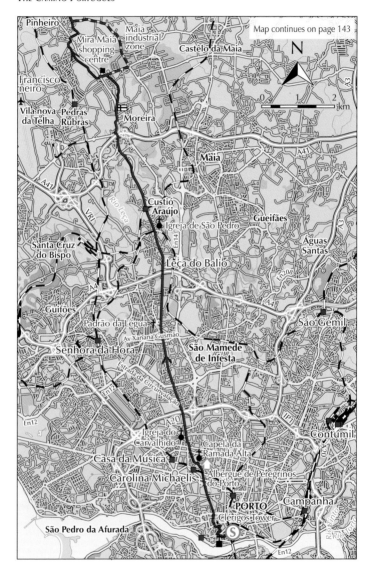

Map continues on page 143

N

0   1   2   km

Pinheiro

Mira Maia shopping centre

Maia industrial zone

Castelo da Maia

Francisco neiro

Vila nova da Telha

Pedras Rubras

Moreira

Maia

A41

Río Leça

VRI

Custió Araujo

Igreja de São Pedro

Gueifães

En14

Santa Cruz do Bispo

Leça do Balio

Aguas Santas

A3

Guifões

A4

Padrão da Légua

Av Xanana Gusmão

São Mamede de Infesta

São Gemil

A41

Senhora da Hora

En12

Estrada da Circunvalação

IP1

En12

A20

Igreja do Carvalhido

Capela da Ramada Alta

Contumil

Casa da Música

Carolina Michaelis

Albergue de Peregrinos do Porto

São Pedro da Afurada

PORTO

Clérigos Tower

S

Campanha

En12

the large building (Porto University). Turn right onto Praça de Parada Leitão and continue towards then past Igreja do Carmo (LHS, 18th century) with beautiful *azulejos* (tiles) covering the side-wall. Keep left and go straight into the shopping/pedestrianised Rua de Cedofeita, passing 17–20th century buildings and cafés. After 1.2km pass Albergue de Peregrinos do Porto (RHS), then take the right fork onto Rua Serpa Pinto, turning left immediately and passing the white

Passing the stunning blue-and-white side-facade of Igreja do Carmo, Porto

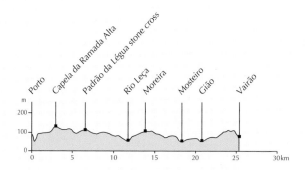

Capela da Ramada Alta (LHS) (**1.9km**). Take the next right onto Rua de Nove de Julho and KSO. Go under an apartment building then under the opposite building and turn left. Shortly afterwards, KSO at the stone cross into Praça do Exército Libertador and pass the blue-and-white tiled **Igreja do Carvalhido** (LHS). **2.7km/3.5km**

KSO into Rua do Carvalhido, which becomes Rua Monte dos Burgos, straight over the multi-lane Estrada da Circunvalação (**1.5km**) into Rua Nova do Seixo, passing Café Cidade do Pão (RH corner, delicious *pastel de nata* sweet pastries). Pass Lidl and Continente supermarkets then KSO across Av Xanana Gusmão (with a Galp petrol station), and after the next traffic lights pass the **Padrão da Légua** (LHS). ◀ **3.1km/6.6km**

A 17th-century stone cross; turn left here for the Coastal Camino Stage 1.

Continue straight, and after 3km pass **Igreja de São Pedro** (RHS, 17th century) in **Araújo**, then shortly afterwards pass **Custió metro station** (Green Line C). KSO for a further kilometre then take the left fork onto the cobbled Rua do Ponte de Moreira, going downhill, then turn left at the end and cross a bridge over the River Leça (**5km**). Continue uphill through a residential area then cross a bridge over the A41 and turn right onto Av de Maria Vieira Neves da Cruz (N107). KSO across a roundabout, pass a Repsol petrol station then turn right at Moreira Cemetery onto the cobbled Rua Mestre Clara into **Moreira**. **6.4km/13km**

After 800m, if you see conflicting arrows, you can either KSO following new wooden-post waymarks along cobbled back-roads (described here) or turn right and follow yellow arrows through the Maia industrial zone, which is 500m longer. Both routes converge at Vilar de Pinheiro.

Following new waymarks, turn left at the junction then pass **Mira Maia shopping centre** and KSO across the roundabout. Turn right at the tower onto Rua de Quires and follow the cobbled road for 1.2km to a T-junction. Turn right and take the first right, then turn left and shortly afterwards carefully cross the N13 into Rua do Sete. Take the first left into Rua Venda, passing fields, then after 200m keep right. (At this point the route is on the edge of **Vilar de Pinheiro**.) ◀ KSO for 500m, then after passing Café Beiracampo keep left and follow this for 1km to reach **Largo da Lameira** square (pharmacy, café, ATM) in **Mosteiro**. **4.9km/17.9km**

The old waymarks join here. For services turn left at the next crossroads.

Continue along Rua da Costinha, ignoring any turns (and passing more cafés) for 1.9km until you reach the paved

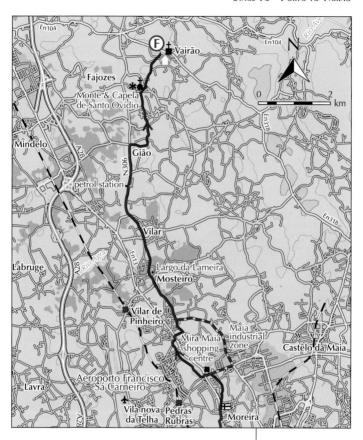

N306. Turn right, carefully following the road for 2km past a **petrol station**, to reach a junction with traffic lights, Camino information board and Café Doce Gião in **Gião (3.9km)**. Turn right here onto Rua da Igreja then after 500m keep left at a 17th-century stone cross. After a further 800m pass Café Tresval (RHS) then KSO to a T-junction with Café Casa Lemos (LHS) and **Monte de Santo Ovídio** in front. ▶ Turn right then turn left. Pass Café Jardim (pilgrim menu) and veer right into Rua das Pedreiras, then after 750m KSO (or take

Capela de Santo Ovidio is on top, on the site of a former Iron Age settlement, with views over the valley to the sea.

Vairão Monastery

the sharp left if not staying at Vairão Albergue) and the stage ends straight ahead at the albergue attached to **Mosteiro de Vairão**. 7.1km/25km

VAIRÃO, 72M, POP. 2643

Vairão's monastery was founded in the 11th century, although with the exception of the side Capela de São João, it mostly dates from the 16th to 18th centuries.

Where to eat: bring food to cook in the fully equipped kitchen, have food delivered from a nearby restaurant, or walk +600m right along the N318 to Café D Miguel, or back 1km to Café Jardim.

Accommodation: Albergue de Peregrinos (Rua do Convento 21, tel 936 061 160 & 966 431 916, www.mosteirodevairao.blogspot.co.uk, 50 beds, kitchen, donation).

STAGE 17
Vairão to Barcelos

Start	Albergue de Peregrinos, Vairão
Finish	Largo da Porta Nova, Barcelos
Distance	30.4km
Total ascent	499m
Total descent	518m
Difficulty	Medium
Time	8–9hr
Cafés	Vilarinho (1.7km), São Mamede (7.1km), Arcos (9.8km), São Pedro de Rates (13.7km), Pedra Furada (21.4km), Pereira (24.1km), Barcelos (30.4km)
Accommodation	Vairão, Vilarinho (1.7km), Arcos (9.8km), São Pedro de Rates (13.7km), Pedra Furada (21.4km), Barcelinhos (29.5km), Barcelos (30.4km)
Note	Barcelos has a famous Thursday market

This is a wonderful yet hilly stage entering Portugal's northern Minho region. The route crosses medieval bridges, passes through historic São Pedro de Rates, provides the perfect lunch-stop in Pedra Furada, and continues through fields, forests and small villages before arriving in Barcelos.

Leaving the albergue, retrace your steps for 180m then take the right fork (the previous stage having come down the LHS). After 500m, when the cobbled road bends left, turn right onto a dirt road through a short section of forest, then turn right at the end onto Rua dos Sobreiros. ▶ Pass mini-market Piposa (RHS) then continue to the N318 and turn left. Soon after, turn left onto the N104, then turn right at the lights, passing the grassy square with cafés in **Vilarinho** (**1.7km**). KSO, now on the N306, passing Café Anjo's (RHS, formerly CJ's). ▶ In 600m turn left onto Rua da Sabariz, then take the right fork. On reaching the N306 again carefully cross over, go down a dirt path and cross **Ponte D Zameiro** (11–12th century) over the River Ave. **3.2km**

For Casa Família Vidal take the next left, Rua do Salteiro 87, tel 252 661 503, 3 rooms, €15.

Turn right here for Casa da Laura, Rua Estreita 112, tel 917 767 307, 8 beds, €15, a lovely private albergue with garden.

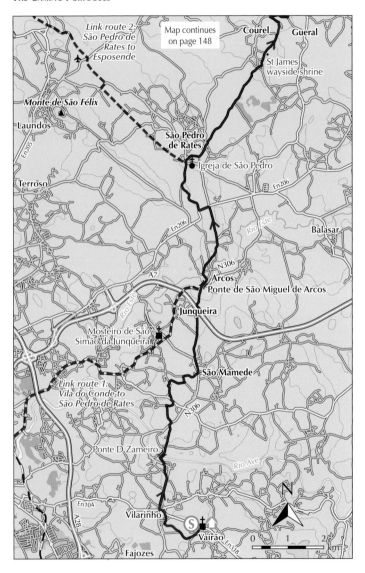

Link route 2:
São Pedro de
Rates to
Esposende

Map continues
on page 148

Courel

Gueral

St James
wayside shrine

Monte de São Félix

Laundos

São Pedro
de Rates

Igreja de São Pedro

Terrôso

En206

Rio Este

Balasar

En206

A7

N306

Arcos

Ponte de São Miguel de Arcos

Rio Este

Junqueira

Mosteiro de São
Simão da Junqueira

São Mamede

Link route 1:
Vila do Conde to
São Pedro de Rates

N306

Ponte D. Zameiro

Rio Ave

En104

A28

Vilarinho

Vairão

En318

Fajozes

0   1   2
km

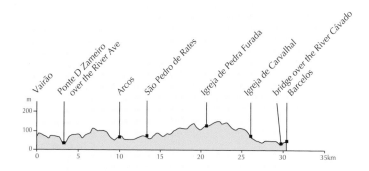

Take the right fork uphill and on reaching the N306 turn right and take the first left at a large blue Camino information sign with *desvio* (detour) waymark. (The detour is strongly recommended and is described here; the alternative is a dangerous road-walk along the busy N306. Both options rejoin in the village of São Mamede.) After taking the left at the 'desvio' sign, continue between fields for 500m to a T-junction and turn right, then follow the arrows along winding lanes for 2km. On meeting the N306 again (and reaching

Ponte de São Miguel de Arcos over the River Este

the end of the detour), turn left then right onto the cobbled Rua de São Mamede through the village of **São Mamede**. Continue to the end, then turn right at Café Moreira (RHS). After 1.2km go under the A7 then downhill, merging right onto the N306 briefly before crossing **Ponte de São Miguel de Arcos** (12th century) over the River Este and heading up into the village of **Arcos. 6.6km/9.8km**

Pass Quinta São Miguel de Arcos (RHS, Rua da Igreja 209, tel 919 372 202, www.countryhotel-quintasaomiguel. com, 10 rooms, €56+, beautiful rooms in an 18th-century house) at the entrance of the village then pass the church, Café Barbosa, and before leaving pass Villa D'Arcos Hotel

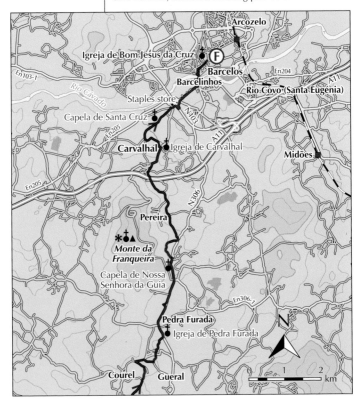

(RHS, Rua da Alegria 38, tel 252 652 041, www.villadarco-shotel.com, 5 rooms, €50+). Pass fields and then a section of forest before reaching a crossroads with the busy N206. Ignore the arrows to KSP and turn left and after 300m, as the road bends left, turn right onto Rua da Bica da Serra and follow this for 1.6km before crossing the old railway tracks into São Pedro de Rates. ▸ Arrive at **Igreja de São Pedro** (RHS, NM). **3.9km/13.7km**

> It's possible to connect to the coastal route by turning left along these old tracks; see Link route 2 for directions.

SÃO PEDRO DE RATES, 65M, POP. 2442

According to legend, St James converted Pedro of Rates to Christianity, appointing him the first Bishop of Braga, but while spreading the word Pedro was martyred. At the end of the 11th century, Count Henrique and Dona Teresa ordered the reconstruction of the primitive church which became part of a Benedictine monastery. Romanesque alterations were made during the 12–13th centuries (visible particularly in the main entrance), then in the 16th century ownership transferred to the Order of Christ. The Núcleo Museológico is next door, closed Sun–Mon.

There's a pharmacy and café 90m further up the road, a mini-market near the albergue and a *padaria* (bakery) and restaurant opposite the BP petrol station.

Accommodation: Albergue de Peregrinos de Rates (Rua Santo António 189, 50 beds, kitchen, donation).

Turn right at the church and go through the square, continuing straight onto the cobbled Rua Direita, then turn left at the end and pass the albergue (LHS). Pass a minimarket (RHS) then go uphill and leave São Pedro de Rates by taking the right fork at the stone cross onto Rua da Ponte do Burrinho. Follow this onto a dirt road through fields and forest for 2km before joining a cobbled road and passing a few houses briefly, then continuing straight onto a dirt road. Pass a **St James wayside shrine** (LHS) (**3.8km**) and after a further kilometre, turn left onto Rua do Ferrado, then turn right at the end onto Rua Central between stone walls. Take the next right onto Rua da Quintão (or KSO for Café Real +50m), then turn left onto a dirt road downhill, through a residential area. On reaching the N306, turn left and shortly afterwards pass **Igreja de Pedra Furada** (RHS). **6.7km/20.4km**

> Pedra Furada is said to have taken its name from the **old stone** (*pedra*) with a hole in the middle (*furada*) next to the church. One legend tells the story of a saint who was buried alive in a stone tomb and, determined to live, used his head to pierce a hole in the stone.

Follow arrows on and off the N306 for 1km before passing Restaurant Pedra Furada (LHS, Rua de Santa Leocádia 1415, tel 252 951 144, www.pedrafurada.com, delicious lunch served daily 12–3pm) then for a further 2km before finally leaving the N306 with a left turn onto Rua dos Cruzeiros. Follow this winding road for 2km through **Pereira** then continuous hamlets before going under the A11 (**5km**). Continue downhill to a junction and turn right into Carvalhal. After 560m turn left at **Igreja de Carvalhal** (RHS) then take the first right onto Rua João Francisco dos Santos. Continue along winding lanes for 1.2km before passing a picnic area and **Capela de Santa Cruz** (LHS). **7.3km/27.7km**

KSO into Rua de Mereces, turning right at the end of the road onto Av de São João, then cross the roundabout, passing a **Staples store**. Follow the road right, around a car dealership (RHS), then turn left and go under the N103. On reaching the roundabout, KSO onto the N205 for 600m to a crossroads, then turn left and downhill into **Barcelinhos**. Before crossing the bridge into Barcelos, pass Albergue Amigos da Montanha and Capela de Nossa Senhora da Ponte. ◀ Cross the medieval bridge over the River Cávado into **Barcelos** and turn left uphill then right towards the Igreja Matriz, passing

A 17th-century reconstruction with ancient stone sinks traditionally used by pilgrims to wash their feet. Turn left here for Albergue Senhor do Galo, at the end of the street.

the open-air archaeological museum (RHS in the ruins of the 15th-century Paço dos Condes. Includes the 14th-century stone cross of Santiago and the cockerel).

The **Legend of the Cockerel** goes that passing through Barcelos on his way to Santiago, a pilgrim was wrongly convicted of a crime and sentenced to be hung. He requested to meet the judge, who was having lunch, and declared that as proof of his innocence, the roast chicken on the table would come to life when he was hung. And so it did. The judge, realising his mistake, rushed to the pilgrim who had miraculously survived. He was freed then later returned to Barcelos and carved the stone cross with an image of the cockerel and Santiago, now in the archaeological museum.

Turn left in front of the church up Rua da Misericórdia, passing the town hall (RHS, built on the site of a 14th-century pilgrim hospital), and turn right onto Rua de São Francisco. Continue into the pedestrianised Rua António Barroso, ending the stage at the domed **Igreja de Bom Jesus da Cruz** in Largo da Porta Nova. **2.7km/30.4km**

BARCELOS, 51M, POP. 122,096

Known for its Thursday market, pottery, and ties to Santiago with the 'Legend of the Cockerel', Barcelos has been hosting pilgrims for centuries. Stroll around and it will be hard to miss one of the giant colourful cockerel sculptures, now a symbol of Portugal. Confalonieri (1594) noted that Barcelos was 'surrounded by walls with a very great bridge of very long arches'.

Tourist office: Largo Dr José Novais 27, tel 253 811 882, www.cm-barcelos.pt, open daily (closed Sundays in winter).

Visit: Igreja de Bom Jesus da Cruz – in December 1504, a cobbler named João Pires saw a black cross appear in the earth so he gathered the locals to also witness the miracle. They erected a stone cross then a small church and the current Baroque domed church was built in 1704. It contains a 16th-century Flemish sculpture of Jesus of the Cross. Torre da Porta Nova (NM), part of the 15th-century town walls, was used as a jail from 1632 until 1932 and now affords free panoramic views. Igreja Matriz (NM), 14th century,

The legendary cockerel stone cross in the outdoor archaeological museum, Barcelos

Romanesque and Gothic with later Manueline and Baroque additions, lined with 18th-century *azulejos* (tiles). Igreja de Nossa Senhora do Terço, part of a former 18th-century Benedictine convent, features a stunning interior lined with blue-and-white azulejos. Feira de Barcelos – held since the 15th century, this famous Thursday market in Campo da Feira has everything from local produce to handicrafts, animals and clothes. Museu de Olaria (pottery), Rua Cónego Joaquim Gaiolas, **www.museuolaria.pt**, closed Mondays.

Specialities: now in the Minho region, the food is typically hearty to match the cooler climate, with many stews and soups like *caldo verde* (potato and cabbage). The wine of the region is *vinho verde* (green wine), referring to 'young' wines, and the slightly sparkling wines can be either red or white.

Where to eat: one of the many restaurants in the lane next to Bom Jesus da Cruz, or for something special try Restaurant Bagoeira (next to Bagoeira Hotel) – the grilled octopus is delicious.

Accommodation (Barcelos): Albergue 'Cidade de Barcelos' (Rua Miguel Bombarda 36, **www.alberguedebarcelos.com**, 20 beds, kitchen, donation). Residencial Kuarenta&Um (Rua Miguel Bombarda 41, tel 932 117 730, **residencial41.wixsite.com/residencial41**, 7 rooms, kitchen, €32.50+, opposite the albergue). ****Bagoeira Hotel (Av Dr Sidónio Pais 495, tel 253 809 500, **www.bagoeira.com**, 54 rooms, €50+, adjacent to the terrific restaurant).

Accommodation (Barcelinhos): Albergue Amigos da Montanha (Rua Custódio José Gomes Vilas Boas 57, tel 253 830 430, **www.amigosdamontanha.com**, 16 beds, kitchen, €8, on the Camino). Albergue Senhor do Galo (Largo Guilherme Gomes Fernandes, tel 253 833 304, 30 beds, €10).

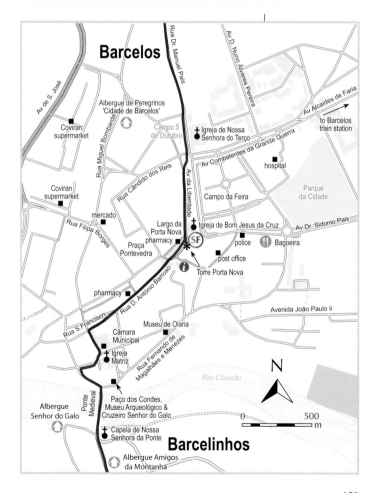

STAGE 18
Barcelos to Ponte de Lima

Start	Largo da Porta Nova, Barcelos
Finish	Largo de Camões, Ponte de Lima
Distance	33.5km
Total ascent	558m
Total descent	581m
Difficulty	Medium
Time	9–10 hours
Cafés	Barcelos, Vila Boa (2.9km), Lijó (5.1km), Tamel São Pedro Fins (9.6km), Aborim (11.2km +220m), Balugães (15.2km +300m), Vitorino dos Piães (21.8km +70m), Seara (27.8km), Ponte de Lima (33.5km)
Accommodation	Barcelos, Lijó (5.1km), Tamel São Pedro Fins (9.6km), Balugães (15.1km), Lugar do Corgo (19.5km), Vitorino dos Piães (21.7km +170m), Facha (24.3km), Ponte de Lima (33.5km)

This is a picturesque but long stage along winding country lanes with a few short forest sections, medieval bridges and one long climb before the albergue in Tamel São Pedro Fins. There's an abundance of excellent accommodation en route.

Continue north from Largo da Porta Nova, passing the Igreja de Bom Jesus, along Av da Liberdade. Pass the park with bandstand (LHS) and go straight into Rua Dr Manuel País. After 500m cross a bridge over the circular road, then at the roundabout take the diagonal right onto Rua de S Mamede, passing restaurant Restaurante Comtradição (LH corner). Keep left onto Rua das Flores, and on reaching the T-junction turn right onto Rua da Lobata. Keep left and take the left fork up Travessa da Igreja, then at Café Central (RHS) turn left onto Rua da Igreja. Pass around the church in **Vila Boa** (**2.9km**) and take the next right onto the cobbled Rua do Espírito Santo, then take the left fork at the **stone cross** (16th century). Go under the railway tracks and turn right, then turn left onto a cobbled road through a small section of forest.

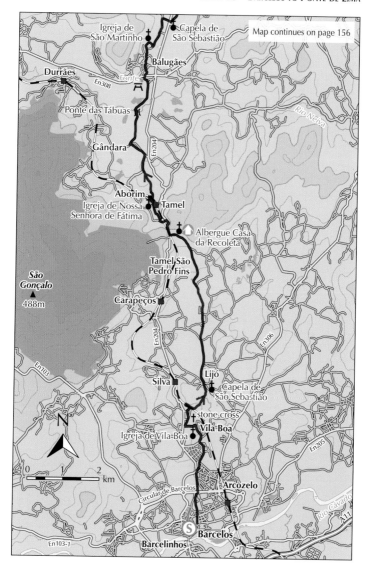

Igreja de
São Martinho

Capela de
São Sebastião

Map continues on page 156

Balugães

Durrães

Fonte

En308

Rio Neiva

Ponte das Tábuas

Gândara

En204

Aborim

Tamel

Igreja de Nossa
Senhora de Fátima

Albergue Casa
da Recoleta

Tamel São
Pedro Fins

*São
Gonçalo*
▲
488m

Carapeços

En204

En306

En103

Silva

Lijó

Capela de
São Sebastião

N

stone cross

Vila Boa

Igreja de Vila-Boa

0 1 2
km

En205

Arcozelo

Circular de Barcelos

Rio Cávado

A11

S Barcelos

Barcelinhos

En103-1

155

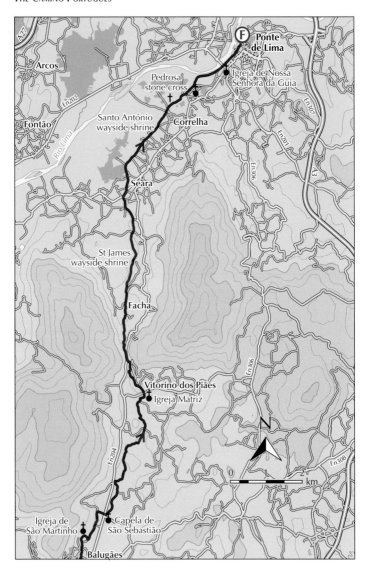

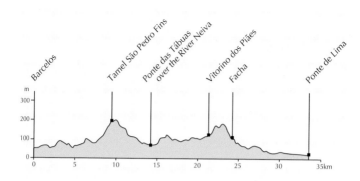

Continue along lanes for 630m before passing Pastelaria Arantes and **Capela de São Sebastião** in **Lijó. 5.1km**

Soon pass Casa de São Sebastião (RHS, Rua dos Caminheiros de Santiago 380, tel 253 884 117, www. coudelariacesarsilva.pt, shared and private rooms, kitchen, €25+), then after 1.2km KSO at a stop sign onto a forest track. After 500m leave the forest and KSO onto a paved road, continuing straight for 2.2km before merging left onto Rua de Nossa Senhora de Portela at a covered cross (LHS). Continue uphill for 550m until you reach Restaurant 2000 (LHS, pilgrim menu, closed Mondays) and take the steps opposite, up and left through the square, passing Capela da Nossa Senhora da Portela (17th century), a stone cross (with Camino motifs) and Albergue de Peregrinos 'Casa da Recoleta' (Rua da Recoleta 100, tel 935 136 811 & 253 137 075, 42 beds, kitchen, €5) in **Tamel São Pedro Fins. 4.5km/9.6km**

Turn right at the end onto the N204 and carefully walk along the shoulder/grass for 500m before turning left at a sign to Quintiães. Take the first right onto the dirt Rua Pa António Costa Rosa, going downhill and veering left onto the cobbled road then passing the large modern **Igreja de Nossa Senhora de Fátima** in **Aborim**. Go down the steps in front of the church, cross the railway tracks and turn right. Take the first left (or KSO +220m for Tamel station with Café Oliveira and ATM) onto Rua de São Tiago, which becomes a dirt road through grapevines. After 800m reach a paved road and turn right, then go left at the end and pass Pastelaria

157

A 16th-century stone reconstruction of the 12th-century wooden bridge; Confalonieri (1594) mentions crossing the stone version.

Rosa Cintilante (RHS). Shortly afterwards turn left onto Caminho de Santiago, and on reaching a T-junction turn left then immediately right onto Rua da Ponte das Tábuas. After 1km cross **Ponte das Tábuas** over the River Neiva. ◀ Turn right and KSO along a dirt road between fields for 950m until you reach a cobbled road and the blue gate of Quinta da Cancela (Cândido Batista de Sousa 275, tel 258 763 079, www.quintacancela.pt, 8 rooms, kitchen, €60+) at the beginning of **Balugães**. **5.5km/15.1km**

For a café and supermarket, turn right along the N308 +300m.

Turn left and pass a *fonte* and picnic table, then turn right and cross the N308 onto the cobbled Rua de Quingustos. ◀ Turn right at the end, then soon afterwards keep right and follow the arrows and 'Igreja Românica' signs for 730m before passing the **Romanesque Igreja de São Martinho** (LHS, 12th century with covered porch). Turn left at the end onto a paved road and continue straight onto a forest road, then turn right, downhill and carefully cross the N204 into Rua da Vila de Sabugueiro, passing **Capela de São Sebastião** (RHS) (**2.4km**). Follow the arrows along small winding roads through fields for 2km before passing Casa da Fernanda (LHS, tel 914 589 521, 10 beds, home-cooked meals, donation, bookings advised – Fernanda and Jacinto are wonderful hosts and this is bound to be a highlight of your Camino). After a further kilometre pass Estabulo Valinhas Guesthouse (LHS, Rua da Fonte Quente 251, tel

Country lanes near Vitorino dos Piães

961 050 955, www.casadevalinhas.com, shared and private rooms in beautifully converted stables, kitchen, dinner available on request), then cross a road into Rua de Jerico. Shortly after, turn right and downhill to the **Igreja Matriz** of **Vitorino dos Piães**. **6.6km/21.7km**

Turn left in front of the church then KSO (or for Casa Sagres +170m, take the next right, Rua do Latão 175, tel 962 916 441, 8 beds, kitchen, €20+) over the small roundabout into Rua de Reborido and go uphill. Turn left onto Rua do Gujo, then first right onto Travessa do Gujo. Follow the arrows for 900m to the N204 again and turn right briefly before turning left onto a parallel dirt road with green and yellow Camino signs. Enter a beautiful stretch of forest for 1km until you join a cobbled road and pass Quinta da Portela (RHS, tel 964 257 171, 14 beds, €25+, meals available with prior request, the multi-lingual owner Han has superbly renovated a large 17th-century house), then Casa de Santiago Guesthouse (LHS, Caminho de Santiago 3158, tel 919 216 557, 5 rooms, €40+ including meals in a design house with sweeping valley views) in **Facha**. **2.6km/24.3km**

Merge right onto the M1259 and shortly afterwards turn left and downhill, veering left onto a cobbled road and passing grapevines and fields. After 600m pass a chapel and **St James wayside shrine** then take the left fork at the stone cross. Continue along winding lanes for 2km, then on reaching the N203 turn right and pass a café and *pastelaria* (pastry shop, both LHS) in **Seara** (**3.5km**). Take the next left onto Rua do Caminho de Santiago and continue along small roads through continuous hamlets for 2.1km before taking the left fork at the **Santo António wayside shrine**. **5.8km/30.1km**

After a further 700m pass the old **Pedrosa stone cross** (LHS, 17th century) then after another 500m cross a bridge and turn left onto Rua do Topo, passing a bandstand and picnic area opposite Capela de Nossa Senhora das Neves. Continue straight onto a path under grapevines around to the River Lima (LHS) then continue beside the river. Go under the N201, pass **Igreja de Nossa Senhora da Guia** (17th century RHS), then go straight through the delightful tree-lined Av dos Plátanos. Pass the tourist office inside the medieval tower then reach the main square with 17th century fountain, Largo de Camões in **Ponte de Lima**. **3.4km/33.5km**

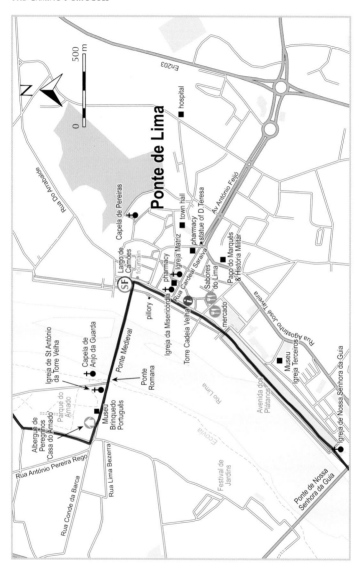

PONTE DE LIMA, 20M, POP. 44,343

Largo de Camões, Ponte de Lima

On the Via XIX Roman road connecting Braga to Astorga and named after its bridge on the River Lima, charming Ponte de Lima is Portugal's oldest village, having received its charter in 1125 from Dona Teresa. During the 14th century the village was fortified with a wall and nine towers (two still remain), and although the bridge was reconstructed, part of the Roman section still remains. The excellent albergue is across the bridge on the RHS.

Tourist office: Torre da Cadeia Velha (part of the old village walls and a prison until the 1960s), tel 258 240 208, **www.visitepontedelima.pt**, open daily (closed weekends in winter).

Visit: Igreja Matriz, 15th century. Historical centre behind the main square. Capela de Anjo da Guarda (NM), thought to be originally 13th century, across the bridge, on the RHS. International Garden Festival (May–October). Fortnightly Monday market beside the river, Portugal's oldest market, first referenced in 1125 by Dona Teresa. Museums: Historia Militar (military), Museu dos Terceiros (sacred art), Museu do Brinquedo Português (toys).

Specialities: *Arroz de Sarrabulho* (rice with pork cuts and blood stew), *lampreia* (lamprey), *leite crème* (crème brûlée), *vinho verde* wines.

Where to eat: Mercado, next to the market, pilgrim menu. Sabores do Lima for traditional meals, opposite the market.

Accommodation: Pousada de Juventude (Rua Papa João Paulo II, tel 258 751 321, **www.pousadasjuventude.pt**, 52 beds, kitchen, €14+, +1km from the square). Mercearia da Vila (Rua Cardeal Saraiva 34–36, tel 258 753 562 & 968 096 554, **www.merceariadavila.pt**, 6 beautifully decorated rooms and a delicious buffet breakfast in the old grocery). Across the bridge: Albergue de Peregrinos 'Casa do Arnado' (Além da Ponte, tel 258 240 200 & 925 403 164, 60 beds, kitchen, €5). Arc My Otel (Largo da Alegria 9, tel 258 900 150, 15 rooms, €45+, modern hotel opposite the albergue).

STAGE 19
Ponte de Lima to Rubiães

Start	Largo de Camões, Ponte de Lima
Finish	Albergue de Peregrinos, Rubiães
Distance	17.9km
Total ascent	575m
Total descent	394m
Difficulty	Medium
Time	5–6hr
Cafés	Ponte de Lima, Arcozelo (3.1km +100m), Revolta (8.4km), Rubiães (17.9km)
Accommodation	Ponte de Lima, Cabanas (14.4km), São Roque (16.6km), Rubiães (17.9km)

Between Lisbon and Porto the Camino often followed the Via XVI Roman road. From Ponte de Lima it follows the Via XIX (connecting Braga to Astorga). This stage crosses Roman bridges and climbs what many consider to be the hardest part of the Camino, over the Portela Grande. ('Bad to pass' is what Confalonieri wrote!) Allow time to take it easy and carry water.

From Largo de Camões, cross the medieval-Roman bridge over the River Lima then pass the albergue (RHS) and take the next right onto a cobbled road. Veer right towards the river then turn left, and shortly afterwards turn left again along a dirt lane. Follow this as it becomes a stone path beside a small stream, then carefully cross the N202 and KSO. Go under the A27, and on reaching a road turn right then left and pass the Romanesque Igreja Paroquial (12–13th century) in **Arcozelo**. **3.1km**

▶ Follow the arrows for 900m as they lead you across the Roman **Ponte do Arco da Geia** over the River Labruja, then go uphill and turn left. As the road bends right, turn left onto a dirt road and shortly afterwards turn left and downhill for 700m before passing Café Pescaria (LHS, open Mar–Oct). Soon go under the A3 (**2.7km**) and turn left onto a dirt track under the highway. Follow the arrows painted on pylons as they lead you to the right of the highway and across a narrow footbridge, then veer to the left, and to the right once more,

Take the next left for Café Casa Veiga +100m.

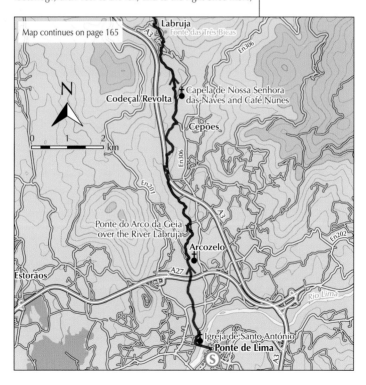

Map continues on page 165

Fonte das Três Bicas, Labruja

then go uphill along a forest road beside the highway. Reach a paved road but turn right to stay on a forest road, which becomes a delightful section of stone path with the sound of the cascading River Labruja (RHS). After 1.2km reach a cobbled road and houses and turn left onto Rua do Santuário do Senhor do Socorro (M522) through Arco. Follow the road for 660m then turn left and uphill, passing **Capela de Nossa Senhora das Naves** opposite Café Nunes (the last café before the climb and until Rubiães) in **Revolta**. **5.3km/8.4km**

Continue along the small road for 1.6km, and on reaching the M522 turn left and take the first right onto Rua da Fonte das Três Bicas. Take the left fork then pass **Fonte das Três Bicas** (RHS, the last chance for water before the climb) and turn left, uphill. Cross the M522 into Rua da Bandeira, then shortly afterwards meet the M522 one last time and turn left then right onto a forest path. The climb up and over the Portela Grande is well marked but take care, especially in wet weather, along the rocky trail. After 1.4km pass a stone cross (LHS, **Cruz dos Franceses**), then after a further 500m reach the pass and a dirt road on **Portela Grande** (408m altitude). **4.5km/12.9km**

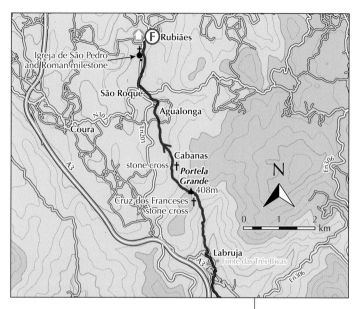

Cruz dos Franceses stone cross on the way up Portela Grande

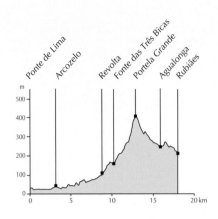

Begin descending steeply (next to a Camino information board) and after 1km pass a stone cross. After a further 500m join a paved road through **Cabanas**. KSO for 1.2km through **Agualonga** and across a stone bridge. After a further 500m go straight across the N301 and shortly afterwards reach the N201 with Repouso do Peregrino directly in front, in **São Roque (3.7km)**.

> **São Roque accommodation:** Repouso do Peregrino (Estrada de São Pedro de Rubiães 2192, tel 251 943 692, 17 rooms, €30+). Quinta das Leiras (Caminhos de Santiago de Rubiães 576, tel +49 174 323 9436, 4 rooms, €26+, multiple languages spoken, pool and garden, on the Camino, free transport to nearby restaurant).

Turn right and pass a pharmacy, then after passing Capela de São Roque (RHS) take the right fork onto a cobbled road at an information sign. Pass Quinta das Leiras and enter a short stretch of forest. Pass a stone cross (turn left here to visit **Igreja de São Pedro**, NM) and shortly afterwards turn left onto the cobbled Caminho de Santiago, reaching Albergue S. Pedro de Rubiães, in **Rubiães. 5km/17.9km**

RUBIÃES, 218M, POP. 512

A peaceful spot with the nearby 13th-century Romanesque Igreja de São Pedro de Rubiães (NM) and Roman milestone (in front of the church).

Where to eat: Café/mini-market S. Sebastião is opposite the albergue and Restaurant Bom Retiro is +500m along the N201.

Accommodation: Albergue de Peregrinos 'S. Pedro de Rubiães' (Estrada de S. Pedro de Rubiães 949, tel 965 053 751 & 251 094 558, 46 beds, kitchen, €8). Ninho – The Pilgrim Nest (Estrada de S. Pedro de Rubiães 695, tel 916 866 372, shared and private rooms, kitchen, €15+, 300m further along the Camino).

STAGE 20
Rubiães to Tui

Start	Albergue de Peregrinos, Rubiães
Finish	Tui Cathedral
Distance	19.5km
Total ascent	320m
Total descent	471m
Difficulty	Easy
Time	5–6hr
Cafés	Rubiães, São Bento da Porta Aberta (4.3km), Fontoura (7.5km), Arão (14.6km), Valença (16.2km), Tui (19.5km)
Accommodation	Rubiães, Pecene (3.7km), Paços (10.1km & 10.8km), Valença (16.2km), Tui (19.5km)
Note	Spanish time is 1hr ahead of Portugal

This is a beautiful stage through forest and woodland. There's one initial short climb to São Bento da Porta Aberta before descending to the historic fort of Valença. Say *adeus* to Portugal and cross the International Bridge over the River Minho to Spain's hilltop city of Tui.

Leave the albergue and continue down to the N201, turning right. Pass Ninho – The Pilgrim Nest (see previous stage for details) then turn left, initially doubling back along a

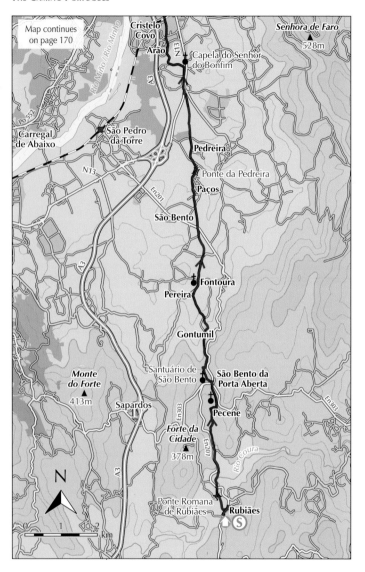

Map continues on page 170

Senhora de Faro
528m

Cristelo Covo

Arão

Capela do Senhor do Bonfim

Rio Miño / Rio Minho

A3

N13

Carregal de Abaixo

São Pedro da Torre

Po 552

Pedreira

N13

Ponte da Pedreira

En201

Paços

São Bento

A3

Fontoura

Pereira

Gontumil

Monte do Forte
413m

Santuário de São Bento

São Bento da Porta Aberta

Sapardos

En303

Pecene

En303

Forte da Cidade
378m

En201

Rio Coura

A3

N

0   1   km

Ponte Romana de Rubiães

Rubiães
S

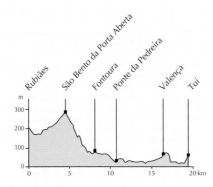

cobbled path. Cross **Ponte Romana de Rubiães** over the River Coura and turn right, then cross the N201 onto a cobbled path, passing café/mercado Ponte Nova. After 560m reach the N201 again and turn right, then right onto Estrada da Bolência. Soon turn left and uphill along a cobbled dirt road. On reaching a T-junction turn right onto a paved road, and shortly afterwards pass Casa da Capela (Pecene Cossourado, tel 913 424 947, www.casadacapela.pt, 9 rooms, kitchen, €65+) next to the chapel in **Pecene**. **3.7km**

After a further 530m reach the N303 in **São Bento da Porta Aberta** and turn left, passing Café Castro (RHS), then turn right onto the N201, passing **Santuário de São Bento** (LHS, 17th century). Turn left onto the cobbled road adjacent to the church then follow a picturesque forest path downhill with views towards Valença. After 1.2km reach a road and turn left downhill through **Gontumil**. Follow the arrows through **Pereira**, turning right onto a narrow stone path beside a small stream before entering **Fontoura**. **3.8km/7.5km**

Pass the church and Taberna da Igreja (RHS) then continue along the road for 800m before turning left onto a dirt road through woodland. After another 800m KSO across the N201 onto the cobbled Caminho de Santiago, then go through **Paços**. Pass Albergue Quinta Estrada Romana (1607 Caminho de Santiago-Paços, tel 933 736 078 & 251 094 125, www.quintaestradaromana.com, 18 beds in a wonderfully restored building, €18 including breakfast) then cross the medieval **Ponte da Pedreira**. **3.2km/10.7km**

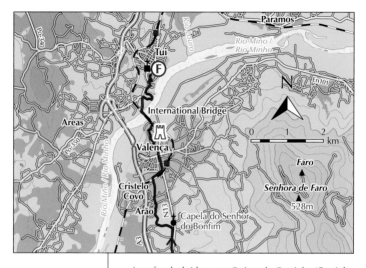

Just after the bridge, pass Quinta do Caminho (Caminho de Santiago-Lugar da Pedreira, tel 251 821 183, www.quin-tadocaminho.com, shared €17+ and private rooms, bar and restaurant) then continue for 2km to the N13 and turn right. Turn left at the roundabout onto a parallel road, then after 550m turn left at **Capela do Senhor do Bonfim**. Follow the road around to the right, turning right at the end (with a stone cross in the road) and pass Café Contrasta (RHS) in **Arão** (**3.9km**). Shortly afterwards, veer left around a tree then right and KSO. After 650m go under the railway tracks and turn right, then pass the bus station and turn right at the roundabout. Take the next left onto Av Miguel Dantas, pass supermarket Minho Super and continue for 350m to a large roundabout and Av dos Bombeiros Voluntários in **Valença**.

5.5km/16.2km ◄ Continue straight across the roundabout, then turn left and uphill on Av dos Combatentes. Enter the **fort** through the Portas do Sol gate and turn right at the end. Take the left fork through the square into Rua Mouzinho de Albuquerque, passing shops, restaurants and Igreja de Santa María, then turn right and pass the Pousada de São Teotonio. Go down the stairs, through the 13th-century Muralha Primitive gate, through a second gate and continue downhill to the road. Turn left and cross the **International**

Turn left here for the albergue (+400m, LHS), passing Hotel Val Flores and Hotel Lara. On leaving the albergue, follow arrows straight into the fort.

VALENÇA, 73M, POP. 14,187

Valença's fort

A walled hilltop village since the 13th century, it was in the 17th century (to protect Portugal from Spanish and later French invasion) that Valença's walls were transformed to their current design with two forts connected by a middle gate. Nowadays it's a shopping magnet – particularly if you want linen or towels! Allow time to wander through the fort, admire the views from the walls and devour one last *pastel de nata*...

Tourist office: Portas do Sol, tel 251 823 329, **www.visitvalenca.com**, open daily.

Visit: the fort, including Capela de Bom Jesus, 17th century, behind a statue of Portugal's first Saint Teotónio. Igreja da S Estevão, 13th century, with a Roman milestone in front. Igreja de Santa María, 13th century, opposite the Pousada.

Specialities: last chance for Portuguese food!

Where to eat: Fatum, literally inside the castle walls; have your last Portuguese meal listening to *fado* music in a beautiful setting. Trattoria Casa Di Mamma, delicious and great-value Italian outside the fort

Accommodation: outside the fort – Albergue de Peregrinos 'S. Teotónio' (Av José Maria Gonçalves, tel 251 806 020 & 961 168 501, 49 beds, kitchen, €8). *Hotel Val Flores (Av Bombeiros Voluntários, tel 251 824 106, **www.hotelvalflores.com**, 31 rooms, €30+). ***Hotel Lara (Av Bombeiros Voluntários, tel 251 824 348, 54 rooms, €40+). Inside the fort – Residencial Portas do Sol (Conselheiro Lopes da Silva 51, tel 965 851 667, **www.residencialportasdosol.com**, 9 rooms, €50+). Pousada de S. Teotonio on the Camino just before leaving the fort (tel 251 800 260, **www.pousadavalenca.pt**, 18 rooms, €100+, with fantastic river views).

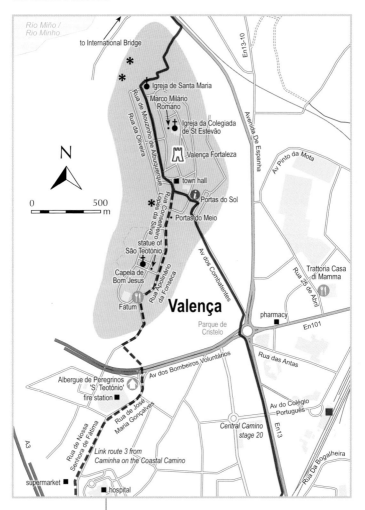

Rio Miño / Rio Minho

to International Bridge

Rua de Mouzinho de Albuquerque

Igreja de Santa Maria

Marco Milário Romano

Igreja da Colegiada de St Estevão

Rua da Oliveira

Valença Fortaleza

En13-10

Avenida De Espanha

Rua Do Pinto da Mota

N

0   500
m

town hall

Rua Conselheiro Lopes da Silva

Portas do Sol

Portas do Meio

Rua 25 de Abril

Trattoria Casa dí Mamma

statue of São Teotónio

Capela de Bom Jesus

Fatum

Rua Apolinário da Fonseca

Valença

Av dos Combatentes

Parque de Cristelo

pharmacy

En101

Av dos Bombeiros Voluntários

Rua das Antas

Albergue de Peregrinos 'S/ Teotónio'

fire station

Rua de José Maria Gonçalves

Central Camino stage 20

En13

Av do Colégio Português

A3

Rua de Nossa Senhora de Fátima

Link route 3 from Caminha on the Coastal Camino

Rua Da Bogalheira

supermarket

hospital

Spanish time is 1hr ahead of Portugal. Int'l dialling code: +34

Bridge over the River Minho into Spain (Tui is visible on the RHS). ◀ **1.2km/17.4km**

Take the first right onto Av de Portugal then turn right at the crossroads with a Repsol petrol station. Pass the

View of Tui across the River Minho from the Pousada de São Teotonio, Valença

****Parador (Av Portugal s/n, tel 986 600 300, www.parador. es, 32 rooms), and on reaching the river (where pilgrims would traditionally disembark by boat) turn left immediately, uphill, winding around the old lanes for 1km to reach Praza de San Fernando with the tourist office and **Tui Cathedral**. **2.1km/19.5km**

TUI, 70M, POP. 16,884

'Tudae' to the Romans, Tui is an ancient Galician provincial capital that was fortified during the 12th century. 'A Bishopric with a rather beautiful church' is what Jérôme Münzer noted in 1494. A visit to the cathedral is highly recommended, as is the view from the cathedral walls across the Minho.

Tourist office: Paseo de Calvo Sotelo 16, tel 677 418 405, **www.tui.gal**, open daily.

Visit: Cathedral of Santa María de Tui, 12–13th century Romanesque with Gothic facade and cloister. After visiting the cloister, climb the stairs for a view of the river and Valença, Praza de San Fernando, **www.catedraldetui. com**, open daily from 10.45am (closed 2–4pm), €5+. Museo Diocesano

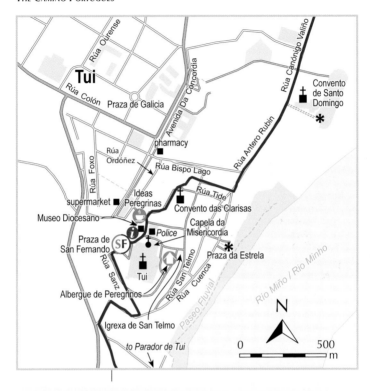

houses archaeological and sacred art in the ancient pilgrim hospital, Praza do Concello, **museos.xunta.gal**. Capela da Misericordia, 16th-century Renaissance. Igrexa de San Telmo, 18–19th-century Portuguese Baroque church, built on the site of San Telmo's house (Tui's Patron Saint). Convento das Clarisas, 17–18th century, built on an existing palace. Convento de Santo Domingo, 14th century, Gothic with two Baroque altarpieces. Behind the convent is a viewpoint of Tui and the Minho. Igrexa de San Bartolomé, 11th century with 16th-century paintings in the main chapel, this is the oldest church in Tui +1.2km further along the Camino.

Specialities: *enguia* (eel), *lampreia* (lamprey) and fish-shaped almond biscuits made by the nuns of Convento das Clarisas.

Where to eat: Café Ideas Peregrinas (along the Camino on the edge of Praza do Concello, one minute from the cathedral) for a warm welcome, delicious healthy meals, charging stations for electronics and a selection of outdoor gear.

Accommodation: Albergue de Peregrinos (Rúa Párroco Rodríguez Vázquez s/n, tel 649 502 704 , 42 beds, €8, behind the cathedral). Ideas Peregrinas (Porta da Pia 1, tel 986 076 330, **www.ideas-peregrinas.com**, shared and private rooms, kitchen, €15+, fresh modern pilgrim-friendly accommodation in a terrific location). **Hotel A Torre do Xudeu (Rúa Tide 3, tel 986 603 535, **www.atorredoxudeo.es**, 8 rooms, €55+, on the Camino). Albergue Convento del Camino (Rúa Antero Rubín 30, tel 690 328 565, **www.conventodelcamino. com**, 43 beds, kitchen, €14+, on the Camino).

STAGE 21
Tui to Mos

Start	Tui Cathedral
Finish	Albergue de Peregrinos, Mos
Distance	23.1km (or 21.9km via the industrial estate option)
Total ascent	352m
Total descent	319m
Difficulty	Easy
Time	6–7hr
Cafés	Tui, Orbenlle (9.2km, on the industrial estate route), O Porriño (17km), Veigadaña (20.5km), Mos (23.1km)
Accommodation	Tui, O Porriño (16.8km), Veigadaña (20.5km), Mos (23.1km)
Note	If starting your Camino in Tui you can pick up a credential from the cathedral. Remember to get two stamps per day from now on as you enter the last 100km to Santiago. Carry extra water if walking the river path to O Porriño.

This stage follows the scenic River Louro through picturesque woodland to Orbenlle, where there is the option of continuing by the river or taking the slightly shorter (and much less pleasant) route through an industrial estate and along the N550. Both routes meet in O Porriño before heading to the peaceful village of Mos.

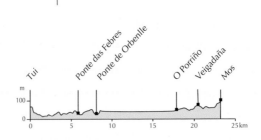

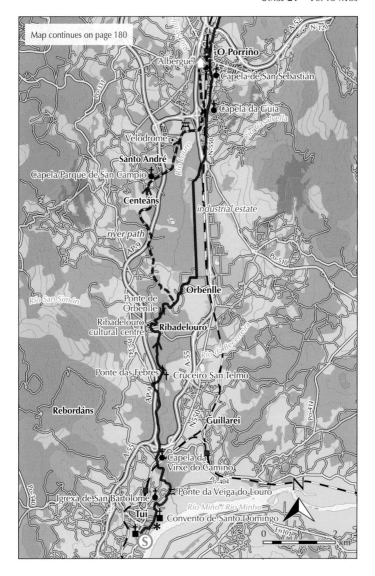

Map continues on page 180

O Porriño
Albergue
Capela de San Sébastián
Capela da Guia
Río Casalvella
Río Louro
Velodrome
Santo André
Capela/Parque de San Campio
Centeáns
industrial estate
river path
AP-9
Orbenlle
Río San Simón
Ponte de Orbenlle
Ribadelouro cultural centre
Ribadelouro
Río da Becerrexa
Ponte das Febres
Cruceiro San Telmo
Rebordáns
Guillarei
N-550
Capela da Virxe do Camino
Ponte da Veiga do Louro
Igrexa de San Bartolomé
Río Miño / Rio Minho
Tui
Convento de Santo Domingo
S

Pilgrim monument and Ponte da Veiga do Louro after leaving Tui

Go up the steps between the tourist office and cathedral, turning left and passing the old pilgrim hospital (LHS) then Ideas Peregrinas (LHS, café, accommodation and outdoor equipment). Turn right at Café KF Central, pass Convento das Clarisas then go through the tunnel, turning left then right onto Rúa Tide. Pass A Torre do Xudeu (LHS) and turn left at the end onto Rúa Antero Rubin. KSO for 630m, passing Albergue Convento del Camino (with viewpoint), then turn right onto Rúa S Bartolomeu. Turn right at the bandstand and ornate stone cross, pass **Igrexa de San Bartolomé (1.2km)** then turn left onto a dirt road. On reaching a paved road, turn right then go straight over a crossroads towards the Roman-medieval **Ponte da Veiga do Louro**. KSO without crossing the bridge, along a dirt road passing fields. Reach a T-junction and turn right then follow the road for 550m, and under the railway tracks. Carefully cross the N550, taking the first right, then at the end of the road pass behind **Capela da Virxe do Camino** (18th century). **3.2km**

Turn left onto the PO-342 and carefully follow the road for 1.7km before going under the AP9. After a further 200m turn right onto a dirt road at a flora/fauna information board and follow the dirt road across the AP9 and into a lovely stretch of woods to **Ponte das Febres** and Cruceiro

San Telmo. ▶ **(2.6km)**. Cross the bridge and turn left along a peaceful woodland track for 1km to join a road in **Ribadelouro**. Cross the PO-2502, passing the **Ribadelouro Cultural Centre** (LHS), and take the first right then turn left at the end, passing five stone crosses. Soon after, turn right onto a rocky path going downhill through woodland and cross the River Louro on the picturesque medieval stone **Ponte de Orbenlle**. Continue for 600m to a T-junction with a painting of Santiago's Pórtico da Gloria in **Orbenlle**. **5.2km/8.4km**

The 'bridge of fevers' was named after San Telmo caught a fever and died here in April 1251.

From Orbenlle there are two options to O Porriño: one along the river path (recommended, and passes near a café after 5km) or the old way through an industrial estate then along the N550 (passes several cafés).

Alternative route along the river path (8.8km)

Turn left at the artwork then after 150m turn left onto a dirt road (there should be an arrow here but it may have been blacked out by those who want pilgrims to continue along the industrial area option. The black paint will be obvious if the yellow arrows have been painted over). ▶ Follow the dirt path downhill and across a bridge (Ponte de Baranco) over the Louro, then go uphill and away from the river between grapevines. Reach a paved road and turn left, then shortly

If you need a café at this point, continue along the industrial route for 700m.

Turn left here for the river path at the beginning of Orbenlle, or go straight on for the Industrial Estate option to O Porriño

afterwards turn right at a small junction. After 150m keep right then take the left fork, going downhill through woods. After 550m reach a paved road and turn right, then just before the underpass turn right onto a dirt road, going uphill then left across the bridge over the AP9. Follow the arrows for 1.8km through **Centeans** and along a green pedestrian path, then past a stone cross at the base of a few steps leading to **Capela de San Campio** (LHS). **4.1km/12.5km**

Cross a bridge over the AP9 then KSO for 800m, passing a sign for Taberna Tia Maria (left +180m) just before passing a **velodrome** (LHS). Turn right at the roundabout, passing a **picnic area**, then go through an underpass and immediately turn left onto a dirt path. Take the right fork to walk beside the river, keeping the river on the RHS for the next 2km until you reach O Porriño **Albergue de Peregrinos** (**4.2km**). Leave the river path here and turn right onto Av Buenos Aires, across the bridge over the river, past a Froiz supermarket and over the railway tracks to a roundabout. Turn left onto Rúa

The industrial estate option joins here.

Ramiranes to continue the Camino (or right for **O Porriño** old town and services). ◄ **4.7km/17.2km**

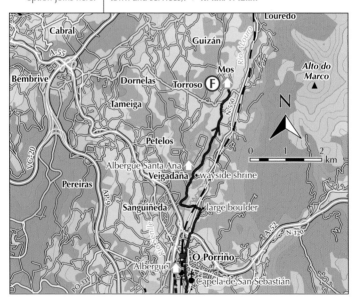

Old way via industrial estate and N550 (7.6km)

Turn left at the artwork then after 700m follow the road right, passing three cafés. Veer left then turn left into an industrial area and KSO for 3.2km to a red pedestrian ramp just before the underpass. Go up the ramp, over the railway tracks, onto the N550 then after 1.4km pass **Capela da Guia** (RHS, 1640). After a further 500m turn left at a Camino waymark, taking the first right and passing Taperia Taberna. Follow the road left, passing **Capela de San Sebastián**, then KSO. Turn left at Igrexa de Santa María then go right and straight on into the pedestrianised Rúa Ramón González and continue to the roundabout. Take the right fork onto Rúa Ramiranes (or turn left for the albergue +300m). ▶ **7.6km/16km**

Along the river path between Orbenlle and O Porriño

The river path joins here.

O PORRIÑO, 36M, POP. 18,508

O Porriño is an industrial and mining town, known for its pink granite. Its old town is particularly pleasant.

Visit: decorative fountain and the palatial town hall (*casa consistorial*) in the old town, both designed by O Porriño local, Antonio Palacios.

181

Where to eat: La Cueva, located in a 16th-century pilgrim hospital next to the town hall in the old town.

Accommodation: Albergue de Peregrinos (Av Buenos Aires, tel 986 335 428, 52 beds, €8). Alojamiento Camino Portugues Hostel (Av Buenos Aires 40, tel 886 133 252, www.alojamientocaminoportugues.es, 60 beds, kitchen, €13+, near the albergue). Hostal Louro (Av Buenos Aires 6, tel 986 112 941 & 669 683 476, www.hostallouro.es, 11 rooms, €22+, near the albergue). *Hotel Azul (Calle Ramiranes 38, tel 986 330 032 & 616 548 193, www.hotelazul.es, 16 rooms, €42+, on the Camino).

Now on Rúa Ramiranes, pass Hotel Azul then a Lidl and Gadis supermarket and KSO over the roundabout. Go under the A52 then turn right through a small tunnel, then left. After 700m turn left at a **huge boulder** (RHS) then carefully cross the N550 and go through a tunnel under the railway. After a further 450m reach a wall of tyres and turn right, then follow the road for 1km before reaching a **wayside shrine** (RHS) opposite Albergue/Café Santa Ana Veigadaña (Camiño Santa Ana 11, tel 986 331 011 & 673 289 491, 16 beds, €12) in **Veigadaña** (**3.5km**). Turn right here, then after 600m veer left and through an underpass. After 1.7km merge right onto a main road then take the first left onto Camino da Rúa, going uphill into **Mos** and passing the Pazo de Mos then Café Flora opposite the albergue. **6.1km/23.1km**

MOS, 101M, POP. 1569

A small village with everything just a few steps away makes this the perfect pilgrim stop. There are two cafés, the 16th-century Igrexa de Santa Eulalia and the grand 18th-century Pazo de Mos.

Accommodation: Albergue de Peregrinos 'Santa Eulalia de Mos' (Camiño da Rúa 3, tel 986 348 001 & 639 300 974, 37 beds, kitchen, €8).

STAGE 22
Mos to Pontevedra

Start	Albergue de Peregrinos, Mos
Finish	Praza da Peregrina, Pontevedra
Distance	29.1km
Total ascent	603m
Total descent	685m
Difficulty	Hard
Time	8–9hr
Cafés	Mos, Saxamonde (6.2km), Redondela (9.5km), Cesantes (12.6km), Arcade (16.3km), Pontevedra (27–29km)
Accommodation	Mos, Saxamonde (6.2km), Redondela (9.5km), Cesantes (12.6km), Arcade (16.3km), Pontevedra (27–29km)

This is a scenic but long stage with three decent hills to climb. There is ample accommodation en route, including Redondela's excellent albergue, and if you like oysters, try to include a meal in Arcade where they're celebrated with an annual festival. Confalonieri (1594) ate in Redondela and noted that the onward route was 'a painful road with pebbles, tiresome mountains and mud,' before spending the night at 'one of the best walled town's in Galicia' in Pontevedra's Convento de San Francisco.

Leaving the albergue, continue uphill then take the left fork at a stone cross. After 400m merge right onto Estrada Alto de Barreiros-Santiaguiño, then after 1km, as the road bends right, KSO onto the dirt Camino da Abilleira, going uphill through woods. At a T-junction turn left onto Camino das Cerdeirinas, then after 800m reach the top of this stage's first hill at a crossroads with a park (LHS). ▶ Cross the road (or turn left for Bar Casa Veiga, +150m) onto a dirt road, passing Camino stone monuments, then soon afterwards pass a Via XIX **Roman milestone**. **3.1km**

The 17th-century Capela de Santiaguiño de Antas is in the park.

After merging right onto the main road EP-2906, pass a playground (RHS) and KSO. After 700m turn left onto Camino de Chan das Pipas, then right at café/restaurant

183

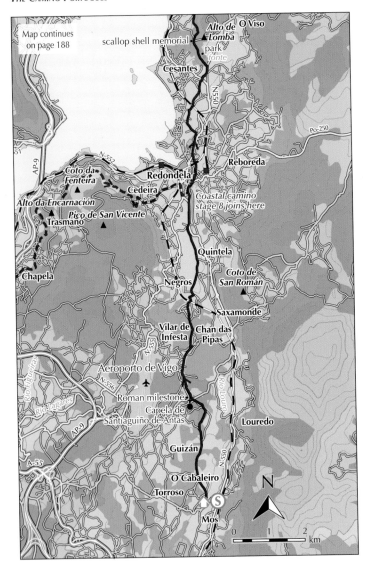

Map continues on page 188

scallop shell memorial

Alto de Lomba

O Viso

park
fonte

Cesantes

N550

Reboreda

Po-250

AP-9

N-552

Coto da Fenteira

Redondela

Cedeira

Coastal camino stage 8 joins here

Alto da Encarnación

Trasmañó

Pico de San Vicente

Quintela

Chapela

Negros

Coto de San Román

Saxamonde

Vilar de Infesta

Chan das Pipas

N-555

Aeroporto de Vigo

N-556

Río Alvedosa

Roman milestone

Capela de Santiaguiño de Antas

Río Louro

N-550

Louredo

Río Lagares

AP-9

A-55

Guizán

O Cabaleiro

Torroso

Mos

N

0   1   2 km

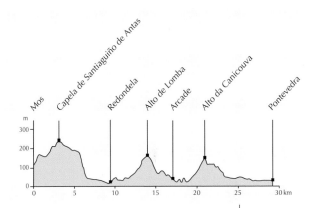

Choles onto a dirt road. Follow this on and off a paved road for 1km to the plateau of **Chan das Pipas**, before a steep downhill on Camino Coto do Gran with terrific views of the valley and Redondela. Shortly after, pass Bar & Albergue Corisco (Saxamonde-Camino Romano 47, tel 986 402 166, www.albergueocorisco.com, shared and private rooms, €15+, pilgrim menu available). **3.1km/6.2km**

Albergue de Peregrinos 'Casa da Torre', Redondela

Continue downhill, passing fields and grapevines for 2km, until you reach the N550. Turn left and cross when it's safe, as you need to take the right fork after 550m onto Rúa do Muro, following a 'Centro Urbano' sign. Soon after this, pass Convento de Vilavella (16th century, now an events centre) then veer left into Rúa Pai Crespo and pass Albergue Santiago de Vilavella (RHS, no.55). Go under the green viaduct and take the right fork, then pass Alvear Suites (LHS, no.30) and restaurants before reaching a roundabout in the centre of **Redondela**. ◄ **3.3km/9.5km**

The municipal albergue is diagonally right across the junction in the old stone 'tower' building.

REDONDELA, 15M, POP. 30,036

A delightful town known for its two 19th-century viaducts, and its cuttlefish! There is a church, fountain and square dedicated to St James.

Visit: Igrexa de Santiago, consecrated by Archbishop Xelmírez (Santiago's first archbishop) in 1114 on his return from Portugal, later rebuilt in the 15th century with subsequent additions. Alameda Park and the 18th-century Fonte de Santiago (fountain) opposite.

Specialities: *chocos* (cuttlefish).

Where to eat: 78 Gastrobar on Rúa Pai Crespo.

Accommodation (all on the Camino): Albergue de Peregrinos 'Casa da Torre' (Casa da Torre-Plaza Ribadavia, tel 986 404 196, 42 beds, €8). Albergue Santiago de Vilavella (Rúa Pai Crespo 55, tel 673 414 752, www.redondelaalbergue.com, 48 beds, €15). A Casa da Herba (Plaza de Alhóndiga, tel 644 404 074, www.acasadaherba.es, shared €15+ and private rooms, 60m further along the Camino from the albergue, RHS). *Alvear Suites (Rúa Pai Crespo 30, tel 986 400 637 & 628 621 864, 10 apartments, €40+).

Redondela is where the Coastal Camino rejoins the Central Camino. If joining from the coastal route, the distance from Redondela to Pontevedra is 19.5km, ascent 445m, descent 430m.

The Camino follows the narrow street to the left of the municipal albergue, Rúa Isidoro Queimaliños. Cross Rúa Telmo Bernardez (or turn right here for Igrexa de Santiago)

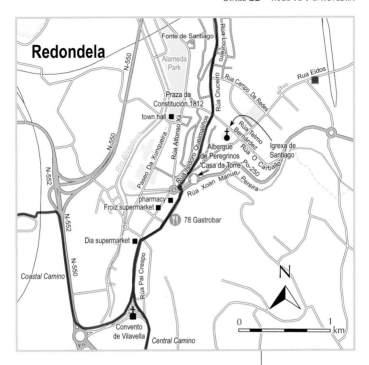

then KSO, going under the railway tracks, downhill and left at the roundabout. Turn right at the N550 and take the immediate left fork onto a parallel road. Follow this as it bends left and uphill, keeping right along the upper fork beside a stone wall. Reach a T-junction and turn right onto Rúa Torre de Calle, going uphill across a bridge over railway tracks then immediately left onto the cobbled Camiño Real de Cesantes and downhill. Continue for 800m to the N550 and Café/ Pension Rustica Jumboli (Estrada Cesantes 13, tel 986 495 066, 10 rooms, €18+) in **Cesantes**. ▶ **3.1km/12.6km**

The next hill is coming up. Carefully cross the N550 onto Estrada do Arieiro, turning left after 400m onto Camino do Loureiro do Viso. Climbing steeply, pass a **park** and *fonte* (drinking fountain) then take the left fork onto a dirt path into the forest. After 560m reach a **scallop shell memorial** and the

For O Refuxio de la Jerezana, turn right +240m along the N550, Estrada do Pereiro 43, tel 601 165 977, 24 beds, kitchen, €15+.

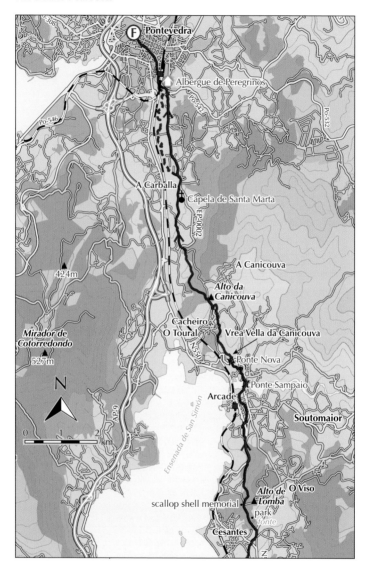

top of the climb up **Alto de Lomba** (162m altitude), then join the road briefly and turn right onto Camino dos Peregrinos. Continue through woods with occasional views of the Vigo estuary for 1.3km, going downhill to the N550 and carefully turning right onto the shoulder. After 600m pass a playground (LHS) then turn left and take the first right onto Rúa das Portas. Continue to the end of the road and turn right, then cross the N550 onto Rúa das Lameiriñas at the top of **Arcade**. **3.7km/16.3km**

ARCADE, 30M, POP. 4540

Arcade is known for its seafood, especially oysters (*ostras*). The centre of town is 700m further along the Camino and most services are on the N550.

Where to eat: Acuna Café (on the Camino), Restaurante Arcadia for seafood (N550).

Accommodation: **Hotel Duarte (Rúa das Lameiriñas 8, tel 986 670 057, 20 rooms, €35+, on the Camino). Albergue Lameiriñas (Rúa das Lameiriñas 8A, tel 986 670 057, 26 beds, kitchen, €12+, modern hostel next to Hotel Duarte). O Lar de Pepa (Calle Ribeiro 1, tel 986 678 006 & 649 494 905, www.olardepepa.com, 9 beds, kitchen, €10). **Hotel-Restaurant Isape (Cr. Soutomaior 36, tel 986 700 721, +400m off-Camino).

Pass Hotel/Café Duarte then Albergue Lameirinas (take the next left for Albergue O Lar de Pepa) and continue downhill. After 600m cross Rúa Rosalía de Castro into Rúa da Coutada, passing Acuna Café (LH corner), then keep right. At the end of the road turn left, crossing the River Verdugo on **Ponte Sampaio**. ▶ Turn left after the bridge then take the first left, going uphill, and follow the arrows as the Camino winds around the small streets for 1km. Cross **Ponte Nova** (a metal-and-concrete version of the original medieval bridge) over the River Ulló. Shortly afterwards reach a warehouse (LHS) and turn right onto what becomes a scenic but strenuous climb, initially along old stones (with wheel indents), known as **Vrea Vella da Canicouva**. **2.6km/18.9km**

After 1.1km KSO across a paved road, continuing uphill. After a further 530m reach another paved road and this time turn right, following the road as it bends right, then turn left onto an old road to reach the top of the climb up **Alto da Canicouva** (148m altitude). Turn right onto a forest

This was the site of the Battle of Ponte Sampaio during the Peninsular War (1809), in which the Spanish were victorious, forcing the French to retreat.

track going downhill and follow this onto a small paved road through a logging area, then pass fields and grapevines. After 1.8km carefully cross the EP-0002 and after a further 1.8km pass **Capela de Santa Marta** (RHS, 17th century, stamp inside). **5.6km/24.5km**

Turn left onto the main road (EP-0002), then at the first left turn (with a Río Tomeza information sign) there are two options: one following the EP-0002 (mostly without a footpath), the other along a peaceful river path. The routes converge near Pontevedra's Albergue de Peregrinos.

Following EP-0002 (2.7km)

Continue along the EP-0002 for 2.3km then cross the round-about and take the first left. Keep left and after 200m go

under the railway tracks. ◄ Soon afterwards, reach Hostal Restaurant Peregrino (LHS) on the outskirts of Pontevedra. The Albergue de Peregrinos is opposite and up the ramp.

Along the Río Tomeza-Río Dos Gafos (3.5km)

The waymarks are limited but so are the turns. Turn left at the information sign then initially keep right and take the left fork down to the River Tomeza, crossing a short stone bridge. Turn right and keep the river on the RHS for 1.2km before crossing a road and passing Ponte da Condesa (RHS). Keep to the main dirt path with the river on the RHS and after 900m cross the stone Ponte Valentim (with a gate in front); the river is now on the LHS. After 630m, just before the underpass, cross a wooden bridge then turn left under the highway. (There may be a detour around here, so follow any new arrows.) Shortly afterwards, go through a tunnel under the railway tracks then reach a paved road and turn left to arrive at Hostal Restaurant Peregrino (LHS) on the outskirts of Pontevedra. The Albergue de Peregrinos is opposite and up the ramp.

From Hostal Restaurant Peregrino, continue along Rúa Ramon Otero Pedrayo to a roundabout and **Pontevedra train station** (RHS), opposite the bus station. Turn left then take the immediate right along Rúa do Gorgullon, passing Albergue Aloxa (RHS). At the end of the road, merge left onto Rúa Eduardo Pondal, taking the first right onto Rúa da Virxe do Camino towards a Froiz supermarket. Turn left at the end onto Rúa Sagasta then turn right onto the pedestrianised Rúa da Peregrina. Shortly afterwards reach Capela da Virxe Peregrina in Praza da Peregrina, in **Pontevedra**'s old town. **4.6km/29.1km**

PONTEVEDRA, 39M, POP. 82,946

'Turoqua' to the Romans, Pontevedra is named after the Roman bridge that crossed the River Lérez until the 12th century, when it was replaced by Ponte do Burgo (which you'll depart on). Pontevedra's old town is a gem, showcasing ancient churches, an excellent provincial museum and beautiful squares with lively tapas bars.

Ravachol the talking parrot (Pontevedra's mascot) belonged to a pharmacist in Praza da Peregrina. He was so popular that when he died during the Carnival in 1913, a large funeral was held. Ravachol's memory is celebrated during the annual Carnival; see if you can find him in Praza da Peregrina!

Tourist office: Plaza de España, tel 986 090 890, www.visit-pontevedra.com, open daily.

Visit: Capela da Virxe Peregrina, 18th century, dedicated to the patroness of Pontevedra; the facade has an image of the Virgin as a pilgrim between San Roque and St James. Museo de Pontevedra, Rúa Padre Amoedo Carballo, www.museo.depo.es, closed Mondays, free entrance. Ruínas de Santo

Capela da Virxe
Peregrina, Pontevedra

Domingo (NM), interesting ruins of the 14th-century Gothic convent. Basílica de Santa María, 16th century, Gothic and Renaissance with a brilliant plateresque facade, €1 entrance for the museum, tower and viewpoint. Convento de San Francisco, 14th century (the facade remains from this time), reconstructed in the 18th century.

Specialities: *empanada de maiz* (stuffed pastry made with corn flour; fillings include seafood, beef and chicken).

Where to eat: Taberna de Felix for great-value tapas. Confitería Solla for all things sweet.

Accommodation: Albergue de Peregrinos 'La Virgen Peregrina' (Rúa Ramon Otero Pedrayo s/n, tel 986 844 045, 56 beds, kitchen, €8). Hostal Peregrino (Rúa Ramon Otero Pedrayo 8, tel 986 858 409, 27 rooms, €30+, opposite the albergue). Albergue Aloxa (Rúa do Gorgullón s/n, tel 986 896 453 & 663 438 770, **www.alberguealoxa.com**, 60 beds, €15+, on the Camino). **Old town:** Slow City Hostel (Rúa Amargura 5, tel 631 062 896, **www. slowcityhostelpontevedra.com**, shared and private rooms, kitchen, €20+, near the Basílica de Santa María). *Hotel Restaurante Rúas (Rúa Sarmiento 20, tel 986 846 416, 22 rooms, €39+).

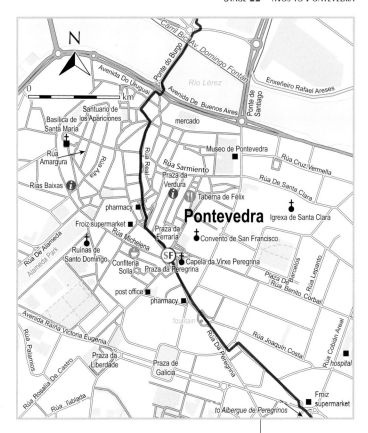

STAGE 23
Pontevedra to Caldas de Reis

Start	Praza da Peregrina, Pontevedra
Finish	Praza Martin Herrera, Caldas de Reis
Distance	21.2km
Total ascent	288m
Total descent	287m
Difficulty	Easy
Time	5–6hr
Cafés	Pontevedra, San Amaro (8.9km), Valbón (11.4km), Tivó (19.4km), Caldas de Reis (21.2km)
Accommodation	Pontevedra, A Portela (9.2km +670m), Briallos (16.4km +350m), Tivó (19.4km), Caldas de Reis (21.2km)
Note	Bring food if you're planning to stay in the albergues of A Portela or Briallos

This is a delightful stage along small roads and through peaceful woods, with one main climb to San Amaro. If time permits, after 15km when the Camino joins the N550 take the 550m detour to the stunning Parque Natural Ria Barosa falls.

Leaving Praza da Peregrina, head north into Paseo de António Odriozola, turning left in Praza de Ferreria. Pass cafés under the arches then turn right at the iron fountain into Praza de Curros Enriquez. Take the left fork onto Rúa

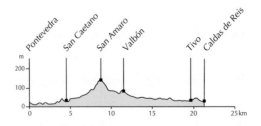

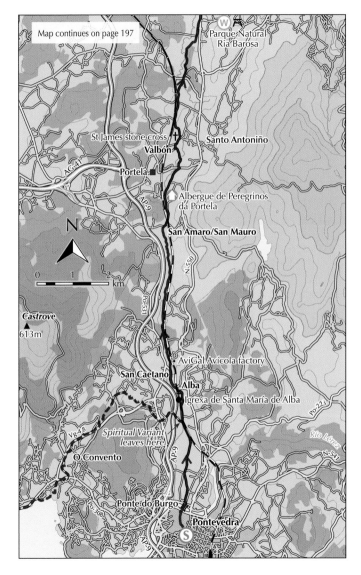

Map continues on page 197

Parque Natural
Ría Barosa

Santo Antoniño

St James stone cross
Valbón

Portela

Albergue de Peregrinos
da Portela

San Amaro/San Mauro

N

0   1   2
km

Castrove
613m

AviGal Avícola factory

San Caetano

Alba

Igrexa de Santa María de Alba

Río Lérez

*Spiritual Variant
leaves here*

O Convento

Ponte do Burgo

Pontevedra

Ponte do Burgo over the River Lérez, leaving Pontevedra

Real, then before reaching the end of the road turn left into Rúa do Ponte and take the first right. Cross the River Lérez over the scallop shell-adorned **Ponte do Burgo** (**600m**) then continue straight. Take the first left onto Rúa da Santina, passing Bar Breoyan. Keep left at the small roundabout and continue straight then onto a dirt road, passing wetlands, until you reach a T-junction. **3.1km**

For the Spiritual Variant (Variante Espiritual) turn left here.

◀ Turn right and go under the railway tracks then take the left fork. After 500m pass **Igrexa de Santa María de Alba** (16th century). On reaching the PO-225, turn left and go under the railway tracks. Carefully follow the busy road through **San Caetano**, then as the road bends left, veer right, passing the **AviGal Avícola factory** (RHS). Take the left fork and KSO as this becomes a dirt road beside the Río da Gándara (LHS), heading gradually uphill through picturesque woods for 3.2km before crossing the railway tracks. Continue uphill into the hamlet of **San Amaro**. **5.8km/8.9km**

Turn right for Albergue de Peregrinos da Portela +670m, Lugar A Cancela, tel 655 952 805, 16 beds, kitchen, €12, eat in San Amaro or bring food to cook.

Pass Café A Pousada do Peregrino then turn left opposite the chapel, passing Café Meson Don Pulpo, and go downhill past a picnic area. Shortly after this, take the lower left fork. ◀ Continue for 1.4km to a T-junction and turn left (onto the PO-0506) then immediately right onto a dirt track. Take the second left and after 600m (and a few more turns) pass Bar Mesón A Eira in **Valbón** (**2.5km**). Soon pass a **stone cross** with an image of St James facing north (LHS) and take the left fork, then turn left. Continue along dirt and quiet roads for 1.5km before crossing a small stone bridge. After a further 2km reach the N550. **6.3km/15.2km**

Turn left onto the N550 then follow the arrows as they direct you on and off the highway (onto safer roads). ▶ After 1.2km pass signs for Albergue de Peregrinos de Briallos (+350m off the Camino, Lugar San Roque, tel 986 536 194 & 662 620 480, 27 beds, kitchen, €8), then after 760m pass **Capela de Santa Lucía** (LHS). After a further 2.2km pass Albergue Vintecatro (Tivo 58, tel 986 539 028 & 659 061 792, 19 beds, €16+, large garden to relax in and on-site bar) in **Tivó (4.2km)**. Pass the fountain and stone cross and continue for 1.2km back to the N550, turning left and passing **Igrexa de Santa María** (12th-century portal). Just before reaching the bridge, pass Albergue/Café Timonel opposite Hotel Acuna then cross the bridge over the River Umia into **Caldas de Reis**. Take the first left onto Rúa Laureano Salgado and pass Hotel Balneario Davila (LHS) with a thermal spring in front and a square opposite, Praza Martin Herrera, where this stage ends. **6km/21.2km**

For Parque Natural Ria Barosa – a picnic area with waterfalls, mills and a scenic walking course – cross over the N550, +550m, or for Café Casa Maruja turn right +50m.

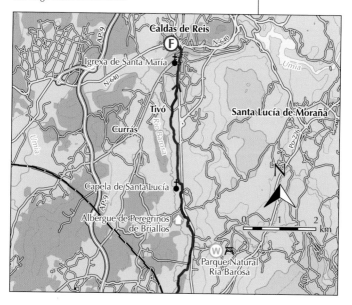

197

CALDAS DE REIS, 25M, POP. 9895

Thermal spring, Caldas de Reis

A thermal spa-town at the confluence of the Umia and Bermaña rivers, Caldas de Reis was known as Aquis Celenis to the Romans. Queen Dona Urraca (Portugal's Dona Teresa's half-sister) lived and gave birth to her son here (King Alfonso VII), and owing to these royal ties, 'Reis' was added to the name. Jérôme Münzer (1494) was impressed with the 'hot sulphurous baths, at an excellent temperature, like the baths of Baden near Zurich'.

Tourist office: Centro Comarcal da Tafona, García Bayón, closed Sunday, tel 665 286 957, **www.caldasdereis.com**.

Visit: Igrexa de Santo Tomás Becket, a church dedicated to the Archbishop of Canterbury who is believed to have passed through in 1167. Gardens beside the River Umia.

Where to eat: Taberna O Muino (atmospheric!). Bar 5 Jotas (next to the albergue).

Accommodation (all on the Camino): Albergue de Peregrinos 'Posada Doña Urraca' (Rúa Campo da Torre 1, tel 638 605 335, 26 beds, €13. Access: continue along the Camino for 250m and the albergue is just across the Roman bridge on the LHS). Albergue Timonel (Calle de la Herrería 3, tel 986 540 840, 20 dorm beds €13+, and 5 private rooms, €20+, kitchen, next to the town hall).

Balneario Acuña (Calle Herrería 2, tel 986 540 010, **www.balnearioacuna. com, 62 rooms, €44+, spa hotel opposite the town hall). Balneario Davila (Laureano Salgado 11, tel 986 540 012, **www.balneariodavila.com**, 26 rooms, €60+, spa hotel).

STAGE 24
Caldas de Reis to Padrón

Start	Praza Martin Herrera, Caldas de Reis
Finish	Igrexa de Santiago, Padrón
Distance	18.6km
Total ascent	298m
Total descent	311m
Difficulty	Easy
Time	5hr
Cafés	Caldas de Reis, Carracedo (5.4km), San Miguel de Valga (12km), Infesta (15.5km), Padrón (18.6km)
Accommodation	Caldas de Reis, O Pino (9.6km +220m), Infesta (15.7km), Herbón (16.2km +3km), Padrón (18.6km)
Note	If you want to arrive for the midday mass in Santiago, consider continuing past Padrón

This is a pleasant stage along small roads and woodland paths through valleys, before following the River Sar into the historic town of Padrón, closely linked to St James. If you'd like a peaceful setting for what may be your last night before Santiago, consider taking the detour to Herbón Monastery Albergue.

From Praza Martin Herrera go straight into Rúa Real, passing the municipal market (LHS), then across the Roman bridge over the River Bermaña (the albergue is on the LHS). Continue along Rúa San Roque, passing the chapel, then turn left onto the N550 (**560m**). Shortly afterwards, veer right onto a small road which soon becomes a dirt path. After 750m go through an underpass then continue along small roads and quiet woodland paths for 3.9km, gradually ascending to meet the N550 in **Carracedo. 5.4km**

Cross the N550 and take a road slightly to the left (Café Esperon is also to the left), then veer right. Soon pass **Igrexa de Santa Mariña** then KSO, passing the bandstand (RHS). Follow the arrows along winding lanes for 1.1km back to the N550, continue straight across then take the first left onto

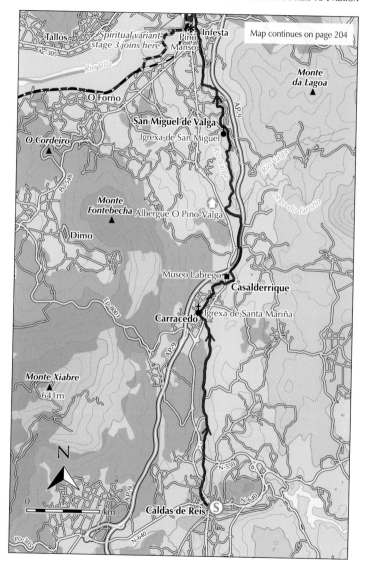

Map continues on page 204

Tallós

Spiritual variant stage 3 joins here

Pino Manso

Infesta

Monte da Lagoa

Río Ulla

O Forno

AP-9

San Miguel de Valga

Igrexa de San Miguel

Río Valga

O Cordeiro

Río Valga

rego do farono

Monte Fontebecha

Albergue O Pino-Valga

Dimo

Museo Labrego

Casalderrique

EP-8001

Igrexa de Santa Mariña

Carracedo

AP-9

Monte Xiabre
641m

N

AP-9

N-550

0 ———— km

Caldas de Reis (S)

N-640

N-640

PO-305

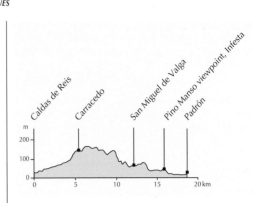

For Albergue O Pino-Valga +220m, turn right onto the N550, LHS, tel 699 831 738, 76 beds, kitchen, €8, Restaurant El Criollo and Camioneros are nearby on the N550.

a dirt path. After 300m pass **Museo Labrego** (WC, vending machines) then continue for a further 700m between the motorway and fields until you reach a paved road. Turn left and cross a bridge over the AP9 (**2.9km**), then immediately turn right onto a dirt path (or KSO +70m for Bar Pardal), again parallel with the motorway. On reaching a paved road, bend left and go uphill away from the motorway, then just before reaching the N550 turn right onto a dirt road. ◄ This

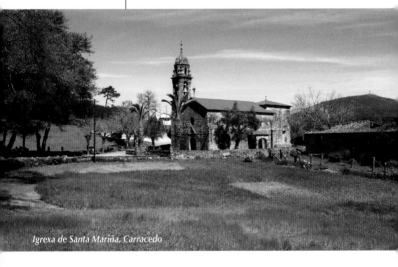

Igrexa de Santa Mariña, Carracedo

becomes an undulating and scenic mossy woodland track. After 1.8km cross a bridge over the River Valga then follow the road around to the left into **San Miguel de Valga**. **6.4km/11.8km**

Pass **Igrexa de San Miguel**, then as the road bends left KSO, passing the now closed Autoservicio San Miguel. Take the first left onto a dirt path and continue along winding lanes for 1.8km to a T-junction with a paved road and an old stone *fonte* (RHS). Turn right and KSO for 1.4km, then cross the busy Rúa Ullán (PO-214) onto Camiño Infesta, going uphill into **Infesta**. Pass the popular tavern 'Mesa de Pedra' (RHS) then the **Pino Manso viewpoint** (LHS) (**3.9km**). ▶ Veer left at the end of the street, then take the lower left fork downhill and pass Cruceiro de San Lázaro (14th century) and the back of Igrexa de San Xulián (built in the 12th century by Archbishop Xelmírez). Reach a T-junction and the option for Herbón's albergue and monastery. **4.4km/16.2km**

For Albergue de Peregrinos de Pontecesures take the next right; the albergue is the second building on the LHS, Estrada das Escolas, Lugar de Infesta, tel 699 832 730, 54 beds, €8.

Herbón detour (3.4km longer than main route)
To stay in the albergue at Herbón's Franciscan monastery, turn right onto Rúa Cantillo, following **red** arrows, and after 150m, when the road forks, KSO (left). After a further 700m pass houses then a fonte (RHS) and shortly afterwards turn left onto a grassy track, going downhill and following this onto a path beside the **River Ulla** (LHS). After 500m go under the AP9 highway and on reaching a road, turn left. Cross a small stream then keep left when the road forks. Soon after, turn left and cross a bridge over the River Ulla then take the first left onto a road by the river. Follow this for 500m as it climbs, passing fields of Herbón peppers, until you reach a stone cross at the entrance to **Herbón Monastery and albergue**. Turn right and go down the driveway; the entrance to the albergue is on the LHS before the church.

Founded in the 14th century, the **monastery** was a school for missionaries during the 18–19th centuries. It was ransacked by the French in the early 19th century then became a convent school in the 20th century. It was the Franciscan monks who introduced the popular Padrón peppers from the Americas, planting them in Herbón, where they still grow today.

Albergue 'San Antonio de Herbón' (Rego da Manga 56, tel 679 460 942, www.amigosdelcamino.com, 30 beds, communal dinner and breakfast, donation, check-in from 4pm).

To continue to Padrón from the monastery and albergue (+2.8km), at the top of the driveway pass the stone cross (LHS) and KSO along the road, following yellow arrows. After 750m turn left at the T-junction onto a main road (AC-242), then go under the AP9 highway. Continue along this road, bending right after 500m, then after a further 500m pass Café Rosalía and a pharmacy and KSO across the railway tracks. Cross a bridge over the **River Sar**, then after passing the Padrón Botanical Gardens (LHS) KSO across the N550 onto Rúa Rosalía de Castro into **Padrón**'s old-town. At the end of the road, look left to see Igrexa de Santiago but turn right to continue on the Camino at the beginning of Stage 25.

To continue on the main route straight to Padrón, at the T-junction turn left onto Rúa Cantillo, cross the railway tracks then turn left before the petrol station and go through a tunnel under the N550. Pass a statue of St James (LHS) then cross **Pontecesures** bridge over the River Ulla. ◄ The Camino continues on a road behind the white electricity tower; follow this for 500m to the River Sar and turn right. Go under the AG11, then pass Albergue Camino do Sar (tel 618 734

Spiritual Variant Stage 3 joins the route at this point.

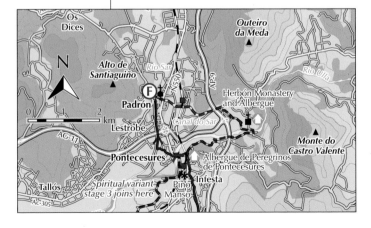

373, www.caminodosar.com, 20 beds, kitchen, €15+) and KSO through the market car park and into the avenue of trees along Paseo do Espolón. At either end of this Avenue you'll pass statues of Padrón's two most famous residents – Nobel Laureate Camilo Jose Cela (1916–2002) and poet Rosalía de Castro (1837–1885); it's behind Rosalía where the stage ends, at the Igrexa de Santiago in central **Padrón**. **2.4km/18.6km**

Paseo do Espolón, Padrón

Roman 'pedron' stone, Igrexa de Santiago, Padrón

PADRÓN, 13M, POP. 9037

Padrón is named after the 'pedron' Roman stone underneath the altar in the Igrexa de Santiago. It was this stone, according to legend, that the boat carrying St James' body and his disciples moored up against before the corpse was transported by ox and cart (provided by Queen Lupa) to a burial site – which Santiago Cathedral was subsequently built on top of. The old pilgrim hospital

205

(15–19th century) next to the church attests to the popularity of the pilgrimage through medieval times. Don't forget to try the famous Padrón peppers in season (May to October): *Os pementos de Padrón uns pican e outros non* – 'Some are hot, others not!'

Tourist office: Av Compostela, tel 646 593 319, www.padronturismo.gal, closed Mondays.

Visit: Igrexa de Santiago – the original church was built in the ninth century by Bishop Teodomiro then rebuilt in the 12th century by Archbishop Xelmírez and the current neoclassical building is a 19th-century reconstruction, but most importantly, underneath the altar is the Roman 'pedron' stone, www.iglesiaenpadron.com, open daily. Fonte O Carme, 16th century – in the niche is an image of Queen Lupa being baptised by St James and below is an image of the boat transporting the deceased apostle's body accompanied by his two disciples. Convento do Carme, 18th century, built on the other side of the River Sar next to the albergue, open daily. Santiaguiño do Monte, rocky hilltop outcrop believed to be where St James would preach and where a spring appeared after tapping his staff on a rock. There is a statue of St James on the rocks, a chapel and fountain. Access: cross

Fonte O Carme, Padrón

the Santiago bridge and turn right, then after 60m turn left up the staircase and climb 125 steps to the top. Casa-Museo Rosalía de Castro, the house where the famous poet spent the last five years of her life, A Matanza s/n, www.rosalia.gal, closed Mondays, €3. Camilo José Cela Foundation, Sta. Maria 22, closed Sat–Sun, €3 with guided tours €2 extra. Botanical gardens.

Specialities: *pementos de Padrón* (Padrón peppers).

Where to eat: Secreto do Vino tapas bar, Rúa Real. A Casa dos Martínez for a special dinner on Rúa Longa.

Accommodation: Albergue de Peregrinos de Padrón +150m (Costiña da Carmen s/n, tel 673 656 173, 46 beds, €8. Access: turn left and cross Santiago bridge then KSO onto the cobbled road, passing Fonte O Carme (RHS). Veer left and the albergue is straight ahead). **Albergue Corredoiras** (Rúa Corredoira da Barca 10, tel 981 817 266, **www.alberguecorredoiras.es**, 17 beds, kitchen, €16+, modern hostel a few minutes further along the Camino). ****Hotel Chef Rivera** (Enlace Parque 7, tel 981 810 413, **www.chefrivera.com**, 17 rooms, €45+, attached to a great restaurant).

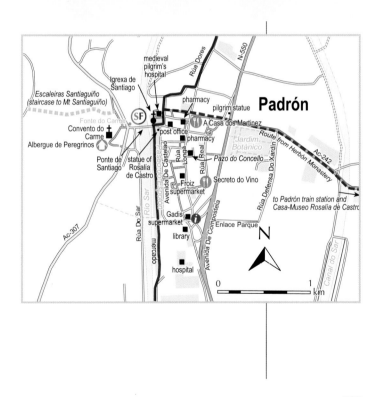

STAGE 25
Padrón to Santiago de Compostela

Start	Igrexa de Santiago, Padrón
Finish	Santiago Cathedral
Distance	24.9km
Total ascent	527m
Total descent	277m
Difficulty	Medium
Time	6–7hr
Cafés	Padrón, A Escravitude (5.9km), A Picaraña (9.2km), Faramello (10.3km), Rúa de Francos (11.7km), O Milladoiro (17.5km), Santiago de Compostela (24.9km)
Accommodation	Padrón, A Escravitude (5.9km), A Picaraña (9.2km), Faramello (10.3km), Teo (10.8km +150m), Rúa de Francos (11.7km), O Milladoiro (17.5km), Santiago de Compostela (24.9km)

This is it, the final 25km... It's not the most relaxing stage, being on and off the N550, but it does pass through quaint hamlets and pockets of woodland. When you arrive in Santiago, allow time to soak in the atmosphere of Praza do Obradoiro before exploring the incredible sites of the UNESCO World Heritage old town.

Destroyed by Almanzor in the 10th century, the church was rebuilt by Archbishop Xelmírez in the 12th century with subsequent renovations. Nobel Laureate Camilo José Cela is buried here.

Leaving Igrexa de Santiago (LHS), pass the old pilgrim hospital then turn right at the end and pass Albergue Corredoiras (no.10). Turn left into Calle de Dolores, cross a bridge over the River Sar then carefully cross the N550 onto Lugar de Pedreda, passing **Igrexa de Santa María de Iria** (**1km**). ◀ Go down the ramp and under the railway line then after 400m turn left at a workshop. On reaching the N550, turn right and continue straight across a roundabout, passing the large ***Hotel Scala (Lugar de Pousa s/n, tel 981 811 312, www. hscala.com, 194 rooms, €50+). Shortly afterwards, turn left onto a small road at another workshop and turn right at the end. Follow the arrows for 1.3km as the Camino winds around small lanes through a hamlet before crossing a short bridge with an old **stone watermill** (LHS). After a further 1.5km reach the N550 again and turn left at the beginning of **A Escravitude**. **5.9km**

Pass Café Rianxeira then the **Santuario da Escravitude**. ▸ Turn right and pass Casa Grande da Cappelañia (LHS, Lugar Esclavitude 3, tel 651 132 591, shared and private rooms). Soon afterwards turn left, passing Igrexa de Santa María de Cruces. On reaching a T-junction turn right then left. After 360m, as the road bends right, turn

Eighteenth-century, Baroque; legend has it that the church was built after a sick pilgrim was cured when he drank from the fountain on his way to Santiago in 1732.

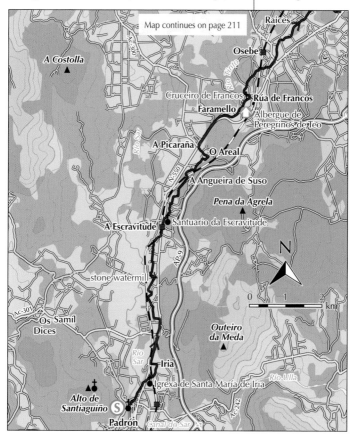

Map continues on page 211

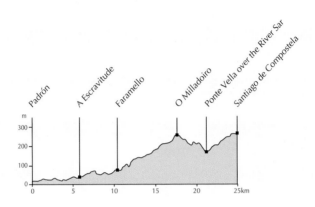

left and then after a further 430m take the lower left fork downhill and under the railway tracks. Turn right and pass through the hamlets of **A Angueira de Suso** and **O Areal**. On reaching the N550 again, pass Café/Pension Milagrosa (Carretera Coruna–Vigo, km75, tel 981 803 119, €10+) on the LH corner in **A Picaraña**. **3.3km/9.2km**

Turn right and pass Pension & Restaurant Glorioso (RHS, Carretera N550, km75, tel 981 803 181, www. pensionglorioso.es, 12 rooms, €20+) then carefully walk along the shoulder of the N550. After 900m, as the road bends right, veer left into **Faramello**. Pass Café O Alpendre do Camino then Albergue-Restaurant La Calabaza del Peregrino (Lg Faramello 5, tel 981 194 244, 40 beds, €15+), and on leaving Faramello pass a playground then take the second left. ◄ After 600m come to a T-junction and turn left to reach the stone cross of **Cruceiro de Francos** (14–15th century, one of the oldest in Galicia) in **Rúa de Francos** (**2.2km**). Turn left at the cross then turn right at the park and shortly afterwards pass between two restaurants including Restaurant-Casa Parada de Francos (Rúa de Francos 43, tel 981 538 004, www.paradadefrancos. com, 12 rooms, €90+). Continue straight onto a paved road then after 640m reach an overpass with blue rails (RHS) in **Osebe**. **3.3km/12.5km**

KSO for Albergue de Peregrinos de Teo +150m, Rúa de Francos s/n, 28 beds, kitchen, €8. Café Casa Javier, +250m further up the road, serves meals.

Turn right and cross the railway tracks then KSO onto a narrow road, taking the second left. Go straight across the junction into Camino de Riotinto and pass Casalonga school then cross a stone bridge. After 260m KSO onto a narrow cobbled path which becomes a dirt path through woodland for 2.3km before reaching a roundabout and the N550. Carefully cross the road and double back along a dirt road then turn right, passing houses. Take the second left then turn right at the end onto a busy road, following this uphill into the built-up area of **O Milladoiro. 5km/17.5km**

Pass Pavillon Polideportivo and Café (LHS) then KSO. ▶ After passing Novo Milladoiro Centro Comercial (shopping centre), veer right onto a dirt track downhill and around to the right. Turn left onto a paved road then after 420m take the right fork onto Covas do Porto, turning right at the end (the highway is now on the left). Turn left and go through the underpass, heading towards and then under another underpass (AG-56), then start uphill, with Santiago views. After 600m reach a junction with a small roundabout (to the left) and turn left then immediately right. Take the second right, going downhill and across a bridge over the

Or, for the modern Albergue Milladoiro +250m, take the next left onto Rúa Buxo, tel 981 938 382, **www. alberguemilladoiro. com**, 62 beds, kitchen, €16.50+.

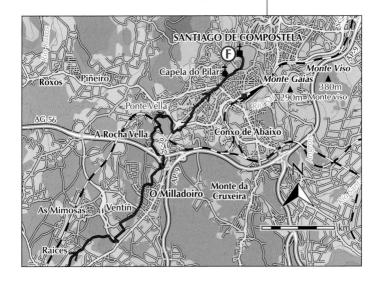

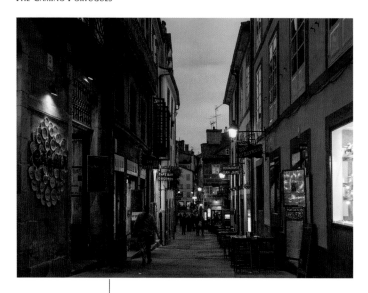

Rúa do Franco, Santiago de Compostela

Praza do Obradoiro's name means 'workshop', in reference to the stonemasons who were working in the square for nine years to create the cathedral's Baroque west facade.

railway tracks. Turn right at the end then cross the River Sar on the stone **Ponte Vella**. **3.6km/21.1km**

There are conflicting arrows here but the recommended route is as follows: turn right onto a woodland path and after 500m go under the highway and turn left. KSO (slightly right) across a road, then shortly afterwards cross a bridge over the highway and pass modern apartment blocks. Follow the road as it bends left at the end of the apartments, then turn right and veer left onto a footpath up to the main road, Rúa da Volta do Castro. Turn right and KSO for 1.6km, passing cafés, shops and across two roundabouts before reaching Alameda Park and **Capela do Pilar** (LHS, 18th century). Walk through the park briefly (or KSO) then cross at the lights into **Santiago**'s old town, veering left onto Rúa do Franco. Pass windows full of delicious seafood before reaching Praza do Obradoiro and the west facade of **Santiago Cathedral**. ◄ **3.8km/24.9km**

Cathedral view from Praza da Quintana,
Santiago de Compostela

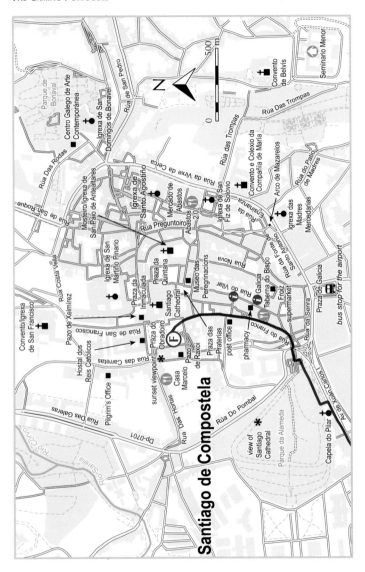

Santiago de Compostela

SANTIAGO DE COMPOSTELA, 266M, POP. 95,800

Congratulations! Feelings of euphoria and accomplishment may be overwhelming, but you're not alone. Look around and you'll see pilgrims from all walks of life who have travelled the various routes to converge here; the energy is palpable.

If you want to follow an age-old pilgrim tradition, enter the cathedral through the south Romanesque entrance in Praza das Praterías, then

1   Admire the Pórtico da Gloria (three arches intricately carved in the 12th century by Maestro Mateo, on the west side). Although it's no longer possible, pilgrims used to touch the Tree of Jesse on the central column underneath a figure of St James; notice the hand imprint. Then on the other side of the column, pilgrims would bump their foreheads three times against the kneeling figure of the sculptor himself, for wisdom!

2   Make your way behind the Baroque high altar and up the steps into the small room to embrace and thank the jewel-encrusted St James.

3   Descend under the altar to the crypt to visit the tomb of St James. Pilgrims Mass is held daily at midday – arrive early if you want a seat!

The Pilgrim's Office is where you present your stamped *credential* to receive the last stamp and Compostela. A certificate of distance is also available for €3. In the same building there is a post office, Renfe and Alsa booking office (train and bus tickets), garden and chapel. Access: from Praza do Obradoiro go down the ramp in front of the Parador and turn right onto Rúa das Carretas; it's on the LHS, no.33, tel 981 568 846, www.oficinadelperegrino. com, open daily 9am–7pm.

Pilgrim House is a non-profit welcome centre created for pilgrims. Services include baggage storage, a communal and quiet space for reflection, Wi-Fi, laundry and more. Rúa Nova 19, www.pilgrimhousesantiago.com, closed Wednesdays and Sundays.

Tourist office: Rúa do Vilar 63, tel 981 555 129, **www.santiagoturismo.com**, open daily. The Galicia tourist office is in the same street, 30–32.

Visit: cathedral (open daily 7am–8.30pm); in addition to the pilgrim traditions already described, don't miss the Holy Door, the entrance is from Praza da Quintana. It's opened during Holy Years, the next is in 2027. The Botafumeiro is a censer full of coal and incense and is operated by eight men called *tiraboleiros* who pull on the ropes, making it swing 17 times, wafting the incense throughout the cathedral. It's used during special occasions or by advance request. Join a guided visit to see the rooftop, permanent museum collections, excavations and more, **www.catedraldesantiago.es**. Standing in Praza do Obradoiro and facing the cathedral, the building on the right is the 17th-century Colegio de San Xerome. Behind you is the 18th-century neoclassical Pazo de Raxoi, where the Tuna musicians play under the arches most evenings. To the left is the former pilgrim hospital, Hostal dos Reis Católicos, now the Parador. Diagonally left is the 12th-century Pazo de Xelmírez, built for the first Archbishop of Santiago, Diego Xelmírez. Praza da Quintana to see the Holy Door and the Pilgrim Shadow (a shadow cast by a pillar onto a corner of one side of the cathedral which looks uncannily like a pilgrim with a hat, staff and backpack) every evening, if you can find it! Alameda Park with a cathedral viewpoint. Museo das Peregrinacións, Praza das Praterías, **museoperegrinacions.xunta.gal**, closed Mondays, currently free. CGAC – Galician Centre of Contemporary Art, designed by Portuguese architect Álvaro Siza Vieira, **museos.xunta.gal**, closed Mondays. Mercado de Abastos, food market, Mon–Sat 7am–2pm.

Specialities: seafood; 'Tarta de Santiago' almond tart (as well as in shops, you can buy it direct from the nuns at Mosteiro de San Paio – enter through the green door on Rúa de San Paio de Antealtares and ring the bell).

Where to eat: a free pilgrim meal at the Parador, in keeping with a tradition started in 1509 when the building was a pilgrim hospital. Available to the first 10 pilgrims daily. Taberna do Bispo on Rúa do Franco for excellent tapas. Casa Marcelo, O Sendeiro or Abastos 2.0 for something special. In many bars you also receive free tapas with your drinks.

Accommodation: (visit the tourist office for a full list of accommodation for all budgets; the following are close to the cathedral): Hospedería San Martín Pinario (Plaza de la Inmaculada 3, tel 981 560 282, **www.hsanmartinpinario. com**, private pilgrim rooms with ensuite and hotel rooms, includes a great buffet breakfast, opposite the cathedral). The Last Stamp (Rúa Preguntoiro 10, tel 981 563 525, **www.thelaststamp.es**, 62 beds, kitchen, €19+, modern hostel). *Hotel Atalaia B&B (Algalia de Arriba 44, tel 981 566 373, **www. atalaiabnb.com**, 10 rooms, €45+, beautiful modern rooms). ***Hotel Rúa Villar (Rúa do Vilar 8–10, tel 981 519 858, **www.hotelruavillar.com**, 17 rooms, €60+, traditional-style rooms in a converted 18th-century building).

COASTAL CAMINO

Boardwalk between Vila do Conde and Esposende (Coastal Camino Stage 2)

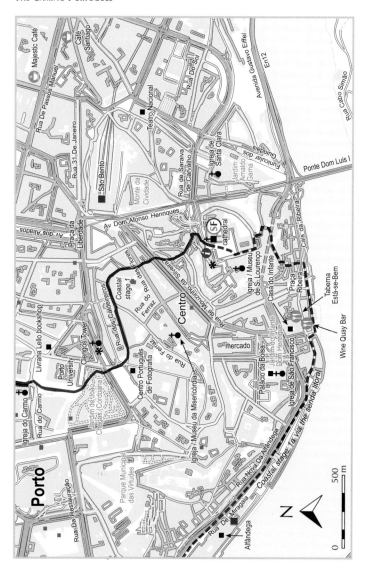

STAGE 1
Porto to Vila do Conde

Start	Porto Cathedral
Finish	Praça da República, Vila do Conde
Distance	28km
Total ascent	301m
Total descent	373m
Difficulty	Medium
Time	7–8hr
Cafés	Porto, Pedras Rubras (12.9km), The Style Outlets (21.5km), Mindelo (23.2km), Areia (25.6km), Vila do Conde (28km)
Accommodation	Porto, airport hotels (12.3km), Azurara (27km), Vila do Conde (28km)

After a short variation at the very beginning, the first stage of the Coastal Camino follows the Central Camino for nearly 6km north out of Porto before branching off at the Padrão da Légua stone cross. It then passes the perimeter of Porto airport and follows cobbled roads through villages and farmland. (There's a scenic alternative from Porto along the Douro and Atlantic; see Stage 1A.)

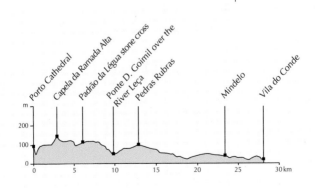

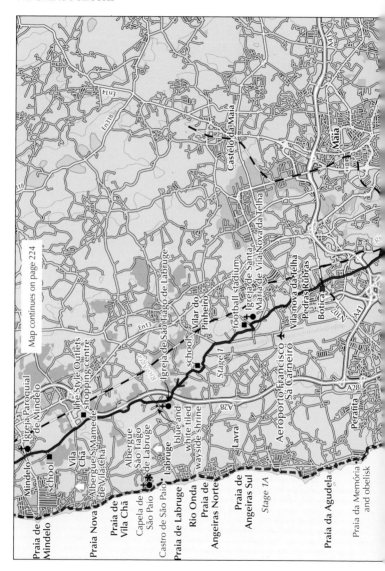

Map continues on page 224

Castelo da Maia

Maia

Igreja de Santa Maria de Vila Nova da Telha

Football stadium

Vilar do Pinheiro

Vila Nova da Telha

Pedras Rubras

Botica

Igreja de São Tiago de Labruge

Aeroporto Francisco Sá Carneiro

Perafita

Stage 7

school

Igreja Paroquial de Mindelo

The Style Outlets shopping centre

Lavra

Mindelo

Vila Chã

Albergue S.Mamede de Vila Chã

Albergue São Tiago de Labruge

Capela de São Paio

Castro de São Paio

blue and white tiled wayside shrine

Praia de Mindelo

Praia Nova

Praia de Vila Chã

Praia de Labruge

Rio Onda

Praia de Angeiras Norte

Praia de Angeiras Sul

Stage 1A

Praia de Agudela

Praia da Memória and obelisk

220

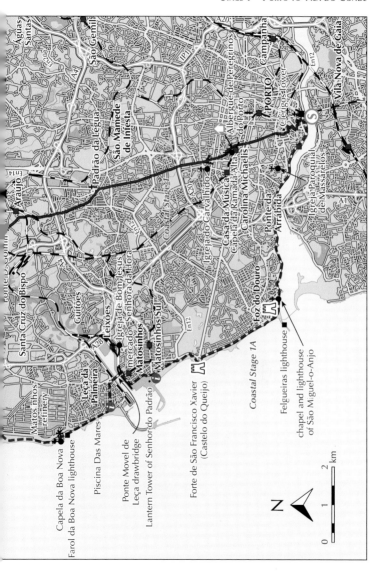

Águas Santas
São Gemil
A20
IP1
A4
Araújo
São Mamede de Infesta
Padrão da Légua
PORTO
Campanhã
Clérigos Tower
En12
Vila Nova de Gaia
Pontes de Jornil
Santa Cruz do Bispo
Guifões
Leixões
Albergue de Peregrinos do Porto
Casa da Música
Capela da Ramada Alta
Carolina Michaelis
A20
Igreja Bom Jesus
mercado
Nossa Senhora da Hora
Igreja do Carvalhido
Matosinhos
Matosinhos Sul
Ponte da Arrábida
Igreja Paroquial de Massarelos
A1
Matosinhos refinery
Leça da Palmeira
En12
Foz do Douro

Capela da Boa Nova
Farol da Boa Nova lighthouse

Piscina Das Mares

Ponte Movel de Leça drawbridge
Lantern Tower of Senhor do Padrão

Forte de São Francisco Xavier (Castelo do Queijo)

Coastal Stage 1A

Felgueiras lighthouse

chapel and lighthouse of São M.guel-o-Anjo

N

0   1   2
km

Facing the cathedral's main (west) entrance, veer left and pass the first Coastal Camino brown/yellow waymark then turn left down the 'Escadas da Sé' steps. At the bottom (WC, RHS) turn left and downhill on Rua Escura then KSO into Rua do Souto. Cross Rua Mouzinho da Silveira into Rua de Afonso Martins Alho then continue straight into Rua dos Caldeireiros. Go uphill then follow the road as it bends left into a one-way street, continuing uphill for 300m to reach the large square of Campo dos Mártires da Pátria. Turn right here, having now rejoined the Central Camino, and see Central Stage 16 for directions for the following 5.8km to **Padrão da Légua** stone cross (LHS, 17th century). **6.6km**

Turn left at the cross onto Rua Senhor then KSO into Rua Fonte Velha, passing Café Magnolia (LHS). After 1km pass Jardim do Largo do Souto (LHS, with benches) and turn

Padrão da Légua stone cross, Custóias: the Coastal Camino splits here

right, heading to and through the underpass, then keep right onto Rua da Cal. After 450m turn left and cross a bridge over metro tracks then go downhill, under the railway tracks. After a further 600m reach a crossroads and take the diagonal right, down to and across the River Leça on the restored **Ponte D. Goimil**. **3.1km/9.7km**

Follow the dirt path back to the road and turn right, then KSO across a bridge over metro tracks, past a group of houses (the last one is Petisqueria das Carvalhas, RHS), and soon fields and eucalyptus trees are interspersed with industrial zones. Cross a bridge over the A41 then after 1km pass Café Lipe (LHS) shortly before Airporto Hostel (LHS, Rua da Estrada 244, tel 229 427 397, shared and private rooms, kitchen, 1km from the airport). Cross the N107 and metro tracks into Rua da Botica and KSO (or take the next left for **Hotel Aeroporto, Rua Pedras Rubras 157, tel 229 428 081, www.hotelaeroporto.com.pt, 27 rooms), passing a blue-and-white tiled chapel next to Praça Exército Libertador in **Pedras Rubras**. **3.2km/12.9km**

> The *praça* is where **Dom Pedro's Liberal army** camped in 1832 after arriving from the Azores on their way to Porto to fight against Pedro's brother Miguel. After two years of fighting, Pedro was victorious and the constitutional charter was restored.

Shortly after the chapel, veer left opposite a Santander bank onto Rua do Prof António Rocha and follow the cobbled road for 1km before crossing the small but busy Rua da Fábrica into Rua da Aldeia. ▶ After 500m turn right at a stone cross onto Rua da Igreja and pass the blue-and-white tiled **Igreja de Santa Maria**, then turn left at the stone cross. Turn right at the end, passing a **football stadium** (**2.4km**), then after 1.1km turn left onto a small paved road (easy to miss) and go under a red-and-white beam. Keep right onto the narrow Travessa da Pena then left and downhill, turning right at the end onto Rua da Botica. Soon afterwards keep left, passing a **school** (RHS), then after 1.2km go under the A28. **5.5km/18.4km**

▶ After 500m reach a T-junction with a **blue-and-white tiled wayside shrine** (LHS) and turn right then keep left. After a further 400m follow the road left and through a pocket of eucalyptus forest, then KSO for 1.9km, passing

Green arrows pointing left here lead to the sea, but fade out after Lavra.

The church over to the left is Igreja de São Tiago de Labruge.

223

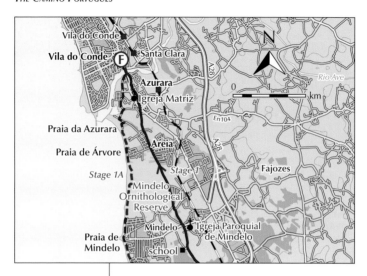

Construction began
in 1502 after King
Manuel visited on
his pilgrimage to
Santiago. Notice
the scallop shells
on the 16th-century
stone cross.

To connect to São
Pedro de Rates
on the Central
Camino from here,
see Link route 1.

Vila do Conde Retail Park. After a further 1.2km veer right at Mindelo **school**. Reach a junction with a café and the **Paroquial Church of Mindelo**. **4.8km/23.2km**

Continue straight into Rua da Estrada Velha, passing a CA bank (RH corner), then keep right and pass supermarket Cruzeiro (LHS). Follow this for 2.2km across a roundabout, through the **Mindelo Ornithological Reserve** to a crossroads (with a café, supermarket, ATM and pharmacy) in **Areia**. Continue straight for a further 1.1km to a large roundabout and the N13, then turn left then first right onto Rua Padre Serafim das Neves into **Azurara (3.8km)**. Pass behind the **Igreja Matriz** (NM). ◄ Continue through the old town then go downhill with views of Mosteiro de Santa Clara across the river. Reach the N13 and turn right, crossing the bridge over the River Ave (traditionally by boat until the 18th century). Once on the other side, if you're on the RHS, take the steps under the highway to reach Praça da República in **Vila do Conde**. ◄ **4.8km/28km**

Mosteiro de Santa Clara, Vila do Conde

VILA DO CONDE, 15M, POP. 79,533

An important shipbuilding port during the Age of Discoveries, Vila do Conde is an attractive riverside city with a rich history, interesting sights and is connected to Porto by the metro red line 'B'. Confalonieri (1594) came here before continuing on to São Pedro de Rates and noted, 'They are trying to make a large bridge that joins the banks of these two populations without the discomfort of the boat … the church is the most beautiful of the Kingdom in grandeur, beauty and proportion.'

Tourist office: two locations – riverfront, Rua Cais das Lavandeiras, tel 252 248 445, open daily; centre, Rua 25 de Abril 103, tel 252 248 473, closed weekends, www.cm-viladoconde.pt.

Visit: Igreja Matriz (NM), 16th century (the existing church's plans were altered after King Manuel visited on his way to Santiago in 1502), features an exquisite Manueline portal by João de Castilho. Opposite is the 16th-century town hall and pillory (NM). The Gothic Mosteiro de Santa Clara, towering over the river, was built by D Afonso Sanches (illegitimate child of King Dinis) and his wife Teresa in 1318. Reconstruction work began in the 18th century but was never finished. Behind is the Igreja de Santa Clara (NM), displaying Gothic, Manueline, Baroque and Rococo styles; also built in 1318, it houses the elaborate tombs of its founders, Afonso and Teresa. Aqueduct (NM), 18th

Aqueduct, Vila do Conde

century, 5km long with 999 arches, built to provide water for the monastery. Museums include the Alfândega Régia-Museu de Construção Naval inside the 15th-century Royal Customs House, highlighting Vila do Conde's important role in shipbuilding during the Age of Discoveries with a replica of a 16th-century ship opposite. Casa de José Régio (poet) and Rendas de Bilros, housing the largest bobbin lace in the world. Friday market behind the albergue.

Specialities: seafood and sweet pastries like *Vila Condenses* and *Pastel de Chila*.

Where to eat: O Mestre in Praça José Régio. Alfândega for seafood overlooking the river. O Forninho for all things sweet.

Accommodation: Albergue de Peregrinos 'Santa Clara' +260m (Rua 5 de Outubro 221, tel 252 104 717, **www.cm-viladoconde.pt**, 25 beds, kitchen, €10. Access: continue along the N13 for 200m then follow as it bends right; it's on the LHS). Naval Guest House (Rua do Cais das Lavandeiras 37, tel 925 693 470, **www.navalviladoconde.com**, €60+, riverfront). ***Hotel Brazão (Av Dr. João Canavarro, tel 252 642 016, **www.hotelbrazao.pt**, 30 modern rooms in a 17th-century building, €45+).

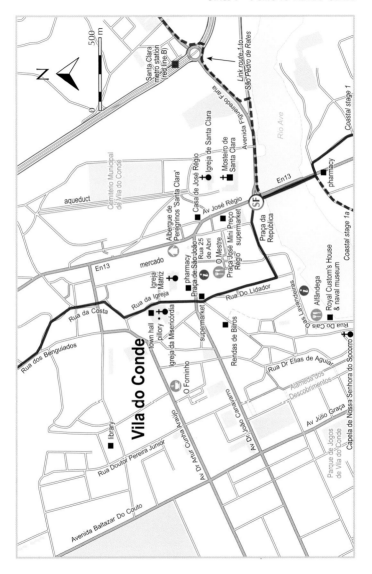

STAGE 1A
Porto to Vila do Conde (via the Senda Litoral)

Start	Porto Cathedral
Finish	Praça da República, Vila do Conde
Distance	33km
Total ascent	209m
Total descent	276m
Difficulty	Easy (but long)
Time	8–9hr
Cafés	Many during the first 12km, then seasonal summer kiosks every 2–3km
Accommodation	Porto, Foz do Douro (5.3km), Matosinhos (10km), Angeiras (22.7km +500m), Labruge (23.5km +900m), Vila Chã (26.1km +600m), Vila do Conde (33km)
Notes	Bus no.500 runs between Porto (Praça da Liberdade) and Matosinhos (Mercado), €2.50. Tram line no.1 travels beside the river between Porto (in front of Igreja de São Francisco) and Passeio Alegre garden, €5.

This scenic alternative follows the River Douro and Atlantic coastline via a series of esplanades and boardwalks known as the Senda Litoral, passing museums, forts and sandy beaches. Route-finding is easy – just keep the water to your left – and there's ample accommodation en route.

From the cathedral's west (main) entrance and facing the tourist office (inside the tower), go diagonally left across the square and down the steps in the corner. Follow the path left then turn right down the steps of Escadas das Verdades. Turn right onto Escadas do Barredo, follow this left then right onto Rua do Barredo, then go left onto Escadas do Barredo, left into Rua dos Canastreiros, then through the arch and reach the lively riverside area of Cais do Ribeira and the **River Douro**. 400m

Turn right, and after 200m turn right again, leaving the river briefly to go up towards a small chapel, then immediately go left onto Rua da Reboleira. KSO into Rua Nova de Alfândega and pass Igreja de São Francisco (RHS, highly recommended). KSO now, passing the Transport and Communications Museum (inside the 'new' 19th-century custom's house), Museum of Port Wine and the **Igreja Paroquial de Massarelos** (RHS, founded in 1394; notice the blue-and-white *azulejo* (tile) panel of San Telmo and Prince Henry the Navigator) (**1.7km**) before going under **Ponte da Arrábida**. **2.6km/3km**

After 2.4km pass the (somewhat hidden) chapel and lighthouse of **São Miguel-o-Anjo** (LHS). ▶ Soon after, reach the Atlantic, passing **Felgueiras lighthouse** opposite Forte de São João de Foz (16th century, one of a number of forts along the coast – this one built to defend the mouth of the Douro) in the upmarket neighbourhood of **Foz do Douro**. **3km/6km**

Dating from the 16th century, this is one of the oldest lighthouses in Europe, with an inscription on the wall facing the river. Opposite is the 19th-century Passeio Alegre garden (WC).

Felgueiras Lighthouse, Foz do Douro

Accommodation nearby: Pousada de Juventude 'Porto' (Rua Paulo da Gama 551, tel 226 163 059, **www.pousadasjuventude.pt**, 160 beds, kitchen, €15+). ***Hotel Boa Vista (Esplanada Do Castelo 58, tel 225 320 020, **www.hotelboavista.com**, 71 rooms, €100+).

Now following beside the sea, after 2.7km pass **Forte de São Francisco Xavier**. Constructed in the 17th century, this fort is known locally as 'Castelo do Queijo' because of the cheese-shape rocky hill it was built on. After a further 1.6km reach **Matosinhos** and the modern beachside tourist office (tel 229 392 412, www.cm-matosinhos.pt, open daily, stamp and WC). **4.3km/10.3km**

MATOSINHOS, 13M, POP. 167,026

Known for its fresh seafood (especially along Rua Heróis de França) and Igreja de Bom Jesus (16th-century church with a granite facade designed by Nicolau Nasoni, housing an ancient wooden sculpture of Christ), Matosinhos is also associated with St James through the story of the Roman Lord, Cayo Carpo. According to legend, after Carpo got married on the beach in Matosinhos in AD44, his horse took off into the sea, taking him to the boat that was carrying St James' body accompanied by his disciples. Carpo was converted to Christianity and when he returned to the beach, both he and his horse were covered in scallop shells so the beach became known as 'Matizadinho' (tinted).

Accommodation: Pensão Central (Rua Brito Capelo 599, tel 229 380 664, **www.pensaocentral.net**, 18 rooms, €40+, great-value modern rooms). Fishtail Sea House (Rua do Godinho 224, tel 229 380 345, **www.fishtail-seahouse.pt**, shared and private rooms).

After passing the tourist office the route leaves the seaside for the next 2.3km to pass around the Leixões Port area. KSO through the park, passing the **Lantern Tower of Senhor do Padrão** (NM). ◀ Turn left onto Rua Heróis de França, entering the seafood restaurant zone. Follow this to the end and around to the right, and after passing the municipal fish market and **Mercado metro station** (blue line A with connections to Porto), cross the River Leça on **Ponte Movel de Leça drawbridge. 1.1km/11.4km**

It's believed a wooden sculpture of Christ washed ashore here from the Holy Land in 124, now housed in Igreja de Bom Jesus.

Turn left at the roundabout onto Rua Hintze Ribeiro and follow this (passing cafés) to the end, reaching Leça da Palmeira **tourist office** (LH corner, Rua de Hintze Ribeiro 13, tel 229 392 413, www.cm-matosinhos.pt, closed Sundays, stamp, WC). Turn right onto Av da Liberdade and continue beside the sea, passing **Piscina Das Mares** (LHS, NM, saltwater pools designed by the famous Portuguese architect Álvaro Siza Vieira in 1966) and **Farol da Boa**

Angeiras fishing huts

Nova lighthouse, then among the rocks pass the trendy Boa Nova Tea House (NM, restaurant also designed by Siza Vieira in 1963) and just to the right, **Capela da Boa Nova**. ▶ **2.9km/14.3km**

Join a boardwalk and pass the refinery then continue along boardwalks and footpaths, passing inviting beaches and interesting sights including **Praia da Memória** beach (**3.7km**) with dunes, café and an obelisk (NM) marking the spot where Dom Pedro and his Liberal army landed in 1832. Nearly 4km later, pass **Praia Angeiras Sul** with Roman salt tanks, a café and colourful fishermen's houses, then after another 800m reach **Praia de Angeiras Norte**.

For the pilgrim-friendly Campismo Orbitur Angeiras (campsite) +500m, leave the boardwalk after the Angeiras Norte information board and turn right onto Rua António Feijó, tel 229 270 571, www.orbitur.com, shared and private bungalows and camp site, €12.50+ in a shared room.

After a further 800m, arrive at **Praia de Labruge**. **9.2km/23.5km**

This is all that remains of a monastery founded here in 1392. There are steps behind the chapel to a viewpoint.

For Albergue 'São Tiago de Labruge' +900m, turn right at the roundabout onto Av da Liberdade and walk for 900m; it's in an old school building on the LHS after the lights. If it's not open, get the key from the nearby Junta de Freguesia, Rua de Labruge 1720, tel 229 284 686 & 961 180 256, www.vis-itviladoconde.pt, 54 beds, kitchen, donation (€10 minimum expected).

KSO and up to the site of the pre-Roman **Castro of São Paio** with ancient engravings, chapel and great views. After 900m, having left the boardwalk and passed a pirate outside the popular Taskuinha bar (RHS), pass a house with mosaics (LHS) and follow the road left onto Rua da Praia into **Vila Chã (2.1km)**. Soon after, reach a square and playground and to continue on the boardwalk by the sea, take the steps to the left of the beach huts onto Rua Alto Dos Varais (or KSO following the arrows +40m for Café Sandra, Rua do Facho 34, tel 919 254 629, 8 rooms, €30+) to reach **Praia Nova**.

For Albergue 'S Mamede de Vila Chã' +600m, walk across the car park and before the boardwalk turn right onto Rua Particular do Facho, left at the end onto Rua do Facho, right onto Rua da Caravela, left at the end, and right onto Travessa do Sol; it's at the end behind the museum, tel 934 379 460 & 229 285 607, www.visitviladoconde.pt, 20 beds, kitchen, €10.

Continue for a further 1.8km to reach **Praia de Mindelo**. **4.4km/27.9km**

At **Praia da Azurara (3.2km)** join the road, then take the boardwalk and turn right onto a cobbled road (with good arrows). Cross a small bridge and turn left onto Rua Francisco Gonçalves Monteiro. At the end of this, reach a paved road and veer diagonally left onto Rua da Junqueira, passing Restaurant Villazur. Follow this for 600m to the N13 and turn left to cross the bridge over the River Ave to Praça da República in **Vila do Conde** (see Stage 1 for details). ◄ **5.1km/33km**

To connect to São Pedro de Rates on the Central Camino from here, see Link route 1.

STAGE 2
Vila do Conde to Esposende

Start	Praça da República, Vila do Conde
Finish	Igreja da Misericórdia, Esposende
Distance	23.8km
Total ascent	146m
Total descent	148m
Difficulty	Easy
Time	6–7hr
Cafés	Vila do Conde, Póvoa de Varzim (4km), summer beach kiosks until Aguçadoura (10.9km), Apúlia (17.5km +700m), Fão (21km), Esposende (23.8km)
Accommodation	Vila do Conde, Póvoa de Varzim (3.8km), Santo André (9.1km), Camping Rio Alto (14.6km +500m), Fão (21km), Esposende (23.8km)
Note	Book accommodation in advance during summer (if not staying in albergues) and carry water after Póvoa de Varzim if walking during low season

This stage joins the seaside after Póvoa de Varzim, following boardwalks and esplanades and passing inviting beaches, sand dunes and old windmills for 8km before heading inland again. After passing agricultural areas the route enters Fão – famous for sweet *Clarinhas* (pastries) – before crossing the River Cávado into Esposende.

▸ Follow the brown Camino plaques on the ground west through Praça da República, straight up Calçada do Lidador and right onto Rua do Lidador. Cross Rua 25 de Abril into Rua da Igreja, then pass the Igreja Matriz with the town hall and pillory opposite. Continue to the T-junction then turn right onto Rua da Costa, following as it bends left and straight across Rua Conde dom Mendo. Veer left onto Travessa do Laranjal and turn right onto Rua dos Benguiados. After 300m KSO across the roundabout with a geometric sculpture. Shortly afterwards, pass the popular Café O Forninho

It's possible to follow the sea between Vila do Conde and Póvoa de Varzim (2.1km longer); simply keep the river then sea to your left.

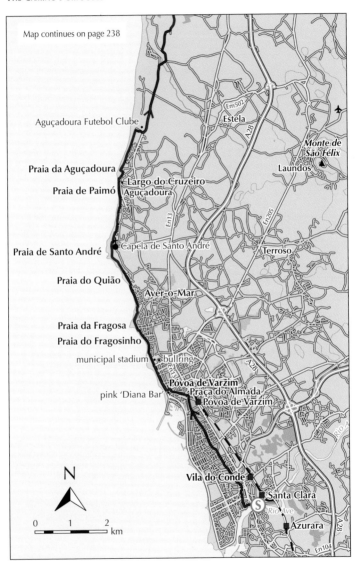

Map continues on page 238

Aguçadoura Futebol Clube

Estela

A28

Em502

Monte de
São Félix

Praia da Aguçadoura

Laundos

Praia de Paimó

Largo do Cruzeiro
Aguçadoura

Em13

En295

Praia de Santo André

Capela de Santo André

Terroso

Praia do Quião

Aver-o-Mar

Praia da Fragosa

Praia do Fragosinho

municipal stadium   bullring

A28

Póvoa de Varzim

Praça do Almada

pink 'Diana Bar'

Póvoa de Varzim

Rio 4

N

Vila do Conde

Santa Clara

S

Rio Ave

0   1   2
km

Azurara

A28

En104

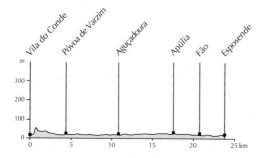

then continue (almost straight) for 2.3km until you're facing a large square with pillory, bandstand and town hall, **Praça do Almada**. Turn left here onto Rua Dr Sousa Campos then KSO, passing Capela de S. Tiago (1582, rebuilt in the 18th century), and join the pedestrianised Rua da Junqueira into the heart of **Póvoa de Varzim**. **4km**

PÓVOA DE VARZIM, 20M, POP. 63,470

This once-small fishing village with a port in use since the 11th century is now a seaside resort with great beaches and the last stop on Porto's metro – red line B.

Tourist office: Praça Marquês de Pombal, tel 252 298 120, www.cm-pvarzim.pt, closed weekends.

Visit: the historic part of town including Praça do Almada. Fortress of Nossa Senhora da Conceição, 18th century, now with restaurants inside.

Specialities: *barquinhos*, *poveirinhos* and *sardinha* sweet pastries from Regata Pastelaria near the albergue at Rua de António Graça 35.

Where to eat: A Taskinha, opposite the fort. Predileto, opposite the albergue.

Accommodation: Albergue de Peregrinos 'S. José de Ribamar' (Av Mouzinho de Albuquerque 32, tel 252 063 964 & 966 501 036, 36 beds, kitchen, donation). Sardines and Friends (Rua da Ponte 4 & 6, tel 962 083 329, www.sardinesandfriends.com, shared and private rooms, kitchen, €16+, behind Igreja de Santiago. **Hotel Avenida (Av Mouzinho de Albuquerque 54, tel 252

683 222, www.hotelavenida-povoa.com, 22 rooms, €40+, one minute from the albergue).

Póvoa de Varzim

Take the right fork past the pharmacy, then turn right onto Rua da Alegria towards the tall church tower. Turn left onto Av Mouzinho de Albuquerque (or turn right for the albergue +100m, pink building LHS), then right at the pink **'Diana Bar'** (a library). You now follow esplanades and boardwalks beside the sea for the next 8km. Along the way, pass Póvoa's **municipal stadium (1.4km)**, **Praia da Fragosa** and a mushroom-like cream-and-orange windmill house (**1.6km**). ◀ Pass **Praia do Quião** with Praia Mestre restaurant (**1km**; rejoin a boardwalk here), Estalagem Santo André (Av de Santo André, Aver-o-Mar, tel 252 615 666, www.hotelsantoandre.com, 78 rooms, €50+) (**1km**), then after a further 1.9km reach **Praia de Paimó** opposite **Largo do**

Moinhos de vento – cylindrical and made of granite with a canvas sail, they were used to grind corn and wheat flour.

236

Cruzeiro (stone cross, playground, cafés and supermarket) in **Aguçadoura**. **6.9km/10.9km**

Join a boardwalk over the dunes towards and then past a windmill, reaching the end of the boardwalk at a large grassy area with a car park and **Aguçadoura Futebol Clube** (**1.5km**). From here you can either take the boardwalk immediately to the right of the football club and follow it for 2.7km to the yellow arrow painted on a rock, going past the entrance to the Estela Golf Club on the way. Alternatively, take the road right, heading away from the sea, then left at the end and follow the cobbled road running parallel with the boardwalk. Either way, the scenery now changes and you pass greenhouses and *masseira* fields. ▶ After 1.9km veer right, then take the next left at a small crossroads. After 330m turn right (yellow arrow painted on a rock) and follow the road through sections of pine and eucalyptus forest. After 1.5km pass **Apúlia football stadium** (RHS) then continue straight across a road into Rua do Pinhal. Turn left at the end onto Rua da Igreja, and soon afterwards pass the **Igreja Matriz of Apúlia**. **6.6km/17.5km**

KSO and across Av da Praia (or turn left for a pharmacy, supermarkets and café) into Rua da Agra. After the initial few turns between houses, continue along the cobbled Rua

Boardwalk, pilgrims and an old windmill near Aguçadoura

A traditional way of farming by digging rectangular depressions into the dunes and piling up the excess sand, creating walls that protect the crops from wind.

237

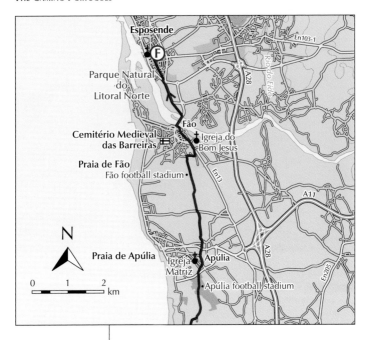

The curious small building (LHS) with the Fão sign was a 19th-century tea house called Casa de Chá.

da Agra, passing fields for 700m until you reach a small T-junction. Turn left then immediately right onto a dirt road through forest, and after 1.1km pass **Fão football stadium** (LHS). Turn right at the small crossroads onto Rua Santo António da Fonte, then left at Fão cemetery, and merge left onto the N13. Shortly after, take the right fork onto Av Dr Henrique Barros Lima. ◄ Pass the Baroque **Igreja do Bom Jesus** (RHS) in **Fão**. **3.5km/21km**

FÃO, 14M, POP. 7301

In the Middle Ages Fão was a large salt producer; there are references to Guimarães Monastery owning its salt mines in 959. In the late 1980s Cemitério Medieval das Barreiras was found nearby, with more than 200 graves dating from the 11–14th centuries.

Accommodation: Pousada de Juventude 'Ofir' (next to Igreja do Bom Jesus in the pink building, tel 253 982 045, **www.pousadasjuventude.pt**, 91 beds, kitchen, €14+).

KSO through Fão, passing a mini-market, Chalé Tapas restaurant (LHS, pilgrim menu and stamp) and Pastelaria Clarinhas (LHS). ▸ Turn right at the Bombeiros Voluntários at the end, then turn left at the river and go up the steps to cross

This is the home of the famous 'Clarinhas' – a pastry shell with *chila* (gourd) filling, invented by the current owner's great grandmother.

Camino Monument, Esposende

the iron Ponte D. Luís Filipe (1892) over the **River Cávado**. Take the first left onto an old road which then joins the main road (with a generous shoulder), Rua da Ponte D. Luís Filipe. Shortly before the roundabout pass Hotel Mira Rio, then turn left at the roundabout and take the first right, passing a Camino monument (RHS). Take the first left onto Rua Narciso Ferreira then KSO for 600m, passing a cemetery, pillory (originally 16th century, has the Manueline armillary sphere on top) and Hostel Eleven (no. 57), and continue straight on into the centre of **Esposende**, ending the stage at Praça do Município, with the town hall (18th century) and Igreja da Misericórdia. **2.8km/23.8km**

ESPOSENDE, 15M, POP. 33,325

Designated a village in 1572 (and welcoming pilgrims at the original hospital since 1579), Esposende has a lovely relaxed atmosphere, delicious seafood, grand buildings built by returning emigrants, and is a popular water sports destination.

Tourist office: Av Eng. Eduardo Arantes e Oliveira 62, tel 253 961 354, **www.visitesposende.com**, closed Sundays, bike hire, WC.

Visit: Igreja da Misericórdia, 16th-century church with later additions including the spectacular Baroque gilded woodcarvings on the ceiling of the Capela do Senhor dos Mareantes. There's also a municipal museum and maritime museum (riverfront).

Specialities: *robalo* (seabass), *polvo da Pedra* (octopus), *Clarinhas* and *Folhadinos* sweet pastries.

Where to eat: O Buraco or Foz do Cávado for great seafood on the riverfront.

Accommodation: Hostel Eleven (Rua Narciso Ferreira 57, tel 253 039 303 & 962 651 485, **www.hosteleleven.pt**, shared and private rooms, kitchen, €11+, bright and modern hostel on the Camino). Esposende Guesthouse (Rua Conde Agrolongo 29, tel 932 832 818, **www.esposendeguesthouse.com**, shared and private contemporarily designed rooms, kitchen, opposite the tourist office). **Hotel Mira Rio (Rua da Ponte D. Luis Filipe 113, tel 253 964 430, **www.hotel-mirario.com**, 13 rooms, €38+, at the entrance to town on the Camino). ***Hotel Suave Mar (Av Eng. Arantes E Oliveira, tel 253 969 400, **www.suavemar.com**, 84 rooms, €60+, +1.3km along the riverfront).

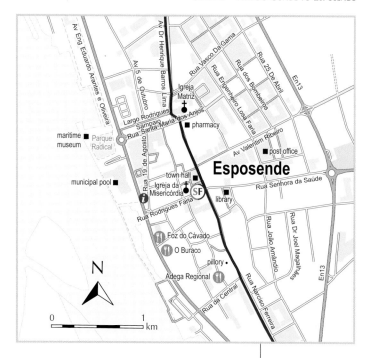

STAGE 3
Esposende to Viana do Castelo

Start	Igreja da Misericórdia, Esposende
Finish	Praça da República, Viana do Castelo
Distance	25.5km
Total ascent	425m
Total descent	378m
Difficulty	Medium
Time	6–7hr
Cafés	Esposende, Marinhas (4.4km), Belinho (8.3km), Chafé (17.7km), Anha (20.2km), Darque (22.6km), Viana do Castelo (25.5km)
Accommodation	Esposende, Marinhas (4.4km), Chafé (18.4km), Darque (22.6km), Viana do Castelo (25.5km)

The Camino heads inland along cobbled roads, passing the albergue in Marinhas and following a picturesque woodland path beside the River Neiva before climbing up out of the valley to Castelo do Neiva's Igreja de Santiago. Short, scenic stretches of forest are followed by a descent to cross the River Lima into Viana do Castelo.

Built originally in 1579 for pilgrims and the sick, the hospital was rebuilt in 1916.

There's a bar further along the road, a restaurant and café if you turn left at the church, and Asdeprovar bakery is back across the N13, open from 6.30am.

Continue straight through Praça do Município into the pedestrianised Rua 1 de Dezembro and straight over onto Av Dr. Henrique Barros Lima, passing the Igreja Matriz. After 400m reach the neoclassical **hospital** (RHS). ◄ Turn left here, then turn right at the end, joining the esplanade by the river. Pass Hotel Suave Mar then the 17th-century **Forte de São João Batista** and lighthouse (19th century). Follow the road as it bends inland, taking the third left onto the cobbled Rua da Agrela, then turn right at Supermarket Coviran onto Av do Praia. Carefully cross the N13 into Av de São Sebastião, passing the Red Cross ('Cruz Vermelha' – check-in here if the albergue is unattended) and **Capela de São Sebastião**, then take the first left and pass Albergue de Peregrinos 'São Miguel' (RHS, Av S. Sebastião, tel 253 964 720 & 967 611 204, 34 beds, kitchen, €10) in **Marinhas**. ◄ 4.4km

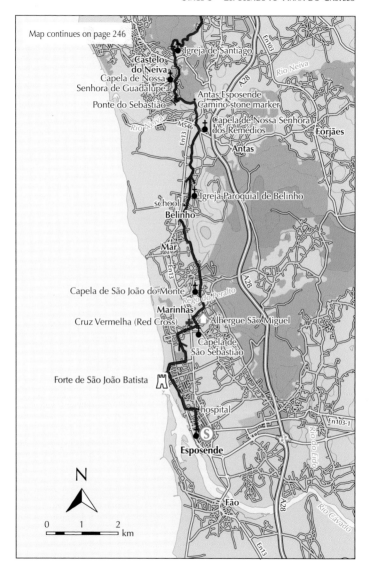

Map continues on page 246

Igreja de Santiago

Castelo do Neiva

Capela de Nossa Senhora de Guadalupe

Antas Esposende Camino-stone marker

Ponte do Sebastião

Capela de Nossa Senhora dos Remédios

Forjães

Rio Neiva

Antas

Igreja Paroquial de Belinho

school

Belinho

Mar

Capela de São João do Monte

Rego do Peralto

Marinhas

Cruz Vermelha (Red Cross)

Albergue São Miguel

Capela de São Sebastião

Forte de São João Batista

hospital

Esposende

Fão

N

0   1   2
km

Rio Neiva

Rio Cávado

Rio do Ério

243

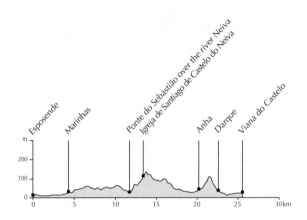

Pass the albergue and turn right at the church, climbing steadily, then turn left onto Rua de São João do Monte. Take the right fork at **Capela de São João do Monte** and follow the road for 2km as it becomes Estrada Velha then Estrada Real, reaching a stone marker in the road. Continue (slightly right) into Rua do Marco do Rei, turning right at the small junction onto Rua Padre Almeida. Pass the Junta de Freguesia (with ATM) opposite the 17th-century stone cross (leading to the Igreja Paroquial) in **Belinho**. **3.9km/8.3km**

KSO for 750m, passing cafés before turning left at the T-junction onto Rua Jose Gonçalves Pereira Barros. Soon after, keep right into Rua Barão de Maracaña then go straight on for 1km, passing the tall stone wall (RHS) of the 16th-century Quinta do Belinho. Reach a T-junction with a chapel opposite and turn left (M546), then after passing a stone cross (RHS) take the second right onto Travessa do Ferreiro. Carefully cross the N13 onto the narrow Rua da Carvalha, then after 470m take the left fork at the **Antas-Esposende Camino stone monument** and follow the peaceful path through woodland for 600m before crossing the River Neiva on the stone **Ponte do Sebastião**. **3.4km/11.7km**

Turn right and uphill into the parish of Castelo do Neiva (named after an Iron Age settlement discovered on the right bank of the river), turning right at a T-junction opposite

Capela de Nossa Senhora de Guadalupe onto Av de Moldes. After 600m reach the N13–3 (turn left for a Coviran supermarket +300m) and turn right then immediately left onto the cobbled Travessa de Santiago. Continue uphill, past the 'Santiago niche', to **Igreja de Santiago de Castelo do Neiva** (**1.7km**). ▶ Turn right onto a dirt road that leads around the back of the church cemetery and onto a lovely forest track. After 1.3km leave the forest and pass a few houses before turning left onto the dirt Rua Caminho de Santiago, heading back into the forest. After 1.1km reach a T-junction with a paved road and turn left, passing a staircase leading to **Capela de Senhora do Crasto** opposite the Benedictine monastery of Mosteiro de São Romão do Neiva (originally 10th century). **4.6km/16.3km**

Take the left fork at the stone cross onto Av do Mosteiro, going up then downhill and left onto the narrow cobbled Caminho da Rebadeira. Turn left, then turn right at the end, then after 300m pass the **cemetery** and reach a crossroads opposite a church (and Café S. Sebastião, RHS) in **Chafé**. Turn left here onto Av da Amorosa, then take the next right (with café) onto Caminho do Campo do Forno. After 600m and a few twists, pass Casa da Reina (LHS, Caminho de Pardinheiro 122, tel 962 893 944, www.casadareina.com,

Ponte do Sebastião over the River Neiva

The church features a dedication to Santiago by the Bishop of Coimbra in 862, making this the oldest church outside of Spain dedicated to Santiago. Stamp, WC.

245

The church is an 18th-century reconstruction; the first references to a church dedicated to Santiago here are from the 14th century. Stamp available.

4 rooms in a beautiful 18th-century house with welcoming owners, kitchen, €80+) then turn right and follow the arrows along winding lanes for 900m before crossing a small busy road into the cobbled Rua do Noval. Take the first left then continue straight for 600m before passing **Igreja de Santiago** in **Anha**. ◄ **3.9km/20.2km**

Turn right onto Av 9 de Julho then take the right fork and immediately turn left onto a cobbled road, passing Café O Nosso. Follow this for 500m up to a T-junction and turn left onto the busy Av da Estrada Real, then KSO for 1.3km up and over the hill. Nearing the bottom of the descent, as the road bends left, KSO onto an old paved road, passing a school (RHS), then continue along a sandy path and go straight across a roundabout onto the N13 into **Darque**. Pass

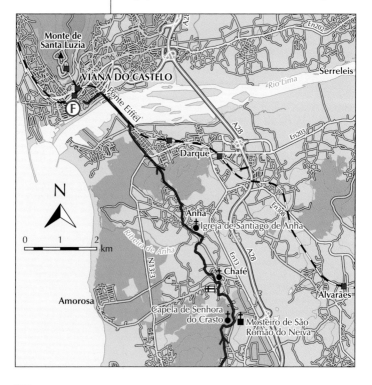

Praça da República, Viana do Castelo

a Galp petrol station and follow the N13 all the way to the River Lima, crossing **Ponte Eiffel**. ▶ **(3.5km)**. At the end of the bridge turn left at the roundabout onto Rua do Gontim, and after passing Igreja das Almas (RHS, originally 13th century) KSO into Rua Mateus Barbosa. KSO into Rua de S. Pedro, taking the first right onto Travessa dos Clérigos, then turn right onto Rua Sacadura Cabral to pass the cathedral before reaching a renaissance fountain (NM) in the charming Praça da República in **Viana do Castelo**. **5.3km/25.5km**

This iron bridge was built in 1878 by Gustav Eiffel and his then partner Théophile Seyrig.

VIANA DO CASTELO, 14M, POP. 88,631

An attractive medieval city by the River Lima with a long maritime history of shipbuilding and cod fishing, watched over by Mt Santa Luzia with its Basílica, Pousada and Iron Age settlement. There are many sights to enjoy (including the pilgrim hospital built in 1468), and sunset from the terrace bar at the Pousada on Mt Santa Luzia is a definite highlight.

Tourist office: Praça do Eixo Atlântico, tel 258 098 415, **www.vivexperiencia. pt**, closed Mondays except Jul/Aug.

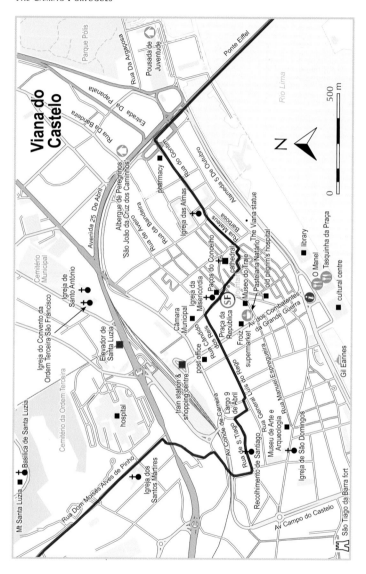

Visit: cathedral, 15th century, Romanesque with Gothic portal. Paços do Concelho (town hall; NM), 16th century, with maritime symbols of a caravel, Portuguese shield and armillary sphere on the outside. Igreja da Misericórdia (NM), 16th century, stunning interior lined with blue-and-white *azulejos* (tiles) and frescoes; the church is attached to the Misericórdia hospital that was built later in the same century. Hospital Velho, 1468, restored in the 16th century, built to accommodate pilgrims. Museu do Traje, ethnographic costume and gold museum, closed Mondays, €2. Museu de Arte e Arqueologia, fascinating collection, closed Mondays, €2. Navio Hospital Gil Eannes Museum, built in 1955 as a hospital ship to support the cod-fleets in Newfoundland, open daily, €5. Monte de Santa Luzia (highly recommended) – take the staircase or funicular to the top (€3 return ticket, operates daily except Mondays Nov–Feb) and visit the Romanesque-Byzantine Basílica de St Luzia, 20th century, open daily, €1 for lift access to the dome. The Pousada (hotel; www.pestana.com) is behind the Basílica, as are the Ruinas da Cidade Velha (NM), remains of an Iron Age settlement later occupied by the Romans, closed Mondays.

Specialities: *Bolas de Berlim* – custard-filled doughnuts from Pastelaria Natário (near Museu do Traje).

Where to eat: Tasquinha da Praça and O Manel by the river near the Cultural Centre.

Accommodation: Albergue de Peregrinos 'S. João da Cruz dos Caminhos' (Igreja do Carmo 1, tel 913 919 455 & 258 822 264, 30 beds, €12+. Access: before reaching the end of the bridge take the steps down (LHS), go under the bridge then turn left; it's in the Convento do Carmo, RHS). Pousada de Juventude (Rua de Limia, tel 258 838 458, www.pousadasjuventude.pt, 74 beds, kitchen, €14+, river-front, 1km from the square). Pensão O Laranjeira (Rua Manuel Espregueira 24, tel 258 822 258, www.olaranjeira.com, 7 rooms and 5 apartments, €35+, beautifully designed family-run accommodation close to the square). **Hotel Laranjeira (Rua Cândido Dos Reis 45, tel 258 822 261, www.hotelaranjeira.com, 29 rooms, €59+, boutique hotel on the Camino). Albergue de Peregrinos (Monte de Santa Luzia, tel 961 660 300, www.templosantaluzia.org). Located on top of Monte Santa Luzia next to the basilica, this hostel has 40 beds and a shared kitchen, €15+.

STAGE 4
Viana do Castelo to Caminha

Start	Praça da República, Viana do Castelo
Finish	Torre do Relógio, Caminha
Distance	26.8km
Total ascent	375m
Total descent	417m
Difficulty	Medium
Time	7–8hr
Cafés	Viana do Castelo, Carreço (8.4km), Âncora (15.6km), Vila Praia de Âncora (18.2km), Moledo do Minho (22.9km), Caminha (26.8km)
Accommodation	Viana do Castelo, Areosa (4.8km), Carreço (8.1 & 9.4km), Vila Praia de Âncora (18.2km), Caminha (26.8km)

This stage follows undulating winding lanes and forest tracks with good waymarks, often with sea and mountain views. There's one main climb before arriving in Vila Praia de Âncora, which has a wonderful beach, then the route takes a flat seaside path before leaving the sea for the last few kilometres to Caminha.

Leaving Praça da República, KSO into Passeio das Mordomas da Romaria (towards Mt Santa Lucia), taking the first left onto Rua Cândido dos Reis. Pass Hotel Laranjeira (no. 45) and continue straight across the avenue into Rua do General Luís do Rego. Turn right at the square, Largo 9 de April, and take the first left into Rua de S. Tiago, passing a statue of Santiago (LHS, on the Recolhimento de Santiago). Take the next right onto Rua do Assento and go down the steps, through the underpass then turn right and take the first left uphill on Rua Portela de Cima. Go through another underpass (under the N13) then go left and uphill on Rua Dom Moisés Alves de Pinho, passing **Igreja dos Santos Mártires**. 1.2km

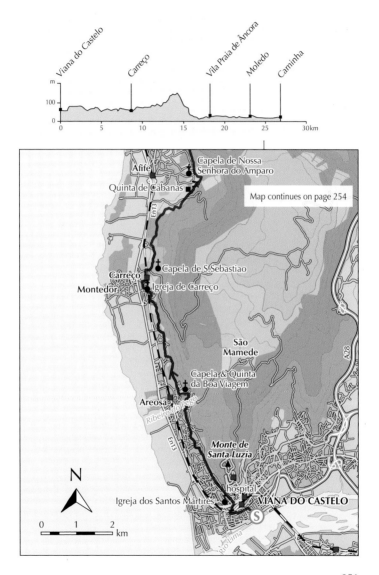

Viana do Castelo

Carreço

Vila Praia de Âncora

Moledo

Caminha

Capela de Nossa
Senhora do Amparo

Afife

Quinta de Cabanas

Map continues on page 254

En13

Capela de S.Sebastiao

Carreço

Igreja de Carreço

Montedor

São
Mamede

Capela & Quinta
da Boa Viagem

Areosa

Ribeira do Pego

En13

Monte de
Santa Luzia

N

hospital

Igreja dos Santos Mártires

VIANA DO CASTELO

S

Rio Lima

0   1   2
km

After 1.3km pass Café Pôr do Sol (RHS), then as the road bends right, turn left onto Rua José Pedro. Take the first right onto Rua Estreita and follow the arrows around the lanes for 460m, then take the diagonal left at a *fonte* (spring, in the middle of the road). After 500m reach the main road again and turn left, going straight across a small roundabout (with metal structure) onto Rua Entre Quintas. After a further 900m of winding lanes, cross a stone bridge over **Ribeiro do Pego** then turn left and pass an old mill (LHS) then a chapel opposite **Quinta da Boa Viagem** (tel 935 835 835, www.quintadaboaviagem.com, shared room and apartments in a 16th-century house with pool and gardens, €40+). **3.6km/4.8km**

Turn right into Rua do Malhão and take the first left. After 600m, as the road bends left, KSO behind a house (LHS), turning right at the end onto Rua da Garita. Follow the arrows for 2km (Casa do Nato +50m KSO to the blue gate, Rua do Moreno 130, tel 258 834 041, www.casadonato.com, 8 rooms, kitchen, €30+) then cross the bridge over railway tracks and turn right down a narrow lane. Soon reach **Igreja de Carreço** (17th century) and turn left in front of the church, going downhill then right at the end onto Av Nossa Senhora da Graça, passing Café Bar Central and mini-market (RH corner – if staying at Casa do Sardão buy food here) in **Carreço**. **3.6km/8.4km**

KSO, then after passing the Junta de Freguesia (with ATM) turn right. Pass Carreço **train station** and turn right, crossing a bridge over the tracks, then take the second left uphill. Pass **Capela de S. Sebastião** and shortly afterwards pass Casa do Sardão Albergue (LHS, Av de Paco 769, tel 961 790 759, shared and private rooms in a lovingly restored 17th-century house, kitchen, €13+, cash only). Follow the arrows onto a forest track for 860m, and once out of the forest turn right onto a path between Casa da Presa and a stone wall. After 1.3km pass **Quinta de Cabanas** (LHS). ◀ Shortly afterwards, cross the River Afife on the stone Ponte de Cabanas. **3.9km/12.3km**

There are references to a monastery here since 564; the current building dates from the early 17th century.

Turn right then left and uphill, turning left at the end onto a cobbled road. Soon after turn right then reach a set of steps (RHS), 'Carreiro de São João', and turn right up the steps, passing behind **Capela de Nossa Senhora do Amparo** (LHS). Continue uphill onto the final forest track for 840m before reaching **two stone crosses**, then turn left (not sharp left). After 400m pass another stone cross then take the dirt road right and downhill for 640m until you pass houses on Rua da

Narrow lanes among stone walls, Afife

Cividade. Turn left at the end and follow the arrows past **Fonte do Crasto**, then at the next junction pass Café O Forno (RHS) at the beginning of **Âncora**. **3.3km/15.6km**

Continue downhill along Rua do Calvário, passing the Junta de Freguesia and a stone cross, then take the right fork onto Rua da Torre. Shortly after, veer diagonally right around a shrine onto a narrow cobbled road then cross the medieval stone slab **Ponte da Torre** over the River Âncora. Cross the N305 into Rua da Barrosa, and as the road bends left KSO then onto a dirt path. ▸ Join a paved road and pass a school

For the 'Dolmen of Barrosa' (NM), megalithic tomb (about 3000BC) with a stone corridor and slab roof, follow the road to the right +100m; it's in the park on the RHS.

Dolmen of Barrosa megalithic tomb

253

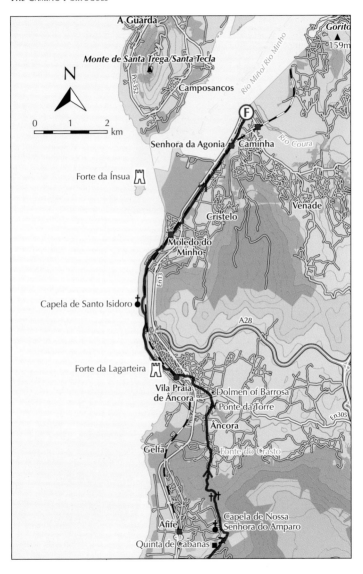

(LHS) then KSO across the roundabout. Pass the municipal swimming pool and follow the road as it bends right, then turn left at the end onto Rua Miguel Bombarda. KSO for 500m to reach the main square, Praça da República in **Vila Praia de Âncora**. 2.6km/18.2km

VILA PRAIA DE ÂNCORA, 21M, POP. 4819

A former fishing village turned popular seaside resort with a 17th-century fort (Forte da Lagarteira), stunning sandy beaches, and dunes accessed by a board-walk over the River Âncora.

Tourist office: Av Dr. Luís Ramos Pereira, tel 258 911 384, www. caminhaturismo.pt, closed Sundays.

Accommodation: ****Hotel Meira (Rua 5 De Outubro 56, tel 258 911 111, www.hotelmeira.com, 52 rooms, €50+, pilgrim-friendly hotel on the Camino). Albergaria Quim Barreiros (Av Dr. Ramos Pereira 115, tel 258 959 100 & 912 525 372, www.albergariaquimbarreiros.pt, 28 rooms, €45+, opposite the beach).

Turn right onto Rua 5 de Outubro, passing Hotel Meira, and just before the fire station turn left onto Rua Celestino Fernandes. Cross the railway tracks and turn right into Rua

View of Mt Santa Tecla in Spain, from Moledo

dos Pescadores then right at the esplanade, passing **Forte da Lagarteira** (17th century). Continue by the sea for 1.8km before passing **Capela de Santo Isidoro** (17th century with covered porch). After passing a stone cross (RHS), follow a dirt road parallel to the railway tracks for 800m then join the cobbled Rua da Estrada Real, passing apartments. Reach the sea again with a view of the pyramid-shaped Mt Santa Tecla (also known as Mt Santa Trega) opposite in Spain and turn right. After 170m turn right again and go through a tunnel under the railway tracks, turning left onto Av Santana. Pass cafés, a supermarket and Moledo do Minho train station in **Moledo. 4.7km/22.9km**

It's possible to connect to Valença/ Tui on the Central Camino from here; see Link route 3 for details.

KSO to a large roundabout and the N13 and take the diagonal left. The railway tracks will soon be on the LHS. KSO for 1.6km before crossing the tracks onto Rua do Pombal, then KSO for a further 1.6km until you reach the main square and clock tower, Torre do Relógio, in **Caminha. ◀ 3.9km/26.8km**

CAMINHA, 17M, POP. 17,069

Situated at the mouth of the River Minho, a natural border between Portugal and Spain, Caminha became a fortified village in the 13th century and there are many vestiges of the medieval walls and town.

Tourist office: next to Torre do Relógio, tel 258 921 952, www.caminhaturismo. pt, closed Sundays.

Visit: Torre do Relógio (NM), 13th century, part of the ancient city walls; the clock was added in 1673. Igreja Matriz (NM), 15th century, late Gothic and Renaissance church. Igreja da Misericórdia, 16th century, Renaissance with Baroque and Rococo interior. Fountain in Largo do Terreiro (NM), 16th century, Renaissance. Forte da Ínsua (NM), on an island at the mouth of the River Minho; a Franciscan Monastery was based here from the 14th century then rebuilt under King Manuel's orders after visiting on his way to Santiago (1502). The current fort surrounding the monastery dates from the 17th century.

Where to eat: cafés and restaurants overlook the main square; Baptista Restaurant is good.

Accommodation: Albergue de Peregrinos de Caminha +500m (Av Padre Pinheiro, tel 914 290 431, 25 beds, kitchen, €10. Access: turn right into the square then along Rua da Corredoura, taking the first left onto Av São João de Deus. Pass supermarket 'Capitolina' (LHS) and the albergue is at the end,

RHS). Muralha de Caminha (Rua Barão de S. Roque 69, tel 258 728 199, 7 rooms, €50+, overlooking the river in front of the Igreja Matriz). ****Design & Wine Hotel (Praça Conselheiro Silva Torres 8, tel 258 719 040, **www. designwinehotel.com**, 23 rooms, €65+, opposite the square).

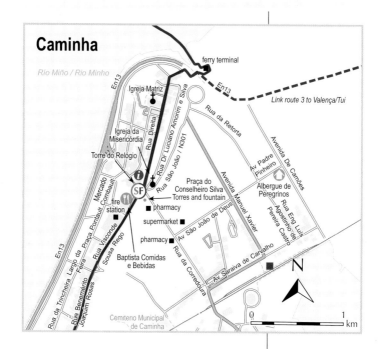

257

STAGE 5
Caminha to Mougás

Start	Torre do Relógio, Caminha
Finish	Aguncheiro Albergue, Mougás
Distance	25km including the 1.5km boat ride
Total ascent	332m
Total descent	331m
Difficulty	Easy
Time	6–7hr
Cafés	Caminha, A Guarda (5.2km), Oia (18.6km), Viladesuso (22.5km +150m), Mougás (25km)
Accommodation	Caminha, A Guarda (5.2km), Oia (18.6km), Viladesuso (22.3km) Mougás (25km)
Note	Check the Santa Rita de Cássia ferry timetable in advance. Fill up on water before leaving A Guarda.

Say *adeus* to Portugal and cross the River Minho to Spain. On the other side, the route follows a scenic forest path to A Guarda. The rest of the stage traces the coastline on small roads, forest and cycle paths, passing through Oia (recommended for lunch) before arriving at Aguncheiro Albergue in Mougás.

Go through the middle of the clock tower onto Rua Direita. Near the end of the street, pass behind the Igreja Matriz, then turn right at the end and take the underpass to the ferry terminal (yellow-and-blue building) to board the **Santa Rita de Cássia ferry**. 500m

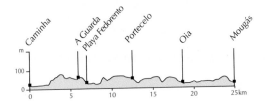

258

Santa Rita de Cássia ferry, tel +351 258 092 564 (Portugal), +34 986 611 526 (Spain), www.caminhaturismo.pt. Cost: €1, duration: 15 minutes.

There is no service on Mondays or at low-tide. The ferry typically operates once an hour from 9/10am–7pm (with a break at 1pm); check for up-to-date information – as at spring 2023 the ferry was not running and its future uncertain. Taxi-Mar operates from the terminal, tel 915 955 827, as does Spanish operator Xacobeo, +34 613 011 226, www.xacobeotransfer.com.

If the ferry isn't operating, enquire at the tourist office/albergue as there are a few locals who will transfer people across the river for around €6 in small taxi boats from near Restaurant Forte da Ínsua (Foz do Minho) +2.5km from the clock tower. Mario Gonçalves is a well-known local who offers this service (tel 931 636 360). Miguel Terra's Taxi Boat Peregrino is another option (tel 913 254 110). (If you take this route and are dropped off on Praia O Muíño, you can follow the Senda Litoral '*sendero azul*' blue coastal trail along a boardwalk then esplanade, keeping the sea on your LHS, all the way to A Guarda (+4.7km). Once you pass A Guarda's port, KSO then go uphill away from the water, passing Hotel Convento de San Benito (RHS). Go straight up the long flight of steps on Rúa Colón, rejoining the Camino in Praza do Reló with the clock tower and tourist office (LHS).) Alternatively, you could walk/taxi across the bridge 16km further up the river at Vila Nova de Cerveira.

Welcome to Spain! ▶ Disembark the ferry in **Camposancos** and turn left, passing a grand old building (RHS), then turn right and uphill. Turn left at the roundabout then continue uphill to a T-junction, turning left briefly

Spanish time is 1hr ahead of Portugal. Int'l dialling code: +34.

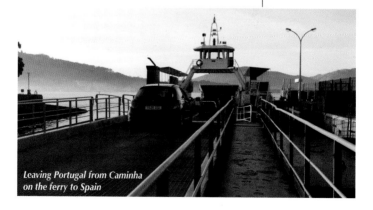

Leaving Portugal from Caminha on the ferry to Spain

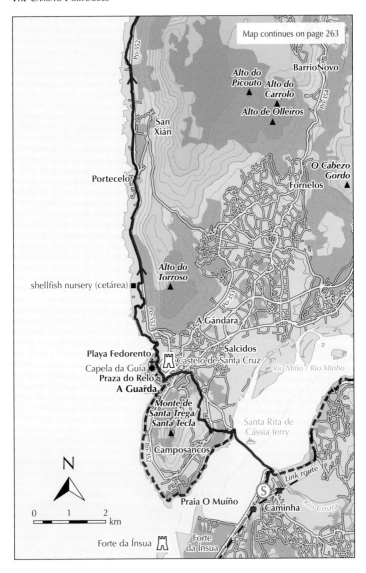

Map continues on page 263

BarrioNovo

Alto do
Picouto
Alto do
Carrolo

Alto de Olleiros

San
Xián

O Cabezo
Gordo

Portecelo

Fornelos

Alto do
Torroso

shellfish nursery (cetárea)

A Gándara

Salcidos

Playa Fedorento

Castelo de Santa Cruz

Rio Miño / Rio Minho

Capela da Guía

Praza do Reló

A Guarda

Monte de
Santa Trega /
Santa Tecla

Santa Rita de
Cássia ferry

Camposancos

N

0   1   2
km

Praia O Muíño

Link route 3

Rio Coura

Caminha

Forte da Ínsua

Forte
da Ínsua

before veering right onto a cobbled road. Take the first right at a stone cross and continue uphill for 500m to reach a right turn onto a stone path into woodland. Follow the arrows along a dirt path for 1km as you skirt around the eastern side of **Mt Santa Tecla**, and at the paved Paseo de Portugal turn left. Pass the sports stadium (RHS) then follow the road as it winds around to a T-junction with Alameda Park (RHS) in **A Guarda**. **4.7km/5.2km**

A GUARDA, 60M, POP. 10,193

A medieval walled fishing village overlooked by the impressive Iron Age settlement on top of Mt Santa Tecla.

Tourist office: Praza do Reló, tel 986 614 546, **www.turismoaguarda.es**, open daily.

Visit: medieval quarter including the 16th-century clock tower in Praza do Reló. Igrexa de Santa María, 16th-century church, Romanesque with an 18th-century Baroque altar and main facade. Castelo de Santa Cruz, 17th century. Mt Santa Tecla hill fort (NM; highly recommended), Iron Age settlement with many stone dwellings. Take the PR-G122–2 hiking trail from Rúa Tui and reach the site after

A Guarda

30 minutes. Allow an extra 5–10 minutes to reach the top with the 12–18th-century chapel, museum, hotel and restaurant.

Specialities: shellfish – especially lobster (*lagosta*).

▶ Turn left onto Rúa Galicia then take the right fork. Shortly afterwards, turn left onto Rúa Vicente Sobrino. Pass Hotel Eli-Mar then at the end veer slightly left and go up a ramp into Plaza de Bautista Alonso. Turn right then take the next right onto Rúa Colón into the centre of the historical quarter, passing the Torre do Reló and tourist office in **Praza do Reló**. Pass Art Café (RHS) and go straight into Rúa de Bernardo Alonso, heading uphill and passing in front of Igrexa de Santa María before veering right and left onto

Before leaving A Guarda, fill up on water for the next 13km to Oia.

Where to eat: opposite the port at one of the many seafood restaurants like
Puerto Guardes.

Accommodation: Albergue de Peregrinos (Rúa Puerto Rico 7, tel 619 258 075,
36 beds, kitchen, €10). **Hotel Eli-Mar (Vicente Sobrino 12, tel 986 613 000,
www.eli-marhotel.com, 17 rooms, €37+, on the Camino). **Hotel Monumento
Convento de San Benito (Plaza de San Benito s/n, tel 986 611 517, **www.
hotelsanbenito.es**, 24 rooms, €48+, a former 16th-century convent).

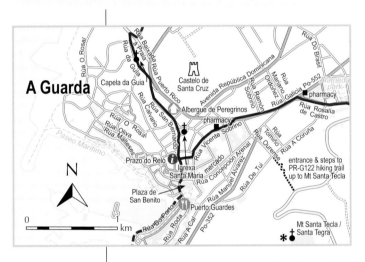

Rúa San Bernardo. KSO (passing behind the albergue, RHS)
then take the left fork at the car dealership, going downhill.
Pass **Capela da Guía** (16th century) then turn right and soon
left onto a road beside a field (LHS). Follow this down a
stone staircase to **Playa Fedorento**. **1.6km/6.8km**

Following the coast, reach **Playa Area Grande** (restaurant, shower and WC) and continue to hug the coastline
as the terrain changes from road to dirt track and rocky
path. After 1.3km pass a large building (RHS) opposite a
shellfish nursery. ◄ Turn right onto a dirt road here, and
just before the main road (PO-552) turn left onto a parallel
dirt path. Follow the arrows as the Camino now alternates
between parallel dirt roads and the cycle path along the
(generous) shoulder of this main road. After 3.7km enter the

*This is a cetárea –
built into the rocks
to act as a hatchery
for shellfish.*

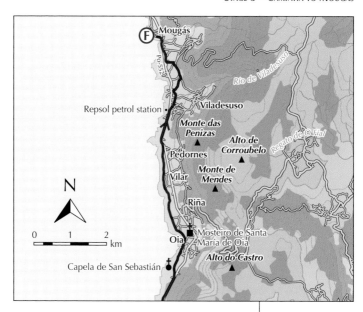

coastal hamlet of **Portecelo** (**5.7km**; there is sometimes a makeshift bar here). After a further 5.3km pass **Capela de San Sebastián** (18th century), then after 600m enter **Oia**, passing Casa Puertas (no. 7, RHS) shortly before reaching the small square with stone cross, Praza da Centinela. **11.8km/18.6km**

Take the path down by the seawall, passing the **monastery**, then turn left to rejoin a cycle path (for Hotel A Raiña, turn right +160m RHS). After 2.6km follow the cycle path left onto the PO-552. Pass Hotel Restaurant Glasgow (Ctra De Baiona, tel 986 361 552, www.hglasgow.com, 65 rooms, €50+) and Alojamiento Camino Portugues Oia Hostel (Rua Serrallo 12, Villadesuso, tel 986 136 906, alojamientocaminoportuguesoia@gmail.com, 30 beds (dorm and private), shared kitchen and laundry) in **Viladesuso** (**3.7km**), then pass a **Repsol petrol station** and follow the cycle path as it turns right onto a parallel road (or KSO +150m for Café Sal de Mar, LHS). After 600m veer right with the cycle path then turn left at the T-junction. Pass a farm and silos (RHS) and turn left past

OIA, 24M, POP. 3100

A quaint seaside village with a couple of restaurants and the standout 12th-century Mosteiro de Santa María de Oia. First referenced in 1137 when King Alfonso VII donated several churches to the monastery, which was Benedictine then Cistercian and commanded great power through the north of Portugal and Galicia.

Tourist office: Praza da Centinela, tel 986 362 225, www.concellodeoia.es, open Jun–Sep, closed Wednesday.

Accommodation: Casa Puertas (Vicente Lopez 7, tel 986 362 144, **www.casapuertas.es**, 8 rooms, €60+, on the Camino). **Hotel A Raiña (Rúa A Raiña 21B, tel 986 362 908, **www.hotelaraina.com**, 12 rooms, €60+, just past the monastery).

a huge pile of stones at a Camino marker, then right onto a paved road. Soon afterwards, turn left and pass a red shed (RHS). Heading back towards the sea, just before reaching the main road, turn right onto the cycle path and follow this for 300m then cross the main road. After crossing the blue pedestrian bridge over the River Mougás, turn left and arrive at the end of this stage in **Mougás**, with a café/restaurant, next-door to Aguncheiro Albergue (Calle O Porto 53, tel 665 840 774, www.aguncheiro.wixsite.com/alojamientoturistico, shared and private rooms, €14+). **6.4km/25km**

Atlantic Ocean views near Oia

STAGE 6
Mougás to A Ramallosa

Start	Aguncheiro Albergue, Mougás
Finish	Hospedería Pazo Pías, A Ramallosa
Distance	16km
Total ascent	341m
Total descent	317m
Difficulty	Medium
Time	4–5hr
Cafés	Mougás, Baiona (11km), Sabaris (14.2km), A Ramallosa (16km)
Accommodation	Mougás (0–4km), Baiona (11km), A Ramallosa (16km)

The Camino continues along cycle paths for a few kilometres before leaving the coast to climb up and around the side of Mt Baredo. After dropping into the village of Baredo the trail climbs once more before descending into the bustling historical town of Baiona and following small roads to A Ramallosa.

Leaving the albergue, continue by the sea, and soon rejoin the cycle path beside the highway. Pass Camping 1ª O Muiño (tel 986 361 600, www.campingmuino.com, bungalows and tents) (**1.5km**), then Camping Mougás (tel 986 385 011, www.campingmougas.com, €14. Private rooms and bungalows available). **4.2km**

After passing Camping Mougás, keep an eye out for the right turn after 600m which leads you away from the coast, marked with an arrow and **blue Camino sign**.

It's also possible – and 1km longer – to reach Baiona via the **coastal cycle path** beside the PO-552. Follow the signs to Baiona and after 6.9km pass the Fortaleza de Monterreal (LHS) then reach the harbour and turn right opposite, along the narrow Rúa Nigrán. Follow this to the end and turn left onto Rúa do Conde to rejoin the Camino.

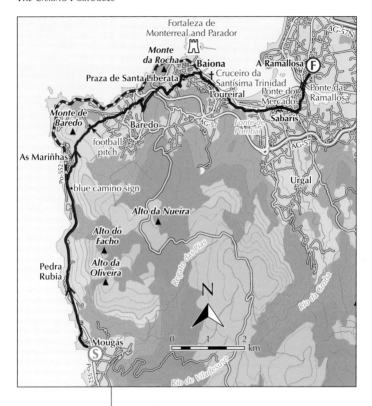

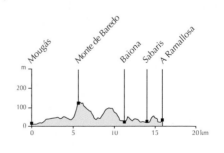

To continue on the main route, however, go through a gate and uphill along an ancient path over rocks with wheel indents, through pine and eucalyptus with sweeping ocean and Cape Silleiro lighthouse views. After 1km go through a second gate then in-between two stone markers. To descend, veer left with a small stone wall on the RHS. After 400m pass a house with a brown gate (LHS), then turn right onto the paved road and pass a **football pitch** (LHS). After a further 850m pass a stone cross then cross a small bridge over the River Fraga. **3.5km/7.7km**

> The boardwalk on both sides of the bridge here is the **Senda Fluvial del Rio Fraga** – a pleasant 760m walkway that passes eight old stone watermills (*molinos/muiños*) and information panels.

Continue uphill, turning left onto a small busy road and passing restaurant 'O'Rizón' before taking the right fork. After the last house (RHS) turn right, doubling back, and continue uphill then turn left at the top onto Estrada de Baredo. KSO and cross a bridge over the AG-57 (don't look down if you're afraid of heights!), then take the first right, passing a playground (LHS) and then keeping right. Follow the winding road downhill, turning left at the faux castle tower (LHS), then continue downhill for 850m until you reach a roundabout. Turn right onto Rúa Dolores Agrelo, pass a football stadium, then take the first left then right through **Praza de Santa Liberata**. Pass the Baroque Capela de Santa Liberata (17/18th century) then the older Romanesque Ex-Colexiata de Santa María (12–14th century, stamp available), turning left opposite this and going down a staircase onto Rúa Manuel Valverde. Turn right onto Rúa do Conde into the historical quarter of **Baiona**. ▶ **3.5km/11.2km**

Take any left now for the harbour.

Continue along Rúa do Conde, following it as it bends right onto Rúa Fonte de Zeta, then bend left and go uphill along Rúa Porta da Villa to reach the Gothic **Cruceiro da Santísima Trinidad**. ▶ Turn left then right onto Rúa Loureiral and shortly afterwards, when the road forks (small roundabout), keep left downhill then straight on. Cross a stone bridge then start uphill, following the road past Fonte de Gafos then **Fonte de Pombal** (15th century, under a stone arch) (**2km**). Continue straight across a roundabout and over the stone Ponte Nova (15th century), then turn right onto

St James is one of the images on this 15th-century covered stone cross.

Fortaleza de Monterreal walls, Baiona

the main road (PO-552). After 250m pass a market (RHS) then cross the stone **Ponte do Mercado** (15th century) over the River Groba into a square with a restaurant and bar in **Sabaris**. **3km/14.2km**

KSO into the small Rúa Ponte, then on the ascent take the left fork onto Viso de Calvos, continuing uphill.

BAIONA, 14M, POP. 12,233

An historic and popular seaside town with the notable Fortaleza de Monterreal, famous for being the port that one of Columbus' fleet 'La Pinta' arrived in, declaring the discovery of America on 1 March 1493. The Cíes islands, part of the Galician Atlantic Islands NP, are located at the mouth of the Vigo estuary; think stunning white sandy beaches and scenic hiking trails (but cold water!). Ferries depart for the islands from Baiona (and Vigo) daily between June and September – you won't be disappointed, even if you only visit for a few hours or a half-day.

Tourist office: at the entrance to the fort, tel 986 687 067, www.baiona.org, open daily.

Visit: Fortaleza de Monterreal (now the Parador), 3km of defensive walls dating from the 11–17th centuries and a popular sunset viewpoint. Caravel Pinta (ship) replica and museum, a fascinating insight into what life was like for the crew on the cramped ship, €2.

Specialities: seafood.

Where to eat: La Boquería, El Patio Pizzeria & Taperia or along Rúa Ventura Misa.

Accommodation: **Pension El Mosquito (Ventura Misa 32, tel 986 385 264, 12 rooms, €40+, harbour front). **Hotel Tres Carabelas (Ventura Misa 61, tel 986 355 133, **www.hoteltrescarabelas.com**, 10 rooms, €35+, central location). ****Parador de Baiona (Av Arquitecto Jesus Valverde 3, tel 986 355 000, **www.parador.es**, 122 rooms inside the fort!). Albergue Estela do Mar, Rúa Laureano Salgado 15, tel 986 133 213, **www.esteladomar.com**, 20 (bunk) beds, shared kitchen and laundry. Another welcome addition to Baiona, this modern albergue is just 400m from Praza de Santa Liberata, towards the fort. Hostel Albergue Baionamar (Calle Venezuela 6, tel 698 165 575, **www. hostelbaionamar.com**, 18 (bunk) beds, shared kitchen. Located just 100m off the Camino, not far from Praza de Santa Liberata, this hostel is a welcome addition for budget accommodation in Baiona).

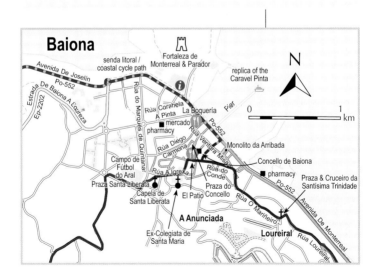

Crossing Ponte da Ramallosa

This 13th-century Romanesque bridge has 10 arches and the cross in the middle features an image of San Telmo, the patron saint of sailors.

Turn right onto Av José Pereira Troncoso then sharp left at a *hórreo* (granary) onto the narrow Camiño do Lindeiro. Keep right onto a paved road, passing a residential area (LHS), then follow the road around to the left. As the road then bends right, KSO onto a narrow road and turn left at the end, then cross the River Miñor on **Ponte da Ramallosa**. ◄ Once across the bridge, take the diagonal right into Rúa Damas Apostólicas, passing cafés and the Centro Comercial Ramallosa shopping centre (with a Gadis supermarket), and KSO to the large gate at the end of the street, which is the entrance to Hospedería Pazo Pías in **A Ramallosa**. 1.8km/16km

A RAMALLOSA, 18M, POP. 4686

A parish in the municipality of Nigrán, A Ramallosa is a seaside town most notable for its medieval bridge.

Where to eat: Various options on Rúa Damas Apostólicas.

Accommodation: Hospedería Pazo Pías (Camino da Cabreira 21, tel 986 350 654 & 638 883 472, **www.pazopias.org**, 62 rooms in a 17th-century palace, €18+).

STAGE 7
A Ramallosa to Vigo

Start	Hospedería Pazo Pías, A Ramallosa
Finish	Rúa Urzáiz, Vigo
Distance	21.5km
Total ascent	506m
Total descent	426m
Difficulty	Medium
Time	6–7hr
Cafés	A Ramallosa, Priegue (6.3km), Coruxo (11.3km), Comesaña (13.9km), Matamá (15.4km), Vigo (21.5km)
Accommodation	A Ramallosa, Saiáns (7.3km +320m), Albergue O Freixo (10.1km +5.2km), Vigo (21.5km)

This is an undulating stage along small roads and scenic woodland paths en route to the outer suburbs of Vigo. The Camino skirts around the edge of Vigo but it's a wonderful city, worth exploring.

Leaving Hospedería Pazo Pías, turn left and continue uphill then bend left onto Camiño da Cabreira. Take the right fork at the old gate of **Casa de A Robaleira**, go under an arch then at the end turn left onto a small but busy road. Shortly afterwards take the right fork at the stone cross onto Rúa Jesús Marzoa. Reaching a square, there are new arrows taking you left on a longer route via Nigrán. Instead, veer right then left around a bandstand (LHS), going downhill and left at the

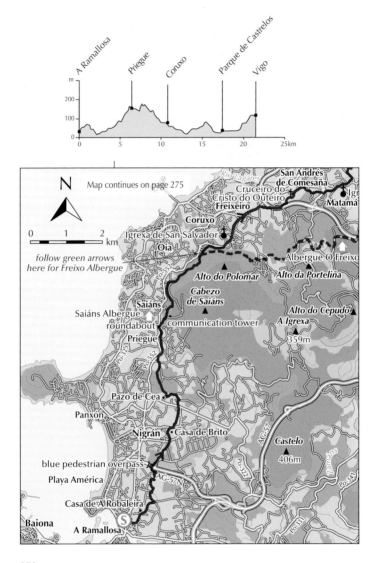

end onto Rúa Soleiro. Keep right at the first fork then right again onto Camiño da Camesella. Reach a roundabout and turn left, then at the next (larger) roundabout cross the **blue pedestrian overpass** over the AG-57N. **2.3km**

KSO through the next roundabout, then after 530m cross a road into Camiño da Rectoral (joining up here with the new longer route via Nigrán). Take the next right, and on reaching a T-junction turn right and then shortly afterwards turn left opposite **Casa de Brito** (RHS, 18th century) onto Camiño da Dehesa. Follow the road right then left around a field, then go across the busy Rúa dos Pazos into Rúa da Nogueira. Take the second left uphill then turn left at the T-junction and after 300m turn right onto an earthen path (if you pass **Pazo de Cea** (RHS) you've gone too far) (**2.8km**). Follow the path uphill through woods for 800m, turning left at the end onto Rúa Condominguez. Shortly after, turn left at the T-junction then right and downhill, turning right onto the PO-552 into **Priegue**. **4km/6.3km**

Pass a pharmacy (RHS) then turn right onto the parallel Rúa Mestra Emerita, heading uphill with views of the Cíes islands until you reach the PO-552 again. ▶ Turn right onto Camino da Cal do Outeiro and walk steeply uphill for 400m, then turn left and pass a **communications tower** and shortly afterwards turn right onto a lush woodland track. After 900m reach a paved road and small junction and turn right. Soon after, turn left back into the woods for 1.1km (the steep descent can be slippery) before passing a small dirt road junction with green arrows.

Albergue O Freixo detour (adds 2.3km)

Turn right here, following green arrows along a forest path for 5.2km to the Albergue O Freixo (Estrada Regueiro-Valadares, tel 986 213 856, www.caminador.es, 5 beds + mattresses, donation). From the albergue, continue for 4.2km to reach the 13th-century Romanesque **Igrexa de Santa María de Castrelos**, then turn left, following a yellow arrow down the steps in front of the church. This road leads to a T-junction; turn right, now with the stone fence of **Parque de Castrelos** on the LHS. After 370m reach a car park and entrance to the park and follow the yellow arrows into the park, keeping right onto a dirt path. After a further 260m reach the River Lagares and rejoin the Camino by turning right, going under the road and following a dirt path beside the river.

For Saiáns Albergue, turn left here at the roundabout +320m, Rúa Eira Vella 4, tel 689 133 973, 10 beds, €10, next to Igrexa de Saiáns. Bar O Bolo serves meals.

Ponte Romana, Vigo

From the dirt road junction with the green arrows, KSO following the yellow arrows for 800m and onto another woodland path before reaching and turning right onto the PO-552 into **Coruxo**. **4.6km/10.9km**

Follow the road for 1.5km, passing **Igrexa de San Salvador** (LHS, 12th century, Romanesque), cafés and a pharmacy, then before passing the Citroen showroom (LHS) turn right onto Camino da Pitasia. Turn left at the T-junction then immediately right, walking under the VG-20 highway, then go left at the roundabout and right onto a dirt road. After 600m of winding streets, pass a series of stone crosses (Via Crucis), passing behind one on a boulder. ◄ Turn left and right onto Estrada Matamá Pazo, then pass Café Anxo and Igrexa de Santo André in **Comesaña**. **3km/13.9km**

This is Cruceiro do Cristo do Outeiro, thought to be one of the oldest stone crosses in Galicia.

KSO, passing picnic tables, then take the next right, turning right at the end onto Camiño de Sanín. Turn left at Café Nautilius (RHS) and after 300m go through an underpass. Turn right at the end onto Camiño da Carpinteira then left at the junction. Shortly afterwards turn right and uphill, veering left into Rúa dos Canteiros towards Café Priton and Igrexa de San Pedro in **Matamá (1.5km)**. Turn left in front of the church onto Camino Real, go straight on into Rúa do Castro, then go left at the end onto Rúa do Roupeiro and downhill. After 220m turn right, then right at the end, at the beginning of an industrial area. Take the next left onto the narrow Camiño de Sabarís, turning right at the end onto the busy Av do Alcalde Portanet. Turn left at Café Ponte Romana and pass the old stone bridge (RHS), then turn right onto a dirt path. Soon after, turn left onto Av Castrelos then turn right into **Parque de Castrelos. 3.6km/17.5km**

> **Parque de Castrelos** is a large park with landscaped gardens, WC, kiosk, and the 17th-century Quiñones de León Pazo-Museo Galician Art Museum, www.museodevigo.org.

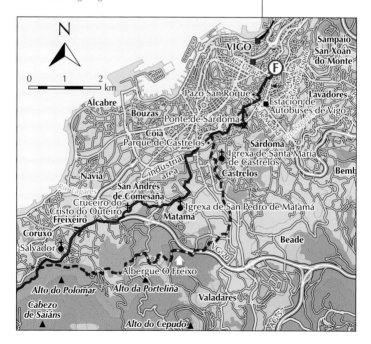

The end of the stage at Rúa Urzáiz, Vigo

The Albergue O Freixo variant rejoins the Camino here.

Follow the arrows in a north-easterly direction through the park, then go under a road and follow a path beside the river (LHS). ◄ After 500m cross Baixada Ponte Nova and continue with the river on the LHS for a further 700m until you reach a graffiti wall (you can also do this stretch on the other side of the river). Turn left and cross a wooden bridge, then the stone **Ponte de Sárdoma** (12th century), then turn left onto the paved road and go through an underpass. KSO uphill to a T-junction, turning right onto Rúa do Carbello. At the next T-junction turn left, then take the first right into Rúa do Loureiro, then KSO across the multi-lane Av de Madrid. Take the first left onto Baixada a San Roque, going uphill and passing the stone wall of **Pazo San Roque** (LHS, 17th-century manor, gardens open to the public). At the top of the steps, turn right onto Rúa de San Roque and follow this for 650m until you reach Av Alcalde Gregorio Espino. Turn left then take the next right onto the pedestrianised **Rúa Urzáiz**, where this stage ends. ◄ **4km/21.5km**

Turn left on Rúa Urzáiz for Vigo's historical quarter and harbour +2km.

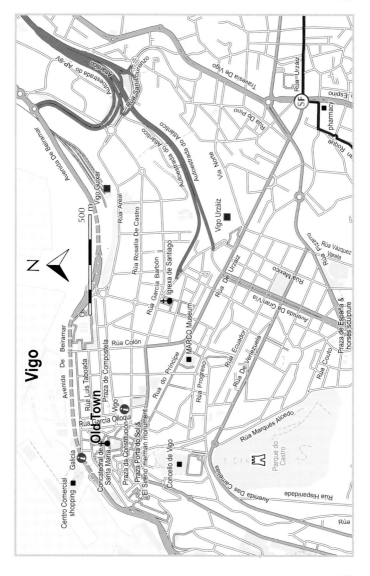

Vigo

N

500 m

Autoestrada do AP-9V
Atlántico
Rúa San Lourenzo
Travesia De Vigo
Rúa Urzáiz
SF
Espino
pharmacy
San Roque
Rúa Do Pino
Autoestrada do Atlántico
Avenida De Beiramar
Vigo Guixar
Rúa Areal
Rúa Rosalía De Castro
Vigo Urzáiz
Via Norte
Rúa Vázquez Varela
Rúa Pizarro
Rúa García Barbón
Igrexa de Santiago
Rúa De Urzáiz
Rúa México
Avenida De Gran Via
Praza de España & horses sculpture
MARCO Museum
Rúa Colón
Rúa do Príncipe
Rúa Progreso
Rúa Ecuador
Rúa Del Venezuela
Rúa Couto
Praza de Compostela
Rúa De Beiramar
Rúa Luis Taboada
Old Town
Avenida De Beiramar
Praza Porta do Sol & El Sireno merman monument
Rúa García Olloqui
Vigo
Concatedral de Santa María
Praza da Constitución
Concello de Vigo
Rúa Marqués Alcedo
Parque do Castro
Centro Comercial shopping
Galicia
Avenida Das Camelias
Rúa Hispanidade
Rúa

VIGO, 107M, POP. 292,817

The most populated city in Galicia and with an ancient history of Celtic and Roman settlements, modern-day Vigo is known for its fishing, canning and ship-building industries. Industrial tourism aside, wander around Vigo and you'll come across numerous modern monuments. The winding lanes of its old town are worth exploration, as are its state-of-the-art museums – and, of course, the nearby Cíes Islands.

Tourist office: López de Neira 8, tel 986 224 757, www.turismodevigo.org, open daily.

Visit: old town (Praza da Constitución, Praza da Almeida, 19th-century neoclassical Concatedral (cathedral church) de Santa María, Praza da Pedra). Parque do Castro with the remnants of an ancient settlement, 17th-century fortress and sunset viewpoint. O Berbes fishermen's quarter with old arched buildings. The merman sculpture 'El Sireno', opposite Porta do Sol. MARCO Museum of Contemporary Art, Rúa do Príncipe 54, www.marcovigo.com, closed Mondays, free entrance.

Specialities: *ostras* (oysters) shucked by the 'Ostreiras' on Rúa da Pescadaria near Mercado da Pedra.

Where to eat: Taberna A Pedra and Bar Chavolas (both in Praza da Constitución).

Accommodation: Hotel Oca Ipanema (Rúa Vázquez Varela 31–33, tel 986 471 344, 60 rooms, €40+, +650m from the stage end). **Near the harbour in the old town** (+1.8km from the stage end): *Hotel Náutico (Rúa Luis Taboada 28, tel 986 122 440, www.hotelnautico.net, 23 rooms, €25+, terrific budget accommodation). **Hotel Compostela (Rúa García Olloqui 5, tel 986 228 227, www.hcompostela.com, 30 rooms, €45+, traditional hotel in a great location).

STAGE 8
Vigo to Redondela

Start	Rúa Urzáiz, Vigo
Finish	Albergue de Peregrinos, Redondela
Distance	14.5km
Total ascent	124m
Total descent	235m
Difficulty	Easy
Time	4hr
Cafés	Vigo, Redondela (14.5km)
Accommodation	Vigo, Redondela (14.5km)

This is a short, easy stage (allowing a morning in Vigo) that mostly follows the Senda da Auga route along small roads and through scenic woodland before descending steeply into Redondela.

Continue east along the pedestrianised Rúa Urzáiz for 520m, passing cafés, pharmacies and a Froiz supermarket, before turning left at A Lonxa seafood market onto Rúa de Toledo. Go straight across the busy Rúa de Jenaro de la Fuente, passing the modern-looking church of **Igrexa de Inmaculada Concepción**. Take the first right then turn left at the small

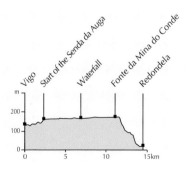

Following part of the Senda da Auga trail between Vigo and Redondela

crossroads onto Rúa Cantabria and go straight across the busy Av do Aeroporto. KSO, passing a playground, then after 500m when the road forks, take the right upper fork onto Rúa de Pouleira. Follow this uphill, merging left onto Camiño da Fonte das Mozas, then take the left fork onto Camiño do Poulo and go downhill along the green-and-yellow **Senda da Auga**. **2.3km**

The Camino now follows the Senda da Auga painted waves (representing the channel that carried water from Eiras dam to Vigo), in addition to yellow Camino arrows, for 9.4km along small dirt and paved roads with terrific sea views and through lush woods.

Follow Camiño do Poulo into Camiño da Traida das Augas. After 1.4km merge right briefly onto Estrada da Madroa before turning left to continue following the waves along Camiño da Traida das Augas. KSO onto Camiño Valeiro then Camiño da Traida, which alternates between a dirt and paved road. After 2km in a section of woods, pass a **waterfall** and picnic table (RHS) (**4.6km**) then KSO through woods interspersed with houses along this delightful flat route. After a further 4.3km on a dirt road in the woods, pass **Fonte da Mina do Conde** (RHS), then soon afterwards meet a paved road and leave the Senda da Auga by turning left onto Camiño Condesa de Torrecedeira, descending steeply. **9.4km/11.7km**

View of Vigo Estuary from the Senda da Auga trail

Reach a crossroads at a stone cross and turn left onto Aldea Cruceiro, passing a **school** (RHS), then keep right at the fork. At the next small crossroads, veer left then take the next right at a stone cross (RHS), quickly turning left between houses onto Camiño das Cardosas. KSO for 600m as this becomes a steep downhill, going under the railway tracks then turning right onto the N550. Carefully cross to the LHS, turning left at the roundabout into Redondela. Pass Convento de Vilavella (RHS, 16th century) and keep left onto Rúa Pai Crespo, passing Albergue Santiago de Vilavella (RHS, no.55). Go under the green viaduct and take the right fork then pass Alvear Suites (LHS, no.30) and restaurants before reaching a roundabout in central **Redondela**. This stage ends at the Albergue de Peregrinos, which is diagonally right across the junction in the old stone 'tower' building. ◀ **2.8km/14.5km**

See Central Camino Stage 22 for more information about Redondela.

To continue, follow Stages 22–25 of the Central Camino.

LINK ROUTES

Mosteiro de São Simão da Junqueira (Link Route 1)

LINK ROUTE 1

Vila do Conde to São Pedro de Rates

Start	Praça da República, Vila do Conde
Finish	São Pedro de Rates
Distance	13.7km
Total ascent	168m
Total descent	131m
Difficulty	Easy
Time	4hr
Cafés	Vila do Conde, Touguinha (4.6km), Junqueira (6.6km), Arcos (9.8km), São Pedro de Rates (13.7km)
Accommodation	Vila do Conde, Arcos (9.8km), São Pedro de Rates (13.7km)

A short stage that cuts inland from the Coastal Camino through Touguinha and Junqueira, joining the Central Camino in Arcos, 4km before São Pedro de Rates. The waymarks are faded but the directions are straightforward along small but often busy roads.

Leaving Praça da República, go under the N13 onto Av Figueiredo Faria with the River Ave on the RHS. Soon after passing the **monastery** (LHS) take the left fork uphill, going straight across the roundabout and metro tracks onto Av Bernardino Machado. Follow this for 1.5km towards then past a large concrete building, turning right at a T-junction

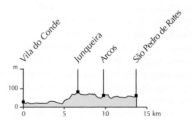

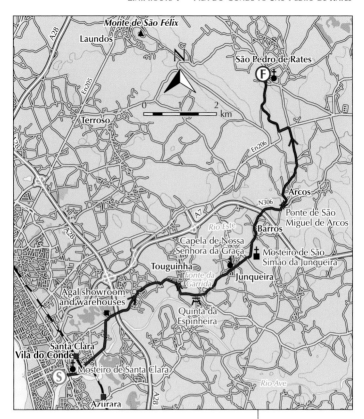

onto Rua da Lapa. Pass the **Agal showroom and warehouses** (LHS) then go under the A28 and KSO, passing cafés. After 900m KSO across a roundabout onto Rua Nossa Senhora do O, through **Touguinha**. After a further 1.1km pass Café Novo and turn right at the crossroads, going over the River Este. **4.8km**

Now on Rua do Rio Este, go uphill, passing picnic tables at the entrance to **Quinta da Espinheira** (RHS), then keep left into Rua Central. Pass **Fonte da Garrida** (LHS) and take the left fork then KSO. After 800m enter **Junqueira** (**1.8km**), passing Café Antunes, **Capela de Nossa Senhora da Graça**

Romanesque bridge over the River Este, Touguinhó

(LHS, 18th century) and Restaurant Casa D'Aldeia (RHS, stamp). On the way out of town pass a pharmacy then continue straight across the busy crossroads with a stone cross in the middle (17th century) onto the N306, and pass **Mosteiro de São Simão da Junqueira**. ◄ Carefully continue along the N306, and after 1.3km cross a bridge over the A7. After a further 700m turn left and cross **Ponte de São Miguel de Arcos** over the River Este, and go up into **Arcos** now on the Central Camino. **5km/9.8km**

Founded in the 11th century, the current church is a 17th-century Baroque reconstruction.

See Central Camino Stage 17 for information on Arcos and continuing on the Central Camino.

LINK ROUTE 2

São Pedro de Rates to Esposende

Start	Igreja de São Pedro de Rates, São Pedro de Rates
Finish	Igreja da Misericórdia, Esposende
Distance	17.2km
Total ascent	98m
Total descent	147m
Difficulty	Easy
Time	4–5hr
Note	There are no cafés/accommodation until Fão (14.4km), which is 2.8km before Esposende

This stage allows you to transfer from the Central to the Coastal Camino after visiting São Pedro de Rates' impressive Romanesque church. The route follows small roads and forest tracks (often muddy) as it moves towards the coast. Keep an eye out for the waymarks.

Retrace your steps from the church back to the old railway tracks at the entrance to São Pedro de Rates and turn right (there's a Coastal Camino tile here). Soon after, pass the old train station building (RHS) and KSO, following the disused tracks and passing fields and farms. After 3.1km reach a paved road and turn right, then after 100m turn left at the **pink house**. This becomes a farm then forest track; continue for 900m before reaching a paved road and the green wire fence of **Aerodromo Povóa de Varzim**. **4.2km**

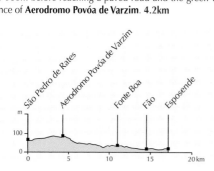

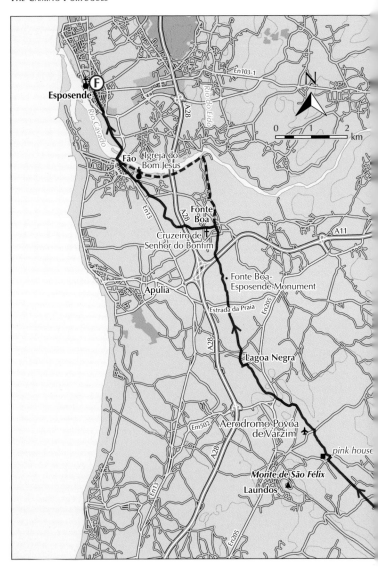

KSO beside the aerodrome fence along a dirt road, then after 800m KSO into Rua dos Crescencios. Shortly afterwards take the left fork, then after 500m reach the N205 and KSO across onto Rua California. Follow this for 1.3km then turn left at a T-junction (there's a bar +450m to the right, opposite the N205) and take the first right onto Rua Senhora da Abadia into **Lagoa Negra (3km)**. Reach a small junction and veer right then left onto Rua da Casa Velha, then take the dirt road to the left of the house, into the forest. After 1.4km KSO across the paved Estrada da Praia, then after 320m veer left then right, passing a factory (LHS). After 300m take the left fork at the stone '**Fonte Boa Esposende**' monument (RHS). **5.6km/9.8km**

Starting from the old railway tracks in São Pedro de Rates

Continue along the forest track for 500m before crossing a bridge over the A11. After a further 600m join the cob-

bled Rua dos Merouços and continue straight onto Rua da Escola into **Fonte Boa**. Take the second left onto Rua de Cima de Vila then pass **Cruzeiro de Senhor do Bonfim** (LHS, stone cross with canopy) and as the road bends right, KSO onto a dirt lane. After 560m cross a bridge over the A28 and join another forest track. Reach a factory (behind a wire fence) and turn right, heading back into the forest. Shortly after, take the left fork then after 500m turn left onto a paved road, passing

São Pedro de Rates

an industrial building (LHS). Take the first right onto Rua da Camareira, turn left at a T-junction, then take the first right onto Rua Campos Morais. Shortly afterwards pass **Igreja do Bom Jesus** in **Fão**, now on the Coastal Camino. **4.6km/14.4km**

An alternative, well-marked route to Fão from Fonte Boa is to KSO rather than take the second left onto Rua de Cima de Vila and follow the arrows north to Rio Cávado and take the pleasant riverside path to Fão fire station. The route is 1km longer.

> See Coastal Camino Stage 2 for information on Fão and continuing along the Coastal Camino.

LINK ROUTE 3
Caminha to Tui

Start	Torre do Relógio, Caminha
Finish	Tui Cathedral
Distance	32.1km
Total ascent	507m
Total descent	464m
Difficulty	Medium
Time	8–9hr
Cafés	Caminha, Seixas (3.5km), Lanhelas (6.7km), Vila Nova de Cerveira (14.8km), Carvalha (20.9km +140m), Alem da Ponte (23km), São Pedro da Torre (24.1km), Cristelo Covo (27.2km), Valença (29km), Tui (32.1km)
Accommodation	Caminha, Seixas (3.5km), Gondarém (10.8km), Vila Nova de Cerveira (14.8km), Valença (29km), Tui (32.1km)

This stage allows you to transfer from the Coastal to the Central Camino, saying goodbye to Portugal in Valença before crossing the International Bridge to Tui in Spain. The first half of the route passes numerous chapels along undulating, winding cobbled roads, relieved by arriving in the small but historic Vila Nova de Cerveira with an excellent youth hostel. The second half is flatter and relatively straightforward along small roads.

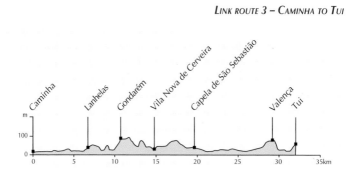

Go through the middle of the clock tower onto Rua Direita and pass behind the Igreja Matriz, then turn right at the end and go through the underpass. Pass the ferry terminal and shortly afterwards cross the bridge over the **River Coura**. Pass a chapel on the other side, then as the road bends left KSO onto a grassy path. Carefully cross the railway tracks onto Estrada das Faias, veering left and going straight on for 900m to the N13 (**2.6km**). Turn right and after passing a stone cross (RHS) take the next right at the car dealership onto

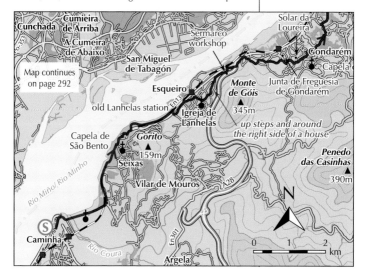

291

Rua Alfredo Cruz. Continue to a square with **Capela de São Bento** (19th century) and cafés opposite in **Seixas**. **3.5km**

KSO onto Rua Arquitecto Miguel Ventura Terra, soon passing behind the beautiful Brazilian-style Palacete Villa Idalina (Largo de São Bento s/n, tel +34 639 154 901, www.villai-dalina.com, 9 rooms), then keep left and downhill. Continue along winding lanes for 550m then go under the N13, over the railway tracks and straight on to the red ecovia nature trail footpath, passing Capela de São Sebastião. After passing the **old Lanhelas train station** (**2.1km**), carefully cross the tracks then the N13 onto Caminha da Rabada, which becomes a dirt road. KSO and turn right at the end onto Caminho de Entre-Muros, veer left onto Rua José António Cancela then turn right at the chapel (and Café S. Sebastião) onto Rua João de Sá, passing two more cafés and the **church of Lanhelas**. **3.2km/6.7km**

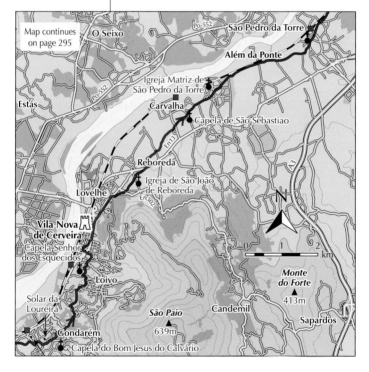

Map continues on page 295

O Seixo

São Pedro da Torre

Além da Ponte

Igreja Matriz de São Pedro da Torre

Estás

Carvalha

Capela de São Sebastiao

Reboreda

Igreja de São João de Reboreda

Lovelhe

Vila Nova de Cerveira

Capela Senhor dos Esquecidos

Loivo

Monte do Forte 413m

Solar da Loureira

Candemil

Sapardos

Gondarém

São Paio 639m

Capela do Bom Jesus do Calvário

1 2 km

Solar da Loureira, Gondarém

Continue along Rua Ilidio Couto, then after 600m of winding streets the arrows direct you up a staircase almost into someone's house. Skirt around the right side and through the backyard until you reach a paved road. Turn right. You then have a choice for the walk to Capela de São Sebastião. A new and well-marked forest track, which initially ascends steeply to take you over the A28 (600m further), or the traditional route on the road. For the traditional route turn left on the road and keep right at the fork. Pass the **Sermarco workshop** before turning right at the end onto Rua do Marco, then go under the A28 and uphill. Follow the arrows for 1.2km then pass Capela de São Sebastião and after a further 560m reach a T-junction and the **Junta de Freguesia de Gondarém**. **3.5km/10.2km**

Turn right onto Estrada de S. Pedro, going uphill past the impressive Baroque house, **Solar da Loureira** (emblazoned with family crests, statues, scallop shell motifs and a fountain) then pass a staircase (to **Capela do Bom Jesus do Calvário**) opposite a driveway leading to ****Hotel Boega (Quinta do Outeiral, tel 251 700 500, www.boegahotel.com, 41 rooms in a 17th-century manor house, €70+). Take the left fork onto the cobbled Caminho de Santiago Outeiral, turn right at the end then left and downhill on Rua do Fulão. Continue along

Art installation and Igreja de São Cipriano, Vila Nova de Cerveira

winding lanes for 2.5km before passing **Capela Senhor dos Esquecidos** (LHS, 18th century with covered porch) (**3.6km**). Turn right after the sports field (RHS), left through the square (with benches), then right at the T-junction onto Rua Das Cortes. Follow the road left and downhill under the N13. Pass the town hall (or turn left here for the Pousada de Juventude hostel +260m RHS) and turn right into the historical centre of **Vila Nova de Cerveira**, arriving at the 16th-century Igreja de São Cipriano. **4.6km/14.8km**

VILA NOVA DE CERVEIRA, 24M, POP. 8852

A delightful riverside town, King Dinis granted its charter in 1321 and a castle was built to defend the frontier village, later reinforced during the 17th century. There are wonderful views from the castle walls and it's possible to see King Dinis' shield above one of the arches.

Accommodation: Pousada de Juventude (E.N.13 Rua Alto das Veigas, tel 251 709 933, **www.pousadasjuventude.pt**, 60 beds, kitchen, €15+). **Hotel Minho Belo (Avenida da Liberdade 414, tel 913 895 317, **www.minhobelo.com**, 18 rooms, €40+, +1km along the Camino).

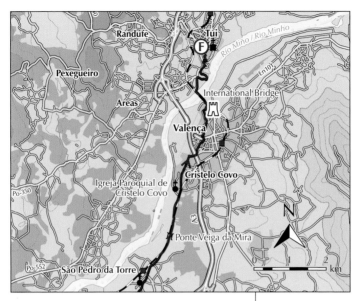

Pass the church and turn right through the square. ▸ Continue into Rua Queiroz Ribeiro and follow this to the N13. Turn left (but cross to the RHS) and after 450m veer right onto Av da Liberdade, passing Hotel Minho Belo (LHS). Take the next right onto the cobbled Rua da Estrada Real then after 400m, at Largo do Meio da Breia, take the right fork onto Rua Nova. Shortly after, keep right then KSO for 900m before passing the gated **Igreja de São João de Reboreda** (Romanesque and Baroque) (**2.7km**). Go downhill to the N13 and turn right then take the first left. Turn right onto Rua de Zurágues then KSO (slightly left) into the cobbled Rua de Carcavelos, which becomes a peaceful forest road. After 800m turn left at the end, then after 430m pass **Capela de São Sebastião** (RHS). **4.9km/19.7km**

KSO into Rua 25 de Abril, then after 1km reach a small crossroads with an old stone fonte and KSO (or turn left for Bar Zina Copus +140m, opposite Largo do Outeirinho) into Rua da Lagoa. Turn left at the end, then right, and go through a small industrial area then KSO. After 1.8km pass Restaurante Sabores D'Aldeia (LHS) in **Além da Ponte**

Notice the 17th-century *fonte* down the steps beside the striking 19th-century green-tiled Brazilian-style palace.

(**3.3km**). After 820m cross a bridge and turn left towards the spire of the **Igreja Matriz of São Pedro da Torre**. Pass the church then Café Mavic and KSO onto Rua do Poço, passing a pharmacy. Continue into Rua Das Cruxes, passing more cafés, then keep right at the stone cross, soon parallel with the railway tracks. After 550m pass picnic tables just before crossing **Ponte Veiga da Mira**. **6km/25.7km**

Join the red ecopista path for 550m then turn left and go under the railway tracks, turning right onto a farm track. KSO for 800m into **Cristelo Covo**, passing the Igreja Paroquial, then after 400m pass a café and mini-market. After a further 400m turn right at the yellow house onto Rua Val Flores, then go under the A3 and left at the roundabout, heading uphill and passing an Intermarche supermarket. Go straight over at the roundabout, pass the Bombeiros Voluntários, and next-door on the corner is the Albergue de Peregrinos in **Valença**. **3km/28.7km**

To continue on to the International Bridge and Tui, KSO across the roundabout up the grassy bank into and through the fort.

> See Central Stage 20 for information on Valença, a map of the town and directions for continuing along the Central Camino.

SPIRITUAL VARIANT

Monasterio de Santa María de Armenteira (Spiritual Variant Stage 1)

STAGE 1
Pontevedra to Armenteira

Start	Praza da Peregrina, Pontevedra
Finish	Monasterio de Santa María, Armenteira
Distance	20.4km
Total ascent	648m
Total descent	397m
Difficulty	Medium
Time	7hr
Cafés	Pontevedra, Campañó (5.6km), Poio (8.8km), Combarro (11.3km), Armenteira (20.4km)
Accommodation	Pontevedra, Campañó (5.6km), Poio (8.5km), Combarro (11.3km), Armenteira (20.4km)
Note	Make sure to fill up on water in Combarro

The Spiritual Variant is an exceptionally scenic route, culminating in an optional boat ride along the route which the boat carrying St James' body and his disciples is believed to have sailed. After splitting off from the Central Camino outside of Pontevedra, this route skirts around the side of Montecelo before arriving at the impressive Poio Monastery. Consider having lunch in the historic seaside village of Combarro before a long climb over Monte Castrove (up to 437m) along small paved and dirt roads, then descending to Armenteira Monastery.

The first 3.1km of this stage follows the Central Camino. Leaving Praza da Peregrina, head north into Paseo de António Odriozola, turning left in Praza de Ferreria. Pass cafés under the arches then turn right at the iron fountain into Praza de Curros Enriquez. Take the left fork onto Rúa Real, then before reaching the end of the road turn left into Rúa do Ponte and take the first right. Cross the River Lérez over the scallop shell-adorned **Ponte do Burgo** (600m) then continue straight across the roundabout. Take the first left onto Rúa da Santina, passing Bar Breoyan. Keep left at the small roundabout and continue

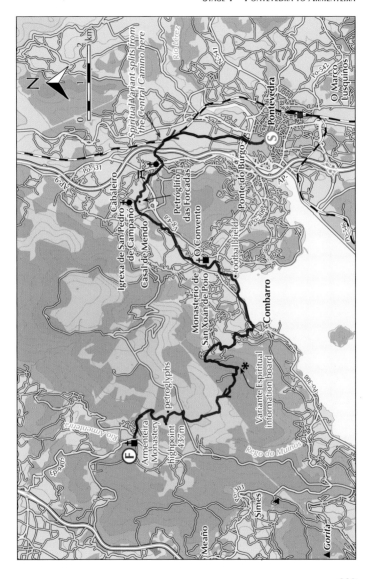

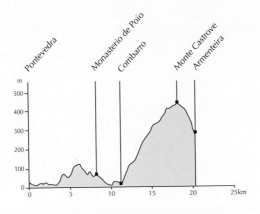

Here the Spiritual
Variant splits off
from the Central
Camino with good
waymarks. .

straight then onto a dirt road, passing wetlands, until you
reach a T-junction. **3.1km**

◄ Turn left and cross old railway tracks then go across a
bridge over the motorway (AP9/E1) and turn left, uphill. After
400m pass a **chapel**, then cross a bridge over the PO-531
and KSO over the next road, going uphill. Follow the arrows
for 600m then pass a fountain and **picnic table** (RHS) shortly
before going through a tunnel under the VG-4.8. Turn left
onto a farm track, passing fields and grapevines for 460m,
then turn right onto a narrow dirt path, going uphill. After
260m reach a road and the 18th-century **Igrexa de San Pedro**
in Campañó. **2.4km/5.5km**

'Petróglifo das
Forcadas' is thought
to be approximately
4000 years old. It
was found 1.7km
away and moved
here in 2015.

Turn left, passing the grassy area with a **petroglyph**. ◄ Pass
Hotel Rural Campaniola with café/restaurant (Cabaleiro 35,
tel 886 166 910, www.hotelruralcampaniola.com, 13 rooms,
€50+) before a square with two more restaurants. KSO for
420m then enter a eucalyptus forest. After a further 420m turn
left at the T-junction, going downhill to the highway (VG-4.8),
and turn right onto a parallel road. KSO for 530m then turn left
and cross a bridge over the highway, then turn right and continue parallel to the highway along a dirt road. After 700m turn
left at a roundabout and shortly afterwards reach **Monasterio
de San Xoán** in Poio. **3km/8.5km**

Monasterio de San Xoán, a former Benedictine monastery, was founded in the 10th century and reconstructed in the 16th century. The Renaissance/ Baroque church was added during the 17–18th centuries. Highlights include the 16th-century processional cloister and the 80-metre long Camino Frances mosaic (made with one million pieces) by the Czech artist Anton Machourek. There's also a 33-metre long *hórreo* (granary) in the grounds, thought to be one of the longest in Galicia. Open daily from 10am (closed Sunday mornings), €1.50. Accommodation: Hospedería Monasterio de Poio (tel 986 770 000, www.monasteriodepoio.es, €43+, 200 rooms, meals available, attached to the monastery).

Monasterio de San Xoán de Poio

Go downhill on Rúa Gonzalo Fernandez, passing Bar Castro, then reach the main road (and Pasteleria Pandemillo) and turn right onto Av San Xoán (PO-308). Just before the roundabout turn left onto Travesia Seara, then take a narrow path uphill on the LHS. After 250m pass behind a **football field** and go across a wooden bridge, then follow a path beside the estuary (LHS) for 600m until you reach the

Combarro Avenida (PO-308) again. There are two waymarked options here (same length):

Either turn left, passing Hotel Combarro, and carefully continue along the Avenida for 750m before turning left onto O Padron into **Combarro**. Or cross the Avenida into Rúa Casalvito and go uphill for 310m before turning left onto Travesia Casalvito, then go downhill for 430m and cross the Avenida onto O Padron into **Combarro**. **2.8km/11.3km**

COMBARRO, 8M, POP. 1786

A quaint historic village with traditional fishermen's houses, eight stone crosses and delicious seafood but most renowned for its *hórreos*. There are no services from here to Armenteira so fill up on water for the climb ahead.

Where to eat: Taberna Leucoiña with a terrace overlooking the sea.

Accommodation: Hotel Xeito (Av de la Cruz 35, tel 986 770 039, **www.hotelxeito.com**, €50+, a few minutes from Combarro's old town). Hotel Combarro (Pontevedra Sanxenxo km5, tel 986 772 131, **www.hotelcombarro.es**, 30 rooms, 900m before Combarro).

Follow the arrows back up to the Avenida and KSO across into Camiño Pedaporta (or turn right for Hotel Xeito). Soon afterwards, turn right at the stone cross onto Camiño do Redondo then bend left, turning right at the end. Keep right and continue uphill, merging right into Camiño Longariña, then take the next left, passing a stone cross and community noticeboard (LHS) on Camiño do Regueiro. Follow the arrows uphill along winding roads for 2.7km before reaching a viewpoint and **Variante Espiritual information board** ('5km to Armenteira'). **3.5km/14.8km**

Take the next left onto a dirt road and follow the arrows as you continue uphill along a forest road for 2.5km before reaching a paved road (CF-102). Turn right, then after 200m turn left back onto a forest road with a sign for 'Petróglifos de Outeiro do Cribo'. After 400m pass the **petroglyphs** (up on the RHS, featuring labyrinths and deer) and reach the **high-point of 437m altitude**. Start to descend and after 1.1km, when the road forks, take the lower left fork downhill. After 340m turn sharp left, doubling back, then turn right and go downhill on a narrow path, crossing a small bridge over a stream. After 400m reach a road and KSO downhill on a narrow dirt path to the end of the stage at **Monasterio de Santa María**. **5.6km/20.4km**

ARMENTEIRA, 278M

The Cistercian monastery was founded by a knight called Ero in the 12th century. According to a popular legend, Ero went for a walk in the woods one day and came upon a bird singing so beautifully that he fell into a trance which lasted for 300 years. The monastery was abandoned in 1837; restoration began in 1963, and in 1989 Cistercian nuns moved in. Vespers are held daily at 7pm before the 7.30pm mass. There's a tourist office inside the monastery (tel 986 804 100, closed Mondays) and a bar and café on the street outside.

Accommodation: Albergue de Peregrinos +650m (Vilar–Armenteira, tel 619 534 087, 32 beds, €10. Access: continue along the Camino down the road between the monastery and Bar O Comercio then turn right onto the gravel path. After 430m reach a T-junction and turn right, then take the first left; the albergue is on the LH corner). Monasterio Cisterciense de Armenteira (Lugar de la Iglesia, tel 627 097 696, www.monasteriodearmenteira.es, 25 beds, €50+).

STAGE 2
Armenteira to Vilanova de Arousa

Start	Monasterio de Santa María, Armenteira
Finish	Pedestrian bridge, Av Galicia, Vilanova de Arousa
Distance	23.5km
Total ascent	190m
Total descent	455m
Difficulty	Easy
Time	7hr
Cafés	Armenteira, Barrantes (6.5km), Pontearnelas (12.6km), San Roque do Monte (19.4km), Vilanova de Arousa (23.5km)
Accommodation	Armenteira, Barrantes (6.5km), Vilanova de Arousa (23.5km)
Note	If planning to take the boat in Stage 3 from Vilanova de Arousa to Pontecesures, call the albergue (tel 633 906 490) in Vilanova de Arousa the day before to confirm the schedule and reserve your spot

This is a stunning stage that follows the Ruta de la Piedra y del Agua ('stone and water route'), passing 51 ancient mills and cascading falls. It then accompanies the River Umia, passing *albariño* grapevines and fields (with a chance for some wine-tasting) before reaching the Ría de Arousa and Vilanova de Arousa.

Continue down the road between the monastery and Bar O Comercio, turning right onto the gravel path. Turn left at the end then immediately right onto the dirt path downhill, joining the lush **Ruta de la Piedra y del Agua (500m)**. Keep the Armenteira river initially on the LHS and follow the white-and-yellow stripe waymarks of the PR-G 170 trail. ◄ After 1.3km cross a small road and continue now with the river on the RHS. After a further 2km pass a sign for 'Aldea Labrega' (slightly off to the left, a sculpture park recreating a Galician village), just before reaching picnic tables and Taberna da Aldea (seasonal). **4km**

Take care, as this first 1.3km along roots and rocks can be slippery.

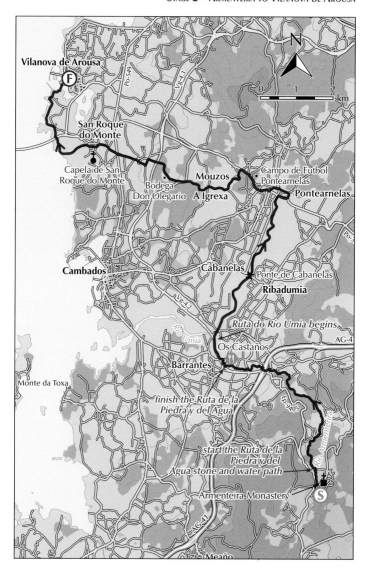

Cascading falls along the Ruta de la Piedra y del Agua

Soon after, pass a WC, then after 700m reach a paved road and roundabout. KSO across then go under the highway (AG-41) and turn right, then left to return to the river, passing grapevines. After 1.3km reach the end of the path and turn right then pass the rustic Os Castaños restaurant and accommodation (Os Castaños 25, tel 986 710 236, www.oscastanos.es, 11 rooms, €35+) in **Barrantes**. **2.5km/6.5km**

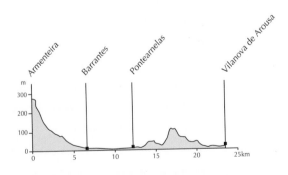

Cross the road towards the brown hut (a seasonal tourist office) and after passing it, turn right to continue beside the river. After 1km cross a road and go through a tunnel, now following the wider **River Umia**. After 2km of passing fields and vineyards, turn left and cross **Ponte de Cabanelas** (**3.1km**) over the river and turn right, continuing by the river. After a further 2.6km turn right and go up and over a wooden ramp (under the bridge) and across the river, then KSO to a roundabout. Turn left (or turn right for Panaderia Puente Arnelas +140m LHS) and cross the medieval bridge then turn left into the small town of **Pontearnelas**. **6.1km/12.6km**

Pass a bar and café (RHS; if they're closed, turn right at the next roundabout for Café Arnelas +120m) then KSO across the roundabout. Turn right at the next roundabout then KSO uphill, passing the **Pontearnelas Campo de Futbol** (RHS), and after a further 500m turn left into Aldea Rio Pequeno. After 200m turn left onto a small dirt path, then follow the arrows for 2.6km along winding roads through the villages of **Mouzos** and **A Igrexa**, through a section of eucalyptus forest, then passing grapevines and **Bodega Don Olegario** (LHS). ▶ **4.7km/17.3km**

The vineyard has friendly owners and special pilgrim wine-tasting prices; tel 678 561 175, www.donolegario.com.

About 550m further on, cross an overpass then turn left at the end. Shortly afterwards turn right at a stone cross. KSO, then after 850m continue straight across the main road (PO-549, cafés left) and after a further 600m take the left fork. Turn right through the square, passing **Capela de San Roque do Monte**, then KSO onto a gravel path, then a narrow road and go straight on for 850m to the Ría de Arousa estuary (**3.7km**). Turn right and follow the path beside the sea for 2.2km, passing idyllic beaches, camp-grounds and Hotel Arco Iris before crossing the pedestrian bridge to Av Galicia in **Vilanova de Arousa**. **6.2km/23.5km**

VILANOVA DE AROUSA, 11M, POP. 10,406

A popular seaside town with alluring white-sand beaches and delicious seafood, this is the birthplace of the famous Spanish writer Ramón María del Valle-Inclán (1866–1936).

Where to eat: Café Reiz is a good-value popular seafood restaurant opposite the harbour.

Accommodation: Albergue de Peregrinos +620m (Pabellón de Deportes, tel 633 906 490, 25 beds, kitchen, €10. Access: after crossing the bridge turn right and follow the esplanade for 550m. After passing the playground reach the modern-looking sports centre where the albergue is located). **Hotel Bradomin (Avenida Juan Carlos I 29, tel 986 561 038, www.hotelbradomin.com, 50 rooms, €50+, 650m from the bridge). *Hotel Arco Iris (Playa del Terron 12, tel 986 555 444 & 669 847 643, www.arcoirisweb.net, hotel, bungalows and camping, 1.5km before the bridge).

STAGE 3

Vilanova de Arousa to Padrón

Start	Pedestrian bridge, Av Galicia, Vilanova de Arousa
Finish	Igrexa de Santiago, Padrón
Distance	27km by boat to Pontecesures then 2.2km walk to Padrón or 34km if walking the whole way
Total ascent	319m (walking option)
Total descent	314m (walking option)
Difficulty	Medium (walking option)
Time	Boat/walking: 1–2hr; all walking: 8–9hr
Cafés	Vilanova de Arousa, Vilagarcía de Arousa (8.4km), Carril (10.7km), O Casal (14.6km), Pontecesures (32km), Padrón (34km)
Accommodation	Vilanova de Arousa (0 to 4.4km), Carril (10.1km), Pontecesures (32km), Padrón (34km)
Note	Limited services if walking. Boat tickets (€25+) should be purchased a day in advance from the albergue; sailing times vary depending on the tide, and the boat departs from the harbour

There are two options for this stage: one is to take the boat along the maritime *Translatio* route, believed to be what the boat carrying St James' body and his disciples sailed along in AD44. Along the way, pass mussel farms, 17 stone crosses and the ruins of Torres de Oeste, before disembarking in Pontecesures and following the Central Camino for the remaining 2.2km to Padrón.

The alternative is to walk, as described below, mainly along roads and a few dirt paths for the first 19km before joining scenic riverside boardwalks by the River Ulla for 3.5km then moving inland through hamlets to reach the River Ulla again in Pontecesures.

For those travelling by boat, after disembarking, follow the footpath with the river on your LHS to Pontecesures bridge and follow the directions from there for the last 2km to Padrón.

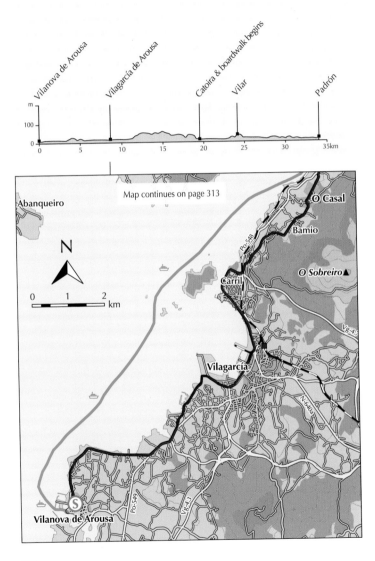

Vilanova de Arousa

Vilagarcía de Arousa

Catoira & boardwalk begins

Vilar

Padrón

Map continues on page 313

Abanqueiro

O Casal

Bamio

O Sobreiro ▲

Carril

Vilagarcía

N

Vilanova de Arousa

To walk the stage, after crossing the pedestrian bridge into Vilanova de Arousa, turn left, passing the harbour (LHS). KSO along Av de Galicia for 700m before turning left onto the main road (EP-9702). KSO, soon beside the water again, then after 1.6km pass *Hotel Playa Las Sinas (Av Las Sinas 31, tel 986 555 173, www.hotellassinas.com). (**2.3km**). After 1.6km turn left at the roundabout onto the shoulder of the PO-549, then after 500m pass ****Hotel Pazo o Rial (Avenida de Vilanova 117, tel 986 507 011, www.pazorial.es, 60 rooms in a 17th-century palace). **4.4km**

Leaving Vilanova de Arousa on the boat to Pontecesures

KSO across the roundabout and after 380m turn left at a Mapfre shop onto Rúa Veiga do Mar, then take the first right onto Travesía Veiga do Mar. Reach the water and turn right, passing the sandy Praia do Preguntoiro, then continue along the bay. After 1.3km enter an industrial wharf area with a cycle lane and street art, then after a further 2km pass the lively marina with fast food restaurants and Parque Miguel Hernández opposite in **Vilagarcía de Arousa**. **4km/8.4km**

Turn left at the next roundabout onto Rosalía de Castro (PO-548) (or KSO +250m for Vilagarcía de Arousa station) and after 300m pass a Mercadona Supermarket (RHS). After a further kilometre pass **Hotel Playa Compostela (Av Rosalía de Castro 138, tel 986 504 010, www.playacompostela.com) then turn right at the next roundabout (with cafés), returning to the water in **Carril** (**2.3km**). Carefully follow the road for 1km, turning left at the large roundabout, then take the first right uphill onto Rúa Salgueiral (PO-192). After 2.8km pass Parrillada la Ponderosa (restaurant) opposite a tavern in **O Casal**, then after a further 1.2km reach the PO-548. **7.4km/15.8km**

Turn right then take the first left, following a maroon 'Camino Real' sign onto a grassy path; the route now alternates between the Camino Real trails and the PO-548 for 2.6km before going under the green viaduct. After the viaduct turn right onto the PO-548 one last time then take the first left onto an initial grassy track which becomes a paved road. Follow the road beside a factory fence (LHS) downhill to the River Catoira, turning left and going under the railway bridge onto a **boardwalk**. Turn right onto a dirt road then continue along dirt roads and boardwalks, soon beside the **River Ulla**. After 900m pass the ruins of **Torres de Oeste**. **4.8km/20.6km**

Passing the Torres de Oeste ruins by boat along the River Ulla

Torres de Oeste is thought to have been built on a pre-Roman site; the remaining two towers and Capela de Santiago date from the 12th century and were part of a large castle with seven towers,

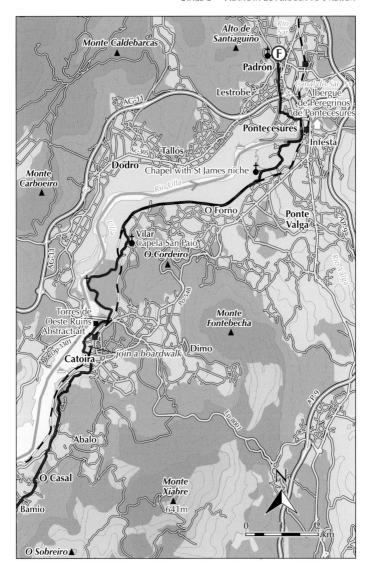

built to defend the mouth of the River Ulla and
Compostela against Norman and Saracen attacks.

Go through the car park and under the road, then continue left along a cobbled path. After 1.6km pass a stone
cross (LHS) and shortly afterwards start uphill, turning left
onto a forest road with painted arrows on a pine tree. After
800m reach a dirt T-junction and turn left, soon passing
grapevines, then go through a small tunnel under the railway
tracks. After a further 400m reach a T-junction with a yellow
house and turn left through **Vilar**. **3.7km/24.3km**

Turn left at the end onto Rúa San Paio, passing **Capela
San Paio** and a stone cross (RHS), then take the next left and
keep right. After 250m meet the railway tracks and turn right
onto a parallel road. KSO, then after 1km follow the road up
and around to the right, crossing a road then continuing back
down to the railway tracks. After a further 1.8km cross to the
LHS of the tracks (**3.5km**), then after 1.3km go under a road.
Shortly afterwards turn right at the roundabout and continue
by the tracks. After 550m follow the road as it bends left,
passing a **chapel** (LHS, with St James in the niche). Turn left
at the yellow house then turn right at house no.93, then keep
left. After 400m reach a warehouse and turn right, then follow the road left, past a sports field (LHS) to the **River Ulla**.
Turn right and follow the river for 900m before turning left to
cross **Pontecesures** bridge. **7.7km/32km**

Here you rejoin Central Camino Stage 24, which continues on a road behind the white electricity tower; follow this
for 500m to the River Sar and turn right. Go under the AG11,
then pass Albergue Camino do Sar (tel 618 734 373, www.
caminodosar.com, 20 beds, kitchen, €15+) and KSO through
the market car park and into the avenue of trees along Paseo
do Espolón. At either end of this Avenue you'll pass statues of
Padrón's two most famous residents – Nobel Laureate Camilo
Jose Cela (1916–2002) and poet Rosalía de Castro (1837–
1885); it's behind Rosalía where the stage ends, at the Igrexa
de Santiago in central **Padrón**.

> See Central Stage 25 for information on Padrón and
> continuing along the Central Camino to Santiago.

APPENDIX A

Facilities tables

Central Camino from Lisbon

Place	Distance between each place	Distance from Lisbon	Albergue/ Hostel	Other accommo- dation	Café/Bar	Restaurant	Mini/ Supermarket	ATM	Pharmacy	Tourist office	Distance to Santiago
Lisbon	**0**	**0**	✓	✓	✓	✓	✓	✓	✓	✓	**621.5**
Parque das Nações	7.5	7.5	✓	✓	✓	✓	✓	✓	✓	✓	614
Sacavém	5.2	12.7			✓				✓		608.8
Granja (+130m)	7.5	20.2			✓			✓			*601.3*
Alpriate	**1.6**	**21.8**	✓		✓						**599.7**
Póvoa de Santa Iria	3.8	25.6			✓						595.9
Praia dos Pescadores	1.4	27			✓						594.5
Alverca	4.2	31.2			✓	✓	✓	✓			590.3
Alhandra	5.6	36.8			✓	✓	✓	✓	✓		584.7
Vila Franca de Xira	**4**	**40.8**	✓	✓	✓	✓	✓	✓	✓	✓	**580.7**
Castenheira do Ribatejo station	4.5	45.3			✓						576.2
Carregado	2.8	48.1			✓	✓					573.4
Vila Nova da Rainha	4.7	52.8			✓	✓					568.7
Azambuja	**7.5**	**60.3**	✓	✓	✓	✓	✓	✓	✓	✓	**561.2**

Place	Distance between each place	Distance from Lisbon	Albergue/ Hostel	Other accommo- dation	Café/Bar	Restaurant	Mini/ Supermarket	ATM	Pharmacy	Tourist office	Distance to Santiago
Reguengo	10.6	70.9			✓						550.6
Valada	2.4	73.3		✓	✓			✓			548.2
Porto de Muge	3.7	77		✓	✓						544.5
Santarém	**15.8**	**92.8**	✓	✓	✓	✓	✓	✓	✓	✓	**528.7**
Ribeira de Santarém	1.6	94.4			✓	✓					527.1
Vale de Figueira	9.9	104.3			✓			✓			517.2
Pombalinho	10.5	114.8			✓						506.7
Azinhaga	4.6	119.4		✓	✓		✓	✓	✓		502.1
Golegã	**7.6**	**127**	✓	✓	✓	✓	✓	✓	✓	✓	**494.5**
São Caetano	5.8	132.8		✓	✓						488.7
Atalaia	5	137.8		✓	✓	✓					483.7
Asseiceira	8.4	146.2			✓		✓	✓			475.3
Casal Marmelo	6.1	152.3			✓						469.2
Tomar	**5.1**	**157.4**	✓	✓	✓	✓	✓	✓	✓	✓	**464.1**
Casais	7.6	165							✓		456.5
Soianda	1	166			✓						455.5
Calvinos	2	168			✓		✓				453.5
Tojal (+180m)	*11.9*	*179.9*			✓						*441.6*
Cortiça	3.3	183.2		✓							438.3
Alvaiázere	**6.7**	**189.9**	✓	✓	✓	✓	✓	✓	✓	✓	**431.6**
Ansião	12.8	202.7		✓	✓	✓	✓	✓	✓	✓	418.8
Venda do Brasil	6.2	208.9			✓		✓	✓			412.6
Alvorge	3.8	212.7	✓		✓						408.8

Place	Distance between each place	Distance from Lisbon	Albergue/ Hostel	Other accommo-dation	Café/Bar	Restaurant	Mini/ Supermarket	ATM	Pharmacy	Tourist office	Distance to Santiago
Rabaçal	**8.9**	**221.6**	✓		✓	✓	✓	✓			**399.9**
Conímbriga	11.1	232.7	✓		✓			✓			388.8
Cernache	6.3	239	✓		✓		✓		✓		382.5
Cruz dos Mourouços	6.9	245.9			✓						375.6
Mesura	2	247.9			✓		✓				373.6
Santa Clara	1.3	249.2	✓		✓	✓			✓	✓	372.3
Coimbra	**1.1**	**250.3**	✓	✓	✓	✓			✓	✓	✓	**371.2**
Adémia de Baixo	6.1	256.4									365.1
Fornos	2	258.4		✓	✓						363.1
Trouxemil	1.3	259.7			✓						361.8
Adões	0.9	260.6			✓						360.9
Sargento Mor	1.1	261.7									359.8
Santa Luzia	1.8	263.5				✓					358
Mala	4.4	267.9			✓						353.6
Lendiosa	1	268.9			✓						352.6
Mealhada	4.8	273.7		✓	✓	✓	✓	✓	✓		347.8
Sernadelo	**1.6**	**275.3**	✓	✓		✓					**346.2**
Anadia (+300m)	6.2	281.5		✓							*340*
Alféloas	2.3	283.8			✓			✓			337.7
Avelãs de Caminho	3.4	287.2			✓	✓					334.3
Aguada de Baixo	4.3	291.5			✓				✓		330
Águeda	**7.4**	**298.9**	✓	✓	✓	✓		✓	✓	✓	**322.6**

Place	Distance between each place	Distance from Lisbon	Albergue/ Hostel	Other accommo- dation	Café/Bar	Restaurant	Mini/ Supermarket	ATM	Pharmacy	Tourist office	Distance to Santiago
Mourisca do Vouga	4	302.9			✓			✓	✓		318.6
Lameiro	5.9	308.8			✓						312.7
Serém	1	309.8			✓						311.7
Albergaria-a-Velha	**5.2**	**315**	✓	✓	✓	✓	✓	✓	✓		**306.5**
Albergaria-a-Nova	7.2	322.2	✓		✓	✓					299.3
Pinheiro da Bemposta	5.2	327.4			✓						294.1
Oliveira de Azeméis	7.6	335		✓	✓	✓	✓	✓	✓		286.5
Salgueiro	3.6	338.6			✓						282.9
Vila de Cucujães	0.9	339.5			✓				✓		282
São João da Madeira	**4.5**	**344**	✓	✓	✓	✓	✓	✓	✓	✓	**277.5**
Arrifana	1.4	345.4			✓						276.1
Malaposta	5.7	351.1		✓	✓	✓					270.4
Souto Redondo	1.8	352.9			✓						268.6
Ferradal	1.7	354.6			✓						266.9
Vergada	2.8	357.4			✓						264.1
Grijó	**5.4**	**362.8**	✓		✓		✓	✓	✓		**258.7**
Perosinho	4.9	367.7			✓						253.8
Rechousa	4.1	371.8			✓	✓	✓		✓		249.7
Vila Nova de Gaia	2.7	374.5	✓	✓	✓	✓	✓	✓	✓	✓	247

Place	Distance between each place	Distance from Lisbon	Albergue/Hostel	Other accommo-dation	Café/Bar	Restaurant	Mini/Supermarket	ATM	Pharmacy	Tourist office	Distance to Santiago
Porto	**3.8**	**378.3**	✓	✓	✓	✓	✓	✓	✓	✓	**243.2**
Araújo	9.5	387.8			✓						233.7
Moreira	4.6	392.4			✓		✓	✓	✓		229.1
Mosteiro	3.8	396.2			✓			✓	✓		225.3
Gião	3.9	400.1			✓						221.4
Monte de Santo Ovídio	2	402.1			✓	✓		✓			219.4
Vairão	**1.2**	**403.3**	✓		✓						**218.2**
Vilarinho	1.7	405	✓		✓		✓	✓			216.5
São Mamede	5.4	410.4			✓						211.1
Arcos	2.7	413.1		✓	✓	✓					208.4
São Pedro de Rates	3.9	417	✓		✓	✓	✓		✓		204.5
Pedra Furada	7.7	424.7		✓	✓	✓					196.8
Pereira	2.7	427.4			✓	✓			✓		194.1
Barcelinhos	5.4	432.8	✓	✓	✓	✓		✓	✓		188.7
Barcelos	**0.9**	**433.7**	✓	✓	✓	✓		✓	✓	✓	**187.8**
Vila Boa	2.9	436.6			✓						184.9
Lijó	2.2	438.8			✓						182.7
Tamel São Pedro Fins	4.5	443.3	✓			✓					178.2
Aborim	1.6	444.9			✓						176.6
Balugães	3.9	448.8		✓	✓		✓				172.7
Lugar do Corgo	4.4	453.2	✓	✓							168.3
Vitorino dos Piães	2.2	455.4		✓	✓						166.1

Place	Distance between each place	Distance from Lisbon	Albergue/ Hostel	Other accommo- dation	Café/Bar	Restaurant	Mini/ Supermarket	ATM	Pharmacy	Tourist office	Distance to Santiago
Facha	2.6	458		✓							163.5
Seara	3.5	461.5			✓						160
Ponte de Lima	**5.7**	**467.2**	✓	✓	✓	✓	✓	✓	✓	✓	**154.3**
Arcozelo	3.1	470.3			✓						151.2
Revolta	5.3	475.6			✓		✓				145.9
Cabanas	6	481.6		✓							139.9
São Roque	2.2	483.8		✓			✓		✓		137.7
Rubiães	**1.3**	**485.1**	✓								**136.4**
Pecene	3.7	488.8		✓	✓						132.7
São Bento da Porta Aberta	0.6	489.4			✓						132.1
Fontoura	3.2	492.6			✓						128.9
Paços	2.6	495.2	✓								126.3
Arão	4.5	499.7			✓						121.8
Valença	1.6	501.3	✓	✓	✓	✓	✓	✓	✓	✓	120.2
Tui	**3.3**	**504.6**	✓	✓	✓	✓	✓	✓	✓	✓	**116.9**
Orbenlle	9.2	513.8			✓						107.7
O Porriño	7.8	521.6	✓	✓	✓	✓	✓	✓	✓		99.9
Veigadaña	3.5	525.1	✓		✓						96.4
Mos	**2.6**	**527.7**	✓		✓		✓				**93.8**
Saxamonde	6.2	533.9	✓								87.6
Redondela	3.4	537.3	✓	✓	✓	✓	✓	✓	✓		84.2
Cesantes	3	540.3	✓	✓	✓						81.2

Place	Distance between each place	Distance from Lisbon	Albergue/ Hostel	Other accommo-dation	Café/Bar	Restaurant	Mini/ Supermarket	ATM	Pharmacy	Tourist office	Distance to Santiago
Arcade	3.7	544	✓	✓	✓	✓	✓	✓	✓		77.5
Pontevedra	**12.8**	**556.8**	✓	✓	✓	✓	✓	✓	✓	✓	**64.7**
San Amaro	8.9	565.7			✓						55.8
A Portela (+600m)	*0.3*	*566*	✓								*55.5*
Valbón	2.2	568.2			✓						53.3
Briallos (+350m)	*5*	*573.2*	✓								*48.3*
Tivo	3	576.2	✓		✓						45.3
Caldas de Reis	**1.8**	**578**	✓	✓	✓	✓	✓	✓	✓	✓	**43.5**
Carracedo	5.4	583.4	✓		✓						38.1
O Pino (+220m)	*4.2*	*587.6*			✓	✓					*33.9*
San Miguel de Valga	2.4	590			✓		✓				31.5
Infesta/ Pontecesures	3.5	593.5	✓		✓						28
Herbón junction (+3km)	*0.7*	*594.2*	✓								*27.3*
Padrón	**2.4**	**596.6**	✓	✓	✓	✓	✓	✓	✓	✓	**24.9**
A Escravitude	5.9	602.5		✓	✓	✓					19
A Picaraña	3.3	605.8	✓	✓	✓	✓					15.7
Faramello	1.1	606.9	✓		✓						14.6
Teo (+150m)	*0.5*	*607.4*	✓		✓						*14.1*
Rúa de Francos	0.9	608.3		✓		✓					13.2
O Milladoiro	5.8	614.1			✓	✓	✓	✓	✓		7.4
Santiago	**7.4**	**621.5**	✓	✓	✓	✓	✓	✓	✓	✓	**0**

Coastal Camino from Porto

Place	Distance between each place	Distance from Porto	Albergue/Hostel	Other accommodation	Café/Bar	Restaurants	Mini/Supermarket	ATM	Pharmacy	Tourist office	Distance to Santiago
Porto	**0**	**0**	✓	✓	✓	✓	✓	✓	✓	✓	**265.3**
Recarei	6.9	6.9			✓						258.4
Santiago de Custóias	0.9	7.8			✓		✓		✓		257.5
Pedras Rubras	5.1	12.9		✓	✓			✓			252.4
Mindelo	10.3	23.2			✓		✓		✓		242.1
Areia	2.4	25.6			✓		✓	✓	✓		239.7
Azurara	1.4	27		✓	✓			✓	✓		238.3
Vila do Conde	**1**	**28**	✓	✓	✓	✓	✓	✓	✓	✓	**237.3**
Coastal Stage 1A											
Porto	*0*	*0*	✓	✓	✓	✓	✓	✓	✓	✓	*270.3*
Foz do Douro	*5.3*	*5.3*	✓	✓	✓	✓	✓	✓	✓		*265*
Matosinhos	*4.7*	*10*		✓	✓	✓	✓	✓	✓	✓	*260.3*
Angeiras	*12.7*	*22.7*		✓	✓	✓		✓			*247.6*
Labruge	*0.8*	*23.5*	✓		✓	✓					*246.8*
Vila Cha	*2.6*	*26.1*	✓	✓	✓		✓		✓		*244.2*
Vila do Conde	*6.9*	*33*	✓	✓	✓	✓	✓	✓	✓	✓	*237.3*
Coastal Camino con											
Póvoa de Varzim	3.8	31.8	✓	✓	✓	✓	✓	✓	✓	✓	233.5

Place	Distance between each place	Distance from Porto	Albergue/ Hostel	Other accommo- dation	Café/Bar	Restaurants	Mini/ Supermarket	ATM	Pharmacy	Tourist office	Distance to Santiago
Aver-o-Mar	3.3	35.1			✓						230.2
Santo André	2	37.1		✓							228.2
Aguçadoura	1.8	38.9			✓		✓				226.4
Apúlia (+500m–1km)	6.6	45.5		✓	✓	✓	✓		✓		219.8
Fão	3.5	49	✓	✓	✓	✓	✓	✓	✓		216.3
Esposende	2.8	51.8	✓	✓	✓	✓	✓	✓	✓	✓	**213.5**
Marinhas	4.4	56.2	✓		✓	✓	✓	✓			209.1
Belinho	3.9	60.1			✓		✓	✓			205.2
Chafé	9.4	69.5		✓	✓						195.8
Anha	2.5	72			✓		✓				193.3
Darque	2.4	74.4		✓	✓	✓					190.9
Viana do Castelo	2.9	77.3	✓	✓	✓	✓	✓	✓	✓	✓	**188**
Areosa	4.8	82.1		✓			✓	✓			183.2
Carreço	3.6	85.7		✓	✓		✓	✓			179.6
Âncora	7.2	92.9			✓		✓	✓			172.4
Vila Praia de Âncora	2.6	95.5		✓	✓	✓	✓	✓	✓	✓	169.8
Moledo	4.7	100.2			✓		✓	✓			165.1
Caminha	3.9	104.1	✓	✓	✓	✓	✓	✓	✓	✓	**161.2**

Place	Distance between each place	Distance from Porto	Albergue/Hostel	Other accommodation	Café/Bar	Restaurants	Mini/Supermarket	ATM	Pharmacy	Tourist office	Distance to Santiago
A Guarda	5.2	109.3	✓		✓	✓		✓	✓	✓	156
Oia	13.4	122.7		✓	✓	✓				✓	142.6
Viladesuso	3.7	126.4		✓	✓						138.9
Mougas	**2.7**	**129.1**	✓		✓						**136.2**
Baiona	11	140.1		✓	✓	✓	✓	✓	✓	✓	125.2
Sabaris	3.2	143.3			✓	✓					122
A Ramallosa	**1.8**	**145.1**		✓	✓	✓	✓	✓	✓		**120.2**
Priegue	6.3	151.4			✓				✓		113.9
Saláns (+320m)	*1*	*152.4*	✓		✓						*112.9*
Coruxo	4	156.4			✓				✓		108.9
Comesaña	2.6	159			✓			✓			106.3
Matamá	1.5	160.5			✓		✓	✓	✓		104.8
Vigo	**6.1**	**166.6**	✓	✓	✓	✓	✓	✓	✓	✓	**98.7**
Redondela	**14.5**	**181.1**	✓	✓	✓	✓	✓	✓	✓		**85.9**
Joins the Central Camino											
Cesantes	3	184.1	✓	✓	✓				✓		81.2
Arcade	3.7	187.8	✓	✓	✓	✓	✓	✓	✓		77.5
Pontevedra	**12.8**	**200.6**	✓	✓	✓	✓	✓	✓	✓	✓	**64.7**
San Amaro	8.9	209.5		✓	✓						55.8
A Portela (+600m)	*0.3*	*209.8*									*55.5*

Place	Distance between each place	Distance from Porto	Albergue/ Hostel	Other accommodation	Café/Bar	Restaurants	Mini/ Supermarket	ATM	Pharmacy	Tourist office	Distance to Santiago
Valbón	2.2	212			✓						53.3
Briallos (+350m)	*5*	*217*	✓								*48.3*
Tivo	3	220	✓		✓						45.3
Caldas de Reis	**1.8**	**221.8**	✓	✓	✓	✓	✓	✓	✓	✓	**43.5**
Carracedo	5.4	227.2		✓	✓	✓					38.1
O Pino (+220m)	*4.2*	*231.4*	✓		✓	✓					*33.9*
San Miguel de Valga	2.4	233.8			✓		✓				31.5
Infesta/ Pontecesures	3.5	237.3	✓		✓			✓			12.4
Herbón junction (+3km to Herbón)	*0.7*	*238*	✓								*27.3*
Padrón	**2.4**	**240.4**	✓	✓	✓	✓	✓	✓	✓	✓	**24.9**
A Escravitude	5.9	246.3		✓	✓	✓					19
A Picaraña	3.3	249.6	✓	✓	✓	✓					15.7
Faramello	1.1	250.7	✓		✓						14.6
Teo (+150m)	*0.5*	*251.2*	✓		✓						*14.1*
Rúa de Francos	0.9	252.1		✓		✓					13.2
O Milladoiro	5.8	257.9	✓		✓	✓	✓	✓	✓		7.4
Santiago	**7.4**	**265.3**	✓	✓	✓	✓	✓	✓	✓	✓	**0**

Spiritual Variant from Pontevedra

Place	Distance between each place	Distance from Pontevedra	Albergue/ Hostel	Other accommodation	Café/Bar	Restaurants	Mini/ Supermarket	ATM	Pharmacy	Tourist office	Distance to Santiago
Pontevedra	**0**	**0**	✓	✓	✓	✓	✓	✓	✓	✓	**102.8**
Campaño	5.6	5.6		✓	✓	✓					97.2
Poio	3.2	8.8		✓	✓		✓	✓	✓		94
Combarro	2.5	11.3		✓	✓	✓					91.5
Armenteira	**9.1**	**20.4**	✓	✓	✓					✓	**82.4**
Barrantes	6.5	26.9		✓		✓					75.9
Pontearnelas	6.1	33			✓	✓			✓		69.8
San Roque do Monte	6.8	39.8			✓						63
Vilanova de Arousa	**4.1**	**43.9**	✓	✓	✓	✓	✓	✓	✓		**58.9**
Vilagarcía de Arousa	8.4	52.3		✓	✓	✓	✓	✓	✓		50.5
Carril	2.3	54.6		✓	✓	✓		✓	✓		48.2
O Casal	3.9	58.5		✓	✓	✓					44.3
Pontecesures	17.4	75.9	✓	✓	✓	✓					26.9
Padrón	**2**	**77.9**	✓	✓	✓	✓	✓	✓	✓	✓	**24.9**
A Escravitude	5.9	83.8		✓	✓	✓					19
A Picaraña	3.3	87.1	✓	✓	✓	✓		✓			15.7
Faramello	1.1	88.2	✓		✓						14.6
Teo (+150m)	*0.5*	*88.7*	✓		✓						*14.1*
Ría de Francos	0.9	89.6		✓		✓					13.2
O Milladoiro	5.8	95.4	✓	✓	✓	✓	✓	✓	✓		7.4
Santiago	**7.4**	**102.8**	✓	✓	✓	✓	✓	✓	✓	✓	**0**

APPENDIX B
Glossary

Essential words

English	Portuguese	Spanish
yes	sim	sí
no	não	no
okay	está bem	bueno/de acuerdo
excuse me	se faz favor	disculpa/perdona
please	por favor	por favor
thank you/ thank you very much	obrigado (m), obrigada (f)/muito obrigado(a)	gracias/muchas gracias
you're welcome	de nada	de nada
sorry	desculpe	lo siento
hello	olá	hola
good morning	bom dia	buenos días
good afternoon	boa tarde	buenas tardes
good evening/good night	boa noite	buenas noches
goodbye	adeus	adiós
today	hoje	hoy
tomorrow	amanhã	mañana
bed	cama	cama
bedroom	quarto	habitación
left	esquerda	izquierda
right	direita	derecha
straight on	em frente	recto/derecho
big	grande	grande
small	pequeno	pequeño
open	aberto	abierto
closed	fechado/encerrado	cerrado

English	Portuguese	Spanish
toilet	lavabos/sanitários/casa de banho/WC	baño/lavabo
women's toilet	WC senhoras	baño de mujeres
men's toilet	WC homens	baño de hombres
Wi-Fi	Wi-Fi	Wi-Fi (pronounced 'wee-fee')
telephone	telefone	teléfono
ATM	ATM/caixa multibanco	ATM/cajero automático
pharmacy	farmácia	farmacia
tourist office	turismo	oficina de turismo
post office & stamps	correios & selos	oficina de correos y sellos
library	biblioteca	biblioteca
bus station	estação de autocarro	estación de autobuses
train station	estação de comboio	estacion de trenes
police	polícia	policía
town hall	câmara municipal	ayuntamiento
church/chapel	igreja/capela	iglesia/capilla
ticket office	bilheteria	oficina de tickets
water (drinkable)	água (potável)	agua (potable)
water (not drinkable)	água (não potável)	agua (no potable)
pilgrim	peregrino	peregrino
pilgrim hostel	albergue de peregrinos	albergue de peregrinos
shoe shop	sapataria	zapatería

Essential phrases

English	Portuguese	Spanish
I don't understand	Não entendo	No entiendo
I don't know	Eu não sei	No lo sé
Do you speak English?	Você fala inglês?	¿Habla usted Inglés?
I don't speak Portuguese/ Spanish	Eu não falo português/ espanhol	No hablo portugués/ español
Please speak slowly	Por favor fale devagar	Por favor, habla despacio
How are you?	Como está?	¿Cómo estás?
Fine thanks. And you?	Bem obrigado(a). E você?	Bien gracias. ¿Y usted?
What is your name?	Como se chama?	¿Cómo te llamas?
My name is...	O meu nome é...	Me llamo...
Where is/ are...	Onde é/são...	¿Dónde es/ son...
Where is the toilet?	Onde é a casa de banho?	¿Donde esta el baño?
How far is it to...?	Qual é a distância para...?	¿Qué distancia hay hasta...?
How much is it?	Quanto custa?	¿Cuánto cuesta?
I have a reservation	Tenho uma reserva	Tengo una reserva
Can I make a reservation for...	Posso fazer uma reserva para...	Puedo hacer una reserva para...
That was delicious	Isto estava delicioso	Eso estaba delicioso
Can I have the bill please?	Posso receber a conta, por favor?	¿La cuenta, por favor?
Do you have Wi-Fi?	Você tem Wi-Fi?	¿Tienes Wi-Fi?
What is the Wi-Fi password?	Qual é a senha Wi-Fi?	¿Cuál es la contraseña del Wi-Fi?
What is the local speciality?	O que é a espe-cialidade local?	¿Cuál es la especialidad local?
Can you show me on the map?	Pode-me mostrar no mapa?	¿Puede mostrarme en el mapa?

Days of the week

English	Portuguese	Spanish
Monday	Segunda-feira	Lunes
Tuesday	Terça-feira	Martes
Wednesday	Quarta-feira	Miércoles
Thursday	Quinta-feira	Jueves
Friday	Sexta-feira	Viernes
Saturday	Sábado	Sábado
Sunday	Domingo	Domingo

Months

English	Portuguese	Spanish
January	Janeiro	Enero
February	Fevereiro	Febrero
March	Março	Marzo
April	Abril	Abril
May	Maio	Mayo
June	Junho	Junio
July	Julho	Julio
August	Agosto	Agosto
September	Setembro	Septiembre
October	Outubro	Octubre
November	Novembro	Noviembre
December	Dezembro	Diciembre

Numbers

English	Portuguese	Spanish
zero	zero	cero
one	um	uno
two	dois	dos
three	três	tres

English	Portuguese	Spanish
four	quatro	cuatro
five	cinco	cinco
six	seis	seis
seven	sete	siete
eight	oito	ocho
nine	nove	nueve
ten	dez	diez
eleven	onze	once
twelve	doze	doce
thirteen	treze	trece
fourteen	catorze	catorce
fifteen	quinze	quince
sixteen	dezasseis	dieciséis
seventeen	dezassete	diecisiete
eighteen	dezoito	dieciocho
nineteen	dezanove	diecinueve
twenty	vinte	veinte
thirty	trinta	treinta
forty	quarenta	cuarenta
fifty	cinquenta	cincuenta
sixty	sessenta	sesenta
seventy	setenta	setenta
eighty	oitenta	ochenta
ninety	noventa	noventa
one hundred	cem/cento	cien

Food-related

English	Portuguese	Spanish
food	comida	comida
breakfast	pequeno almoço	desayuno
lunch	almoço	almuerzo
dinner	jantar	cena
dessert	sobremesa	postre
bakery/cake shop	padaria/ pastelaria	panadería
market	mercado	mercado
hot	quente	caliente
cold	frio	fría
rice	arroz	arroz

English	Portuguese	Spanish
salad	saladaen	salada
eggs	ovos	huevos
bread	pão	pan
potatoes	batatas	patatas
soup	sopa	sopa
tuna	atum	atún
beef	carne de vaca	carne de vaca
chicken	frango	pollo
pork	carne de porco	cerdo
lamb	cordeiro/borrego	cordero
fish	peixe	pescado
ice cream	gelado	helado
cheese	queijo	queso
fruit	fruta	fruta
orange	laranja	naranja
apple	maçã	manzana

Drinks

English	Portuguese	Spanish
still water	água sem gás	agua sin gas
sparkling water	água com gás	agua con gas
with/without ice	com/sem gelo	con/sin hielo
orange juice	sumo de laranja	zumo de naranja
black coffee	abatanado	café solo
espresso	café/bica	cafe espresso
coffee with milk	café com leite	café con leche
milk	leite	leche
tea	chá	té
beer	cerveja	cerveza
white wine	vinho branco	vino blanco
red wine	vinho tinto	vino tinto

APPENDIX C
Useful contacts

Tourist offices

Central Camino – Portugal
(dialling code +351)

Lisbon
Praça do Comércio
tel 210 312 810
www.visitlisboa.com
daily 10am–7pm
or
Rua Jardim do Regedor 50
tel 213 472 134

Vila Franca de Xira
Rua Alves Redol 7
tel 263 285 605
www.cm-vfxira.pt
(Mar–Nov) Mon–Fri 10am–6.30pm, Sat
10am–1pm & 2–6.30pm

Azambuja
Rua Engenheiro Moniz da Maia 29
tel 263 400 476
www.cm-azambuja.pt
Daily 9am–6.30pm

Santarém
Rua Capela Ivens 63
tel 243 304 437
www.cm-santarem.pt
Mon–Fri 10am–6pm, Saturday, Sunday and
holidays 9.30am–1pm & 2–5.30pm

Golegã
Rua Dom Afonso Henriques
tel 249 979 002
www.cm-golega.pt
Mon–Fri 10am–4pm

Tomar
Av Dr. Cândido Madureira
tel 249 329 823
www.cm-tomar.pt
daily 9.30am–12.30pm & 2–6pm

Alvaiázere
Praça do Município
tel 236 650 690
www.cm-alvaiazere.pt
Mon–Fri 9am–5.30pm

Ansião
Praça do Município
tel 236 670 206
www.cm-ansiao.pt
Mon–Fri 9am–12.30pm & 2–5.30pm

Coimbra
Largo da Portagem
tel 239 857 186
www.cm-coimbra.pt
Mon–Fri 9am–6pm, weekends 9.30am–1pm
& 2–5.30pm

Águeda
Largo Dr. João Elisío Sucena
tel 234 601 412
www.cm-agueda.pt
Mon–Fri 10am–1pm & 2–6pm.

São João da Madeira
Torre da Oliva, Rua Oliveira Júnior 591
tel 256 200 204
turismoindustrial.cm-sjm.pt
Mon–Fri 9am–12.30pm & 2–6pm,
Sat 10am–12.30pm & 2–6pm, Sun
10.30am–12.30pm & 2.30–6pm

Porto
next to the cathedral: Terreiro da Sé
tel 223 326 751
www.visitporto.travel
daily May–Oct 9am–8pm and Nov–Apr
9am–7pm
or
centre: Rua Clube dos Fenianos 25
tel 300 501 920
www.visitporto.travel
daily May–Oct 9am–8pm, August 9am–9pm,
Nov–Apr 9am–7pm

Barcelos
Largo Dr José Novais 27
tel 253 811 882
www.cm-barcelos.pt
(15 Mar–30 Sep) Mon–Fri 9.30am–6pm,
Sat & Sun 10am–1pm & 2–5pm (Sunday
closed at 4pm); (1 Oct–14 Mar) Mon–Fri
9.30am–5.30pm, Sat 10am–1pm & 2–5pm,
Sunday closed

Ponte de Lima
Torre da Cadeia Velha
tel 258 240 208
www.visitepontedelima.pt
daily 9am–12.30pm & 2–5.30pm (closed
weekends from end of September to April)

Valença
Portas do Sol
tel 251 823 329
www.visitvalenca.com
Mon–Fri 9am–5pm & Sat–Sun 9am–12.30pm
& 1.30–5pm

Central Camino – Spain (+34)

Tui
Paseo de Calvo Sotelo 16
tel 677 418 405
www.tui.gal
(Apr–Sep) daily 9.30am–1.30pm & 4–7pm;
(Oct–Mar) 10.30am–1.30pm & 4–7pm,
closed on Mondays

Pontevedra
Plaza de España
tel 986 090 890
www.visit-pontevedra.com
(summer) Mon –Sat 9.30am–2pm &
4.30–8.30pm, Sun and holidays 10am–2pm
& 5–8pm; (winter) Mon–Sat 9.30am–2pm &
4.30–7.30pm, Sun and holidays 10am–2pm

Caldas de Reis
Auditorio Municipal, C/ Román López
tel 986 540 110 (ext 5)
www.caldasdereis.com
(Jun–Sep) daily 10am–2pm & 4–8pm
or
Ayuntamiento de Caldas, Ferrería 1
(Oct–May) Mon–Fri 9am–3pm

Padrón
Av Compostela
tel 646 593 319
www.padronturismo.gal
(summer) Tues–Sat 9am–9pm, Sun & holidays
10am–1.30pm; (rest of the year) Tues–Sat
10am–2pm & 4.15–7pm, Sun & holidays
10am–1.30pm

Santiago de Compostela
Rúa do Vilar 63
tel 981 555 129
www.santiagoturismo.com
(May–Oct) daily 9am–7pm; (Nov–Apr) daily
10am–6pm

Coastal Camino – Portugal (+351)

Porto
next to the cathedral, Terreiro da Sé
tel 223 326 751
www.visitporto.travel
daily May–Oct 9am–8pm, Nov–Apr
9am–7pm
or
centre, Rua Clube dos Fenianos 25
tel 300 501 920
daily May–Oct 9am–8pm, August 9am–9pm,
Nov–Apr 9am–7pm

Matosinhos
Av General Norton de Matos
tel 229 392 412
www.cm-matosinhos.pt
Mon 1–7pm, Tues–Sat 9.30am–7pm, Sun and
holidays 10am–1pm

Leça da Palmeira
Rua de Hintze Ribeiro 13
tel 229 392 413
www.cm-matosinhos.pt
Mon 9.30am–3.30pm, Tues–Sat 9.30am–7pm

Vila do Conde
riverfront: Rua Cais das Lavandeiras
tel 252 248 445
www.cm-viladoconde.pt
daily 9am–7pm
or
central: Rua 25 de Abril 103
tel 252 248 473/4/5
Mon–Fri 9.30am–12.30pm & 2–6pm

Póvoa de Varzim
Praça Marquês de Pombal
tel 252 298 120
www.cm-pvarzim.pt
Mon–Fri 9am–7pm

Esposende
Av Eng. Eduardo Arantes e Oliveira 62
tel 253 961 354
www.visitesposende.com
Mon–Fri 9am–12.30pm & 2–5.30pm, Sat
9am–12.30pm & 2–5.30pm

Viana do Castelo
Praça do Eixo Atlântico
tel 258 098 415
www.vivexperiencia.pt
(Mar–Jun & Sep–Oct) Tues–Sun 10am–1pm &
2–6pm; (Jul-Aug) daily 10am–7pm; (Nov–Feb)
Tues–Sun 10am–1pm & 2–5pm

Vila Praia de Âncora
Av Dr. Luís Ramos Pereira
tel 258 911 384
www.caminhaturismo.pt
Mon–Sat 9.30am–1pm & 2–5.30pm

Caminha
Praça Conselheiro Silva Torres
tel 258 921 952
www.caminhaturismo.pt
Mon–Sat 9.30am–1pm & 2–5.30pm

Coastal Camino – Spain (+34)

A Guarda
Praza do Reló
tel 986 614 546
www.turismoaguarda.es
Open daily

Oia
Praza da Centinela
tel 986 362 225
www.concellodeoia.es
Easter and Jun–Sep, Mon–Sun 10am–8pm,
closed Wednesday

Baiona
C/Jesús Valverde
tel 986 687 067
www.baiona.org
(Jul–Aug) Mon–Sun 10am–3pm & 4–9pm;

(rest of the year) Mon–Sat 10.30am–2pm &
3.30–6.30pm, Sun 11am–2pm & 4–6pm

Vigo
López de Neira 8
tel 986 224 757
www.turismodevigo.org
Mon–Sun 10am–5pm

Transport

Portugal

Air

Lisbon airport
www.aeroportolisboa.pt

Lisbon airport bus
www.carris.pt

Porto airport
www.aeroportoporto.pt

Porto airport bus
www.stcp.pt

Rail

Comboios de Portugal
(national rail operator)
www.cp.pt

Bus

Eurolines (long-distance)
www.eurolines.com

Rede Expressos (long-distance)
www.rede-expressos.pt

InterNorte (long-distance)
www.internorte.pt

Metro

Lisbon metro
www.metrolisboa.pt

Porto metro
www.metrodoporto.pt

Spain

Air

Vigo-Peinador airport
www.aena.es

Vigo-Peinador airport bus
www.vitrasa.es

Santiago airport
www.aena.es

Santiago airport bus
www.tussa.org

Rail

Renfe (national rail operator)
www.renfe.com

Bus

Alsa (long-distance)
www.alsa.es

Avanza (long-distance)
www.avanzabus.com

Monbus (long-distance)
www.monbus.es

Tussa (Santiago local)
www.tussa.org

Luggage transfer

Porto–Santiago

Tuitrans
www.tuitrans.com

Camino Facil
www.caminofacil.net

Tui–Santiago

Paq Mochila
www.elcaminoconcorreos.com

Weather

Portugal

Instituto Português do Mar e da Atmosfera (IPMA)
www.ipma.pt

Spain

Agencia Estatal de Meteorológica (AEMET)
www.aemet.es

APPENDIX D
Further reading

Nigel Cliff, *The Last Crusade: The epic voyages of Vasco da Gama* (Atlantic Books, 2013)

Roger Crowley, *Conquerors: How Portugal forged the first global empire* (Faber & Faber, 2015)

José Hermano Saraiva, *Portugal: A companion history* (Carcanet Press, 1997)

Fernando Pessoa, *The Book of Disquiet: The complete edition* (Serpent's Tail, 2017)

José Saramago, *Journey to Portugal: A pursuit of Portugal's history and culture* (Harvill Press, 2002)

José Saramago, *The Elephant's Journey* (Vintage, 2011)

Luis Vaz de Camões, *The Lusíads* (OUP Oxford, 2008)

Foreign-language books

Giovanni Battista Confalonieri, *Viaje de Lisboa a Santiago en 1594*, Spanish translation by Jose Guerra Campos (Instituto Padre Sarmiento, 1964)

Jérôme Münzer, *Voyage en Espagne et au Portugal (1494–1495)*, French translation by Michel Tarayre (Les Belles Lettres, 2006)

DOWNLOAD THE ROUTES
IN GPX FORMAT

All the routes in this guide are available for download from:

www.cicerone.co.uk/1196/GPX

as GPX files. You should be able to load them into most formats of mobile device, whether GPS or smartphone.

When you go to this link, you will be asked for your email address and where you purchased the guide, and have the option to subscribe to the Cicerone e-newsletter.

www.cicerone.co.uk